DATE DUE

963568			
11-19-92			
ILL: 9135038	NO RENEWALS	SAV	MAR 2 6 1994
ILL # 2212898			

Demco, Inc. 38-293

AUTHORITY CONTROL

Principles, Applications, and Instructions

AUTHORITY CONTROL

Principles, Applications, and Instructions

by
Doris Hargrett Clack

AMERICAN LIBRARY ASSOCIATION

Chicago and London 1990

Designed by Charles Bozett

Composed in Times Roman on a Penta-driven
 APS-μ 5 phototypesetting system by
 Impressions, Inc.

Printed on 50-pound Glatfelter, a pH-neutral
 stock

The paper used in this publication meets the minimum requirements of
American National Standard for Information Sciences—Permanence of
Paper for Printed Library Materials, ANSI Z39.48-1984. ∞

Library of Congress Cataloging-in-Publication Data

Clack, Doris H.
    Authority control : principles, applications, and instruction / by
 Doris Hargrett Clack.
       p. cm.
    Bibliography: p.
    Includes index.
    ISBN 0-8389-0516-1 (alk. paper)
    1. Authority files (Cataloging) 2. Authority files
 (Cataloging)—Data processing.   I. Title.
 Z693.3.A88C58 1989
 025.3'222—dc20   89-33240

Printed in the United States of America.
93 92 91 90   5 4 3 2 1

To Harold, Harold Levi, and Herek
with love

Contents

Figures

Preface

The purpose of this book is to bring together in one source information about the basic principles and practices of authority control in libraries. Although the body of literature is growing, it is scattered and largely theoretical in nature. There are very few practical guides available to provide direction to follow through on the theoretical base. This book is designed to fill that void.

AUTHORITY CONTROL: PRINCIPLES, APPLICATIONS, AND INSTRUCTION covers both theoretical and practical aspects of authority control; emphasis, however, is on the practical. A sound theoretical base is provided throughout the work to ensure a thorough understanding of the practice.

The theoretical aspects include a discussion of major issues facing the profession today concerning authority control and an in-depth review of current trends in automation. Emphasis here is on work being done by the four major bibliographic utilities and commercial vendors. The major cooperative projects that are having an impact on the direction of authority control are discussed. Library and information science educators and students should find the theoretical aspects of the work particularly useful for study and discussion.

The practical aspects include both general and specific principles for guidance in creating the physical record. The principles set forth for controlling the intellectual record are applicable to manual or online systems. The procedures described are specific enough for libraries to produce a manual of operations to meet their own individual needs yet remain within the framework of standards used by the Library of Congress.

Concepts are graphically explained with examples, charts, diagrams, and other appropriate illustrations to eliminate any ambiguity that could easily exist in a technical work. Information is presented in the order that tasks are performed in establishing name, uniform title, series, and subject authority records.

The basic principles for establishing references that provide control over variant forms of entry headings are succinctly and clearly discussed. These principles are compatible with the standards set forth in *Anglo-American Cataloguing Rules*, second edition, 1988 revision (*AACR2-88*) and the Library of Congress cataloging policies.

The limitations of this book must be recognized. Advancements in technology that may have an impact on authority control systems are being made constantly. Descriptions of automated systems are, therefore, current only to the time of publication. Also, it is assumed that the reader has a working knowledge of descriptive and subject cataloging. Many of the principles in this book are based on *AACR2-88*, but there is no attempt to provide instructions in the application of the rules of choice and form of entry except in the context of authority work.

My deepest appreciation is extended to the Library of Congress for giving me the privilege of working in the Processing Department to learn firsthand the rules, regulations, and processes of authority control as practiced there. For this privilege I especially thank Lucia J. Rather, John D. Byrum, Jr., and Eugene Walton. Within the Descriptive Cataloging Division of the Processing Department at the Library of Congress, special thanks go to Beecher J. Wiggins and Suzanne Ligget who took me into their sections without hesitation and gave me the freedom to explore in depth the full range of descriptive cataloging and authority control work that fell within the parameters of my interests.

The freedom to explore would not have been so meaningful without the superb guidance of Margaret "Maggie" R. Smith, whose knowledge of *AACR2*, Library of Congress rule interpretations (RIs), and the Library of Congress cataloging procedures (DCMs) is astounding. Without her patience, critical reviews, and meticulous evaluations, I could not have developed the skill in cataloging "LC's way" at a level sufficient to prepare this guide. Also, from her I developed a renewed appreciation for standardization and an understanding of the massive responsibility the Library of Congress has assumed in providing leadership to the national library community for bibliographic organization in general and authority control in particular. Having the opportunity to work with Maggie was one of the most rewarding experiences I have ever had during the thirty years of my professional career.

Special assistance in the preparation of the manuscript came from many people. Maggie Smith reviewed all of the examples in the names and series sections to ensure their accuracy and appropriateness. Her critical review gives the work added authenticity and worth. Mary Lou Miller, Subject Headings Editor in the Subject Cataloging Division of the Library of Congress, reviewed the examples in the section on subject authorities. Her comments and suggestions were invaluable in maintaining the high standards set for this work. Veronica M. Gillespie, MARC Bibliographic Conversion Specialist of the Library of Congress, reviewed the section on the MARC format. Valuable information was supplied by Sally H. McCallum, Head of the Network Development and MARC Standards Office at the Library of Congress; Arnold Wajenberg, University of Illinois; Jean M. Peck, University of California, Berkeley; and Gerald O'Sullivan, New York Public Library.

Special appreciation goes to Deborah S. Crosby of Strozier Library at Florida State University and Veronica M. Gillespie of the Library of Congress who supplied me with hundreds of examples of authority records for use in this work; to the late Harold Goldstein, former Dean of the School of Library and Information Studies at Florida State University, who supported me in my quest for a sabbatical so that I could pursue work on the manuscript full time; and to Harold Levi Clack for his assistance in the preparation of the artwork. Also, I appreciate the speed and accuracy of Linda Zingale who meticulously typed the manuscript and paid attention to all of the little details with the zeal of a seasoned cataloger. I also owe special thanks to my friend and colleague Charles W. Conaway, who assumed responsibility for my manuscript while I was out of the country. He protected it as he would his own. He accurately transmitted my revisions with all deliberate haste to the publisher without a hitch. Last, but certainly not least, special thanks go to my husband, Harold, whose moral support, understanding, and caring made it all possible.

Chapter 1

Fundamentals of Authority Control

Interest in authority control is intensifying as libraries advance from the traditional manual catalog to the online catalog. Before the advent of online catalogs, many libraries merely paid lip service to the concept of authority control; others saw little need to allocate already scarce resources to such activity and never thought of it as a priority.

It was commonly believed that all bibliographic retrieval problems would be solved once the computer was introduced into the cataloging process. There was a misconception that careful attention to the integrity of bibliographic records was not necessary in an online catalog. Some libraries attempted to convert uncontrolled bibliographic data from their old manual files into machine-readable form to produce online catalogs. It was believed that with the computer a catalog could be produced that would be flexible and that could retrieve any information in machine-readable form. Of course, actions based on these misconceptions proved to be very costly and resulted in a reprioritizing of library activities. The computer does provide the online catalog with considerable flexibility; however, flexibility without the integrity achieved by authority control produces a very inefficient file.

Definition of Authority Control

What is authority control? It is a technical process executed on a library catalog to provide structure. Uniqueness, standardization, and linkages are the foundation of authority control.

Authority control of a library catalog is maintained through an authority file that contains the terms used as access points in the catalog. The access points that determine the structure of the catalog may be real entry headings on bibliographic records or cross references. In library catalogs the entry headings under control generally consist of personal and corporate names, uniform titles, series, and subjects.

A particular set of operations must be carried out on every name, uniform title, series, or subject before it is ready to go into the catalog as an access point. The operation involves research, the creation of standardized forms of access points, and linkages to variant forms. As a result of meticulous research, a name is unique, that is, distinguishable from other names that may be candidates for inclusion in the catalog at some later date.

Authorities in the field define authority control in different ways. Schmierer says that determining access points and recording the decisions about the choices may be defined as authority control. She lists three major activities associated with authority control:

1. collecting, recording, and maintaining authority data,
2. verifying, and
3. using established, authorized forms as access points in the library catalog.[1]

Hagler and Simmons define authority control as "the name given to the function of discovering all available evidence relative to the naming of a person, body, topic, etc., and then establishing an access point and cross-references according to some rule."[2] Avram says "authority control is a process for ensuring consistency of headings in a library catalog."[3] Martin defines authority control as "the set of procedures which determines the use of consistent names and terminology in the face of pseudonyms; changing names; changing subject terminology; and changing relationships between and among scholarly disciplines, corporate bodies and governmental agencies."[4] From Elias and Fair comes this definition: "Authority control is the process by which the same or related names, phrases, or titles are brought together in a particular place in the catalog."[5]

To summarize, authority control is the process of ensuring that every entry—name, uniform title, series, or subject—that is selected as an access point for the public catalog is unique and does not conflict, by being identical, with any other entry that is already in the catalog or that may be included at a later date. A network of references is the frame that holds it all together.

Purpose

To understand the purpose of authority control, one must first be familiar with the nature of library catalogs, what their primary functions are, and how they are put together to ensure that those functions are carried out expeditiously. This section will discuss the purpose of authority control and relate it to library catalogs. It will explain why merely formatting an entry heading to fit a standard set of rules cannot be construed as establishing authority.

In 1876 Charles Ammi Cutter characterized a catalog as "merely an index to the library, giving in the shortest possible compass clues by which the public

1. Helen Schmierer, "The Relationship of Authority Control to the Library Catalog," *Illinois Libraries* 62 (September 1980): 602.

2. Ronald Hagler and Peter Simmons, *The Bibliographic Record and Information Technology* (Chicago: American Library Association, 1982), p. 181.

3. Henriette D. Avram, "Authority Control and Its Place," *Journal of Academic Librarianship* 9 (January 1984): 331.

4. Susan K. Martin, "Authority Control: Unnecessary Detail or Needed Support," *Library Issues: Briefings for Faculty and Administrators* 2 (January 1982): 2.

5. Cathy Ann Elias and C. James Fair, "Name Authority Control in a Communication System," *Special Libraries* 74 (July 1983): 289.

can find books."[6] He went on to enumerate the functions of the catalog. His *Objects* are classic statements of the functions that library catalogs are expected to fulfill:

1. To enable a person to find a book of which either the author, title, or subject is known.
2. To show what the library has by a given author, on a given subject, in a given kind of literature.
3. To assist in the choice of a book as to its edition (bibliographically); as to its character (literary or topical).[7]

In other words, the catalog serves both a finding function and a collocation or assembling function. The Council of Library Resources defines a catalog as

> a set of bibliographic records under control of authority files which describes a set of resources contained in collections, libraries, networks, and so forth. It is the instrument by which bibliographic control is maintained and by which the relationship between individual bibliographic records can be indicated. . . . The catalog may include other types of records as well, such as cross references and on-order information.[8]

The Finding Function

According to Cutter's *Objects*, library catalogs serve two basic functions. The first function helps a user to learn what materials are in the library collection and where they are located. This is known as the finding function. In order for the catalog to fulfill this function, it must offer access to the names of authors, titles, and subjects stored there. This function satisfies the needs of those users searching for a simple, discrete item. This function, however, can satisfy the needs of library users only part of the time. If a user knows a particular name of an author, a search of the catalog under that name will allow the user to find the work if the library owns a copy. The same holds true if a particular title or the subject of a particular work is known. A search of the catalog under the particular title or subject will allow the user to find the material if it is in the library's collection.

The finding function emphasizes the individual bibliographic record. Bibliographic records are surrogates for the items they describe. Each description represents a unique, physical item in the collection. The creation of individual bibliographic records involves a mechanical process of following a prescribed set of rules. With the *Anglo-American Cataloguing Rules*, second edition, 1988 revision (*AACR2-88*) as the agreed-upon set of standards and with the physical item in hand, there is little disagreement on what represents an acceptable de-

6. Charles Ammi Cutter, *Rules for a Dictionary Catalog*, 4th ed., rewritten (Washington, D.C.: Government Printing Office, 1904), p. 11.

7. Ibid., p. 12.

8. "An Integrated Consistent Authority File Service for Nationwide Use," *Library of Congress Information Bulletin* 39 (July 11, 1980): 244–248.

scription. Trained professionals can easily create unique bibliographic records that can unambiguously identify an item in a collection. The rules have been internationally accepted and, with minor variations, result in fairly uniform descriptions around the globe.

The Collocation/Assembling Function

The second function of the catalog is to enable the display of the works of a given author, works on a given subject, and the manifestation of various editions of a work in a library collection. This is known as collocation or the assembling function. Of the two functions, authority control is more closely related to collocation/assembling than to finding.

The collocation/assembling function satisfies the majority of the needs of users a majority of the time. It helps the user who approaches the catalog with incomplete information about an author, an edition of a work, or a subject. The consistency resulting from collocation makes the catalog much easier to use than uncontrolled files because it does not make too many academic demands upon the user.

NAMES

Collocation emphasizes entry headings and reference structure. The choice and form of entry, like bibliographic description, are based on *AACR2-88*. More intellectual judgment, however, is required to make effective choices than is required to create a bibliographic description.

A user may know a particular name used by an author. The author, however, may have written under several different names or may have used several different forms of a name. A library may choose to use every name or it may choose to use only one of the many names associated with the author. In order to find a particular item by the author, the user will need to know every name used by that author or the one name that the library elected to use. Many library users will come to the library not fully equipped with either of these pieces of information. To facilitate the user's search, the library will need a reference network of variant names linked together to assure that the user gets complete information. The linking in the network of references may be obvious as in a manual catalog or it may be transparent as in an online catalog.

Each record is related to every other record in the catalog. This relationship is made obvious by a network of references or by the juxtaposition of records in the catalog. Library users cannot expect to know the rules of choice and form of entry that provide structure; therefore, it is essential that the structure be consistent and readily apparent.

UNIFORM TITLES

Collocation brings together all editions of a work owned by a library through the use of uniform titles. A work may become known by various titles since publishers do not necessarily use the same title for a work. During the cataloging process, the identity of a work is captured and labeled to facilitate the collocation or assembling function. A uniform title may be assigned as the gathering device for relating the various editions of the work.

Library users may request any undefined edition of a work instead of a particular edition. They may not know the specific edition needed or that other editions are available. Some users may be fully satisfied if they get any one of several manifestations of a particular work. Others may want or need a particular edition. An effective catalog will reveal to users all the editions of a work that equally meet their needs or that could meet their needs better. Users are better served when the catalog brings to their attention related editions about which they may not have been aware.

Some users may erroneously assume that the library does not own a particular edition of a work if it is not displayed in the catalog or on the shelf with the others. They may even assume that it does not exist at all. It may not occur to them that the various editions have not been efficiently collocated. They may not be aware of the existence of other editions that could very well serve their needs if the edition sought is out on loan or is not on the shelf for some other reason. Collocation gives them choices from which they may make satisfactory substitutions when the edition they seek is not available. Some industrious user may attempt a truly thorough search and waste valuable time browsing an uncontrolled catalog since there is no way to know when an unsuccessful search should be terminated.

SERIES

Series authority files document the decisions concerning accepted practice and provide a record of established precedence of treatment. It is important for the treatment of series to be consistent to facilitate access and retrieval. Consistency of treatment means that all parts of a series follow the same treatment whether the decision is to group them all under the series title, classify them together as a collection, or disperse them throughout the collection. Ensuring uniformity in treatment is the function of series authority control.

SUBJECTS

In theory, the function of subject authority control is to ensure the use of consistent vocabulary that exactly matches both that of the user and that of the document. In practice, authority control ensures consistency in the vocabulary and the reference structure used in the catalog.

A controlled vocabulary and a controlled set of supporting references are important components of a subject access system that effectively connects the varied vocabularies of users to a subject catalog. The reference structure directs the users from narrower, broader, related, or synonymous terms to the controlled vocabulary of the catalog. If the terms from a controlled vocabulary are properly assigned to documents, then authority control ensures that all materials on a given subject are collocated under the same subject term. The adequacy of any subject authority control system is as much dependent on the quality of application as it is upon the quality of the system itself.

Major Issues

With the introduction of any new procedure or product of the magnitude of online catalogs, unresolved issues will naturally surface. With an increase in the number of online catalogs being used or planned for, libraries are having to assess their positions on authority control. As a result, numerous issues, both theoretical and practical, relating to authority control have been raised. New issues will continue to arise as long as new technological developments enable library catalogs to change. The following discussion covers major issues relating to authority control that have arisen as a result of the renewed interest in the concept and the process. They are the persistent ones that seem to elude consensus and fail to succumb to new developments. Some suggestions are made; however, no solution offered can be considered the only one that works.

The Necessity of Authority Control

The flurry of activity going on at the national level relating to the Linked Systems Project (LSP) suggests that local libraries have no need to be concerned with authority control. A cooperative system that links the databases of the Library of Congress (LC) with those of the Research Libraries Information Network (RLIN) and the Online Computer Library Center (OCLC) has just been inaugurated. A library that belongs to either RLIN or OCLC will have its bibliographic records validated automatically for the proper form of access points before they are added to the database. This validation supposedly will ensure a controlled file at the local level. To suggest that libraries at the local level need not be concerned about authority control because of the linked file service is to fail to recognize the potential for inconsistency within the files of the linked system even with validation. It also fails to consider the nature and the needs of hundreds of libraries outside the linked system since they are not affiliated with a bibliographic utility.

The possibility exists for inconsistent entry headings to be entered into the file and remain there over an extended period of time until detected by a diligent file user. The format of such inconsistent entries may defy automatic detection by the computer. In any process where human judgment is involved, potential for error exists. The computer only validates the results of the human decision to choose a particular entry heading or reference. It does not make the initial decision.

Libraries outside the linked system must assume greater responsibility for the integrity of their catalogs than do those libraries that are affiliated with a bibliographic utility. Usually their catalogs are neither as large nor as dynamic. They make authority control decisions often without access to the very latest information such as LSP provides. They are not alerted as frequently to changes in access points used locally that may not be compatible with those in the national-level files. Some of the incompatibilities may be the result of conscious decisions to deviate from known standards in order to support local needs. It is important that a library weigh carefully the value of the returns accrued from incorporating local idiosyncrasies into its authority control system against the advantages of supporting national standards.

Data in authority files do not remain static. They are dynamic and in a constant state of change. They change for a wide variety of reasons. When the contents of the collection shift, expand, or contract, authority files are affected. When the cataloging code changes, or is revised or reinterpreted, the authority file must change to reflect the new code. Also, as authors, creators, and responsible corporate bodies change their names, comparable changes will be necessary in the authority file. For a library to make adequate use of the national files, knowledge of the functions of authority control is mandatory. A thorough understanding of the procedures and practices of authority work is also necessary. One must be aware of the areas of potential problems and workable solutions.

Even if the basic authority information is available from the national files, such information must be transferred to a local catalog to meet local needs. Libraries at the local level certainly do need to be concerned about authority control.

Authority Control in an Online Environment

Since the computer can be programmed to create many different displays from a wide variety of search keys, the question of authority control in an online environment has been raised. A computer can retrieve information rapidly and accurately. It is not dependent on entry words, linear order, or static formats. Its flexibility is one of its greatest assets. So why authority control?

The speed, accuracy, and flexibility that characterize computers are the results of human intervention. The decision about what constitutes a personal name for a particular individual is predetermined by a human mind. Prior knowledge of the varied names, of the order of the words in the names, and of the links that tie them all together is a human function. Without selection of uniform names there would be chaos, with or without electronic access. All the computer does is manipulate data provided by human beings.

Standardization

Standardization is a prerequisite of quality control, the principal goal of authority control. Standardization requires that libraries use a common set of standards and follow a common set of procedures to develop structure in their catalogs. Standardization may benefit bibliographic files at the national level at the expense of local needs.

National-level authority records are the fullest possible and are constantly being reviewed and updated. They usually contain all relevant names identified in reference and other sources. Many of such authority records contain information that is irrelevant in the catalogs of some local libraries. Less full records with more relevant variants are usually sufficient for most local catalogs. Some libraries find that irrelevant authority information does not reduce the integrity of the catalog while others find it difficult to integrate such information into their catalogs.

The issue of relinquishing local needs for the sake of standardization will need to be carefully analyzed and all factors considered. Cost factors, convenience, and probable impact on service to users should be of primary importance.

Networks and Authority Control

Participation in any type of network situation requires cooperation. Local authority files must be able to interface with those of the network. The library in a networking environment must be flexible enough to handle external influences. It may be necessary to change a great many entry headings initially in order for the interface to take place. The library may lose control over decisions regarding modifications to the system. Advantages and disadvantages will vary from library to library, depending on how closely the library adheres to the latest cataloging rules, how many variations the local system requires, and how willing the library is to give up its own autonomy.

Quality Control

Quality control in authority files is as much an issue as quality control of bibliographic records was before the advent of networking. Libraries can get high-quality bibliographic records from a wide variety of sources. The bibliographic utilities offer high-quality bibliographic records or the capability to improve on those that are less than ideal. Libraries that depend on commercial vendors for their bibliographic records also get quality records since many vendors market LC cataloging copy. Other libraries employ highly trained personnel who are familiar with the cataloging rules and can create high-quality records with ease.

Measures for quality control in authority files have not reached the level of quality control for bibliographic records. There is no widely used set of standards for creating authority records. The essential information to be contained in an authority record has not yet been standardized nor has the most efficient format for displaying such information been determined. There are no standards that measure the quality of authority records; however, any authority record that identifies the established name, title, or subject and all relevant references may be considered a quality record.

There is no common understanding of the level of authority control that would best suit a particular type or size of library. Many libraries consider the consistency of the entry headings that come with purchased bibliographic records as quality authority control. Other libraries create their own authority systems without giving consideration to the resulting level of quality control. Some systems have authority control only for frequently used headings with references. Others use simplicity as the criterion for inclusion or exclusion. Entries that are considered simple are under no control. Problems could develop from such a policy since it is difficult, if not impossible, to determine if or how long an apparently simple heading will remain so.

Integrated Files

The validity of establishing files by use or type of heading is being questioned. This issue is a primary concern for manual authority files. In an automated environment, there is no question about the value of an integrated authority file system that includes names, series, and uniform titles as well as subjects. In a manual file, division into intrinsic types seems workable if desired. When all types of headings reside in the same file, however, maintenance is facilitated and a greater level of uniformity is achieved. Separate subject authority files may be more tolerable than separate name files. It may be argued that the high frequency of need to use references with subject headings justifies separate subject authority files.

Questions have also been raised regarding the desirability of establishing authority files separate from bibliographic files. Once a library has decided to integrate or to divide the various types of authority records, it must decide how to relate the authority file to the bibliographic records. Controlling the access points to those bibliographic records is the primary function of the authority file.

Authority files and bibliographic files may be separate or they may be integrated. It follows from their purposes that in a manual system authority files and bibliographic files are separate and distinct. In automated systems the two files may be separate, which requires at least two operations to effect changes to access points. Changes made to headings in the authority file must also be made in a separate operation in the bibliographic file. If the files are integrated, they are interactive. The changes made to authority records in the file effect global changes to all relevant access points and bibliographic records. The reality is that some libraries are comfortable with separate files because that is the system they initially developed, have worked with, and can afford. The ultimate goal, however, should be to build an integrated system with the capability to create global changes in one operation.

Costs

Authority control is expensive; however, no control is even more so. Included in the cost of authority control are personnel, equipment acquisition and maintenance, and supplies. The time spent searching, typing, proofing, and filing is another cost factor. Costs are also accrued for making changes and resolving conflicts. Many libraries do not consider these as costs because they are usually not included as such in the budget. They are absorbed in the expenditures for normal operational routines.

There is a cost for a successful search by a user and for a failed one. Failure has significant financial implications for a library. The more rigorous the process of authority control, the more successful will be the searches in a file. An automated system will improve the integrity of the files and will speed up operations, but there is no evidence that actual dollar figures will be reduced. The greatest potential savings will be in reduced duplication and redundancy.

Summary

Interest in authority control is increasing, primarily because of experiences with online catalogs. Before the advances in computer technology made online catalogs possible, only a few libraries were concerned about rigorous authority control. Some gave mere lip service to the idea of authority control. Many more got along without it. To many libraries, therefore, authority control is a new concept.

Authority control ensures that the entry headings in a library catalog are unique and do not conflict with existing headings or with those that may be included at a later date. Entry headings are usually for personal and corporate names, uniform titles, series, and subject headings. The form and structure of these entry headings determine the form and structure of the catalog as a whole. The structure of the catalog must be rigorously controlled to ensure consistency and uniformity, which facilitate its use by those who are unfamiliar with the rules.

Because more libraries than ever before are establishing and maintaining authority files, more attempts at cooperation in authority control—as with bibliographic control—are being made. There will be problems in beginning any cooperative venture that must be solved before a smooth and effective operation can evolve. Experience and cooperative efforts in authority control have raised numerous issues, many of which remain unresolved. These issues have ranged from questions of validity to concerns over the best way to achieve control. Although computerizing the process has created new kinds of problems, there is little doubt that from automation will come some workable solutions.

Chapter 2

Automation and Authority Control

Automation has had a tremendous impact on libraries and their operations. It introduced bibliographic utilities. It brought new vendor services. It made cooperation the benchmark of bibliographic control. It brought online catalogs into libraries and authority control to the fore. This chapter discusses the effects of automation as it relates to authority control. These effects include the authority control activities of the four major bibliographic utilities, the role of vendors in promoting authority control, and the major cooperative efforts undertaken to support and expand authority control at the national and international levels.

Bibliographic Utilities

Bibliographic utilities have had a significant influence on libraries and their activities relating to authority control. The four major bibliographic utilities are the Online Computer Library Center (OCLC), the Research Libraries Information Network (RLIN), the University of Toronto Library Automation System (UTLAS), and the Western Library Network (WLN). These utilities have encouraged improvements in authority control through their automation activities.

Online Computer Library Center

The Online Computer Library Center (OCLC) is the oldest and largest of the major bibliographic utilities. Begun in 1971 as a shared cataloging system for libraries in Ohio, OCLC now serves thousands of users through broker networks located in various regions of the United States and abroad.

The Online Cataloging Subsystem is the primary service used by member libraries. It is through this subsystem that many libraries maintain authority control over records in their own catalogs.

The database, which is the heart of the network services, comprises records created by member libraries and those from Library of Congress (USMARC) machine-readable cataloging tapes. Quality control of records going into the database depends on the adherence of member libraries to the published standards. Though OCLC encourages its members to adhere to the standards, members still have considerable freedom and flexibility to adopt local rules, within the parameters of *AACR2-88*, to meet local needs without machine intervention.

The network makes available a noninteractive online authority file in MARC format. The authority records are generated and maintained by LC. They are made available to OCLC—and any other interested organization—on a subscription basis through the LC MARC Distribution Service for Name Authorities (MDS–Name Authorities). OCLC offers access to this LC authority file as a service to its members. The records displayed as the result of an authority file search may be viewed only. They may not be added to, deleted, or changed by a member. Because the authority records are generated by LC and the entries in the OCLC bibliographic database are generated primarily (approximately two-thirds) by OCLC members, there often are variances in both choice and form of entries between the two files. OCLC members are encouraged to follow the standards and to consult the LC authority file when establishing access points; nevertheless, because the two files are not interactive, their access points are not always consistent. Of course, members are encouraged to report any errors found in either file to the OCLC staff.

Research Libraries Information Network

The Research Libraries Information Network (RLIN) was established in the spring of 1975 to support the cataloging and other technical processing activities of its members. It evolved from the automated system developed by Stanford University known as BALLOTS (Bibliographic Automation of Large Library Operations Using a Time Sharing System). The current parent organization for RLIN is the Research Libraries Group (RLG). Stanford remains RLIN's head-quarters and maintains the computer system. Originally there was no automated authority control. RLIN has since added an authorities subsystem consisting of two large files of authority records that allow RLIN members to retrieve records from both the LC name authority file and the New York Public Library authority file.[1] Records included are for personal and corporate names, uniform titles, topical subjects, geographic names, and name-title combinations.

Members can search the authorities database using standard RLIN indexes for personal names, corporate/conference name words or phrases, title words or phrases, subject headings or heading subdivisions, Library of Congress card numbers, classification numbers, and unique record IDs. Users can also retrieve records by combining elements from several indexes and using Boolean operators. A notable RLIN feature is its subject and keyword searching capability that includes truncation of words and phrases. Another special feature is the browsing and sampling capability to aid in the formulation of specific search queries.

University of Toronto Library Automation System

The University of Toronto Library Automation System (UTLAS) began as a unit of the University of Toronto Library where library automation activities

1. "RLG's RLIN Authorities Subsystem Ready for Searching," *Information Technology and Libraries* 2 (June 1983): 218.

took place. One project of the unit was to develop a cataloging support system.[2] The product developed was a computer-output microfilm (COM) catalog, but it had no authority control. Online access began in 1978 and the library made cataloging support services available to other libraries. It was then that the need for some measure of authority control became apparent. The National Library of Canada, the University of Toronto, and a consortium of nineteen libraries worked together to address the question of authority control. They defined standards, set parameters, and planned for the future. The result was a fully integrated authority control system that would meet the needs of a community with varied library needs.

Western Library Network

In 1967 the State Library of Washington created a central database for the production of a COM union catalog and card sets for a group of academic and public libraries within the state.[3] The Western Library Network (WLN) has since expanded its services and its boundaries to include more than three hundred libraries located throughout the Pacific Northwest. In addition, WLN makes its software available to interested libraries and other organizations.

The WLN database supports online shared cataloging and other WLN products such as catalog cards, MARC records on magnetic tapes, and COM and compact disc–read-only memory (CD-ROM) catalogs. Its more than four million bibliographic records and four and one-half million authority records come from its member libraries which contribute through its Input/Edit System, and from MARC tapes from the Library of Congress. Other sources include the National Library of Canada and the National Library of Medicine tapes. WLN accepts LC records and policies as the network standards.

Authority control is the heart and major strength of the WLN database. A component of its Bibliographic Subsystem, which provides catalog support services, authority control is achieved through the online manipulation of author, uniform title, and subject authority records in a vocabulary file (VOC) attached to bibliographic records.

Basic to authority control in the WLN system are the bibliographic file and the subfield key file linked to the VOC file. The VOC file contains conference headings, uniform titles, author-title series, and personal and corporate names created according to a preferred set of standards. As each new incoming biblio-

2. Jack Cain, "The UTLAS Authority System," in *What's in a Name? Control of Catalogue Records Through Automated Authority Files*, edited by Natusuko Y. Furuya (Toronto, Ont.: University of Toronto Library Automation Systems, 1978), pp. 71–95; Eric Antilla, "Authorities at UTLAS: Concepts and Facilities," in *What's in a Name? Control of Catalogue Records Through Automated Authority Files*, edited by Natusuko Y. Furuya (Toronto, Ont.: University of Toronto Library Automation Systems, 1978), pp. 55–70.

3. Ruth Patterson Funabiki, Ingrid Mifflin, and Karen Corlee, "Use of the WLN Authority Control System by an ARL Library," *Library Resources & Technical Services* 27 (October/December 1983): 391–394; Jo Calk, "On-line Authority Control in the Washington Library Network," in *What's in a Name? Control of Catalogue Records Through Automated Authority Files*, edited by Natusuko Y. Furuya (Toronto, Ont.: University of Toronto Library Automation Systems, 1978), pp. 135–159.

graphic record is entered into the database, its headings are identified and compared to the headings in the VOC file. If there is a match, the bibliographic record has its headings stripped off and each replaced by a corresponding internal sequence number (ISN). Then the bibliographic record becomes a part of the database. If there is no match, a new VOC authority record is created and assigned an ISN. The heading in the bibliographic record is then replaced with an ISN corresponding to that assigned to the VOC record. The heading is then replaced in the bibliographic record with the ISN for the new VOC record.

Bibliographic records store only ISNs and not the text of the headings. This means that one VOC record can actually be attached to several bibliographic records. Of course, a heading is displayed in full when it is searched in either the VOC file or the bibliographic file. When a record is reassembled for online display, the ISNs are used to gather the corresponding authorized headings from the VOC file into the bibliographic records. Changes made to headings in the VOC file will automatically cause global changes to matching headings in the bibliographic file.

In addition to being linked to records in the bibliographic file, VOC records are also linked to each other through the cross reference structure. Cross references are added to the VOC file as the result of records input by member libraries; however, all data generated by a member library are first reviewed by the WLN staff before they become a permanent part of the database. Only WLN staff may activate the system to input data of any kind directly into the system.

The system reciprocally generates references automatically in response to the input of regular references. Two categories of references in the file used to assist in the retrieval of bibliographic records are (1) regular cross references initiated by participants and (2) internal control references, system-generated references created automatically whenever a regular cross reference is input.

The input of a *see* reference automatically generates a *use for* reference, and a *see also* reference generates a *refer from* reference. Reciprocally, a *use for* reference automatically generates a *see* reference, and a *refer from* reference generates a *see also* reference.

These references not only serve as guides to users of the database, but they are also used to search the VOC file. Modifications to be made to multiple headings may be done only through *see* references in the VOC file. *See* references, therefore, must be valid, up-to-date, and compatible with the authority structure used by the Library of Congress.

References are also used to identify unauthorized and new headings from bibliographic records being added by participating libraries and to prevent such headings from entering the database directly. Only highly trained authorized participants can add to the database or suggest modifications.

The links between the VOC file and the bibliographic file make global updates possible. When a heading in the VOC file is changed, all the bibliographic records linked to it are also changed. Unauthorized headings that match *see* references are automatically changed to the authorized form. Headings are returned to the originating library if they match *see* references that point to more than one authorized form or to a general *see* reference note, or if a heading requires human review for some other reason.

In 1985, WLN installed a new program to check for unauthorized headings going into the database.[4] The new update system, Fixed Links to Unauthorized Headings (FLUH), replaces all unauthorized headings in a bibliographic record with authorized headings before the record enters the database. Before the installation of FLUH, the Input/Edit program facilitated the detection of bibliographic records by member libraries but it did not detect outdated or incorrect headings added from magnetic tapes such as those from the Library of Congress or the National Library of Medicine. The new program is now able automatically to identify and correct unauthorized headings in bibliographic records loaded to the database from any source.

Vendors

Regarding automation, libraries contract with commercial vendors to do for them what they cannot do for themselves.[5] They may lack skilled personnel to do the work or they may not have the financial resources to acquire the necessary equipment.

COM catalogs and online catalogs share a common genesis—bibliographic records coded in machine-readable form. When the records are filmed and distributed on microfiche or in some other microform, a COM catalog results. To produce an online catalog, bibliographic records are stored on magnetic tapes or discs. In either case the records are entered into a file from which they may be searched and retrieved through controlled access points.

Authority control in COM and online catalogs can be equally comprehensive and rigid. Because COM catalogs are not online and interactive, the process of maintaining control is more involved, time consuming, and inherently slower than in an online catalog. The vendor who assumes responsibility for producing a COM catalog works from a bibliographic file in machine-readable form on tapes either supplied by the library or produced by the vendor from library-supplied bibliographic data. The vendor verifies all access points against its authority file produced to clients' specifications, its own authority file, or from LC authority file tapes. Paper printouts of new headings and changes in old ones, including references, are sent to the client library for verification and for

4. Fumiko H. Coyne, "Automated Authorities Maintenance at the Western Library Network," *Technical Services Quarterly* 5, no. 1 (1987): 33–47.

5. It is beyond the scope of this work to provide a primer on library systems, computer products for libraries, and vendors that sell them. For this information readers are referred to the following sources: The excellent series by Robert M. Mason, "Mason on Micros," appearing as a regular feature column in *Library Journal*; Joseph R. Matthews, *Choosing an Automated Library System* (Chicago: American Library Association, 1980); Emily Gallup Fayen, "The Online Public Access Catalog in 1984: Evaluating Needs and Choices," *Library Technology Reports* 20 (January-February 1984): 7–59; and *Commercial COM Catalogs: How to Choose, When to Buy*, compiled by the Catalog Use Committee, Reference and Adult Services Division, American Library Association (Chicago: American Library Association, 1978). For further information about vendors, see Joseph R. Matthews, "Competition and Change: The 1983 Automated Library System Marketplace," *Library Journal* 109 (May 1, 1984): 853–860. Also write to the vendors for information about their systems, services, and products.

its records. Corrections of inconsistencies and inaccuracies usually must wait to be displayed in a later issue of the catalog. The success of this arrangement depends on factors such as the reliability of the vendor, clearly defined specifications of the needs of the library, and speedy and open communications between the partners. Of course, both the library and the vendor must have a full understanding of and a commitment to authority control.

Authority control in an online catalog is extended to access points, both the vocabulary terms and the references to them, at the time a bibliographic record is created. When a bibliographic record is loaded into the online catalog, its access points are automatically checked against an authority file to validate the form of entry. The specific process of validation varies according to the storage system used to link bibliographic records to authority records. Also, the design of an authority control system for online catalogs can vary widely from system to system. Some systems create new authority records automatically for headings new to the bibliographic file. Some make global changes to all relevant headings in one operation. Some systems have a built-in flagging system that identifies certain headings or authority records to be reviewed for editing and authorization. In any case, the validation process in online catalogs is simple, fast, and accurate. Above all, the records never leave the premises and all processes relating to their creation and maintenance remain under the control of the library.

An online catalog may be a module of a vendor-supplied integrated turnkey system. Turnkey systems are "ready made" systems sold to any library wanting to purchase one. Since the system is not made exclusively for the purchasing library according to its own specifications, the library must often adjust its needs to the capabilities of the system.

Some turnkey systems have excellent authority control components with the capability to review and edit headings, trace references, and make global changes. Some have the flexibility to allow a library to define its own authority control indexes and to set numerous other parameters to meet specific needs.

Libraries are employing commercial firms to produce COM and online catalogs. Some vendors have integrated turnkey systems that can perform multiple library functions such as acquisitions, cataloging, serials control, circulation, interlibrary loan, reserves, and electronic mail, among other things. If a COM or an online catalog is to be produced, the library should make sure that some form of authority control is included. Most vendors subscribe to USMARC tapes for authorities and bibliographic records. Vendors, therefore, have access to LC-approved records for personal, corporate, and geographic names; uniform titles; series; and subjects; and to bibliographic data for monographs, serials, and select audiovisual materials.

The quality of authority control may vary widely from one vendor to another. Some vendors rely solely on LC tapes for authorities as the master file against which they check access points on bibliographic records received from their customers. They accept as valid only those that match a record in the LC file. Other vendors use the LC tapes as the basis for their own authority file. Access points on new bibliographic records are checked against their own authority file. Matches are considered valid while nonmatches are held for review by staff before being added to the file.

Some other vendors accept original cataloging from their customers but may consider all access points to such records as temporary or provisional until validated. Some vendors permit their customers to create their own headings for the authority file although they may consider such headings as temporary or provisional until validated against an LC record. Some vendors accept any headings formulated from their customers' bibliographic records as valid as long as they adhere to *AACR2-88* standards. Others may be more permissive in their requirements—or may have no particular requirements at all regarding standards.

In library catalogs a cross reference structure interrelates headings. The structure may be visible to the user or transparent. Some vendors provide all cross references while others supply *see* references only or no references at all. A customer with an online catalog is usually supplied with computer tapes containing the latest cross references so that the library may integrate them immediately into its online system. A customer with a COM catalog must wait for the vendor to incorporate the latest cross references in the next version of its catalog.

Vendors usually ensure the accuracy of the customer's catalog or database. In addition to transforming old forms of headings and adding references, they will usually make other corrections such as in spelling, abbreviations, and the like.

Some libraries need to convert the bibliographic records in their card catalogs into machine-readable form in preparation for automating some library function such as circulation or for creating a COM or online catalog. Usually such retrospective bibliographic records display a variety of cataloging practices and minimal authority control. Many libraries contract with a vendor to do their retrospective conversion for them since this is probably the cheapest and the fastest method of getting the job done.

Bringing the various access points under some measure of control is probably the most important and time-consuming aspect of any retrospective conversion project. A library may decide to do its own authority work before sending its manual files to a vendor for conversion, but more often the vendor assumes total responsibility for bringing all records up to standard and for doing all authority work.

Procedures vary from project to project, library to library, and vendor to vendor, but basically the process involves the use of an authority file and a bibliographic source database against which the manual records and their access points are matched to create a database of the library's holdings. Some vendors may subcontract out the authority aspect of the conversion project to other vendors who have greater facility in authority work. Sometimes two vendors will co-contract with a library to do a conversion project with the understanding that one vendor will assume responsibility for the authority work while the other does the remainder of the work. This arrangement facilitates communication between all parties concerned. Communication is of extreme importance in any vendor/library relationship.

Some vendors deal primarily with retrospective conversion. Different vendors handle old headings on a customer's records in different ways. Some vendors will retain old headings on the MARC records that they process. Others will update them to *AACR2-88* or to LC's latest form. If a vendor uses the former method, the customer's catalog will be outdated before it is completed.

Cost is one of the principal reasons that a library chooses to contract with a vendor for a catalog. Costs of vendor services vary as widely as their offerings. Their price estimates are based on such factors as services rendered, growth rate of the file, proposed use of the database, and the amount of prior planning done.

Many libraries regard automation as a panacea for problems of authority control. Some of them have successfully developed automated authority control systems of their own that they are now making available to other libraries. When planning for an online catalog or for automating other library functions, more libraries than ever are exploring the capabilities of systems that are already available on the market. Current technology has made turnkey systems an affordable option, but the component least likely to be fully developed or effective, if it exists at all, is authority control. With some research and development on their part, some libraries have produced rather sophisticated systems that meet their needs at far less cost than a custom-made system built by a vendor to specifications. The current trend is for these libraries to turn to commercial vendors to market their products since marketing can be rather expensive and time consuming. Vendors are learning from these new relationships and are becoming more sophisticated and skilled in their work with authority control.

Cooperative Ventures

Sharing bibliographic data is a common practice in the library community. The growth and development of a variety of online databases have encouraged cooperative ventures in authority control to facilitate the sharing of bibliographic data across diverse systems. The cooperative ventures discussed here are those that have had the greatest impact in helping libraries provide better service to their users.

National Level

NATIONAL COORDINATED CATALOGING OPERATIONS

Plans for an online catalog must include considerable attention to the requirements for authority control. When LC began to plan for its online catalog, authority control ranked high on the list of priorities and automated authority control was essential. To build an authority file in machine-readable form of the size and quality that was needed to support its bibliographic database, LC initiated a cooperative venture with the Name Authority Cooperative (NACO), currently known as National Coordinated Cataloging Operations.

The initial goal of NACO was to create a national authority system that would accommodate the needs of all libraries. Attempting to prove the viability of a national authority system, NACO's immediate goals were to facilitate the transformation of the LC authority file into a nationwide authority data system and, thus, to reduce the duplication of effort being done in libraries throughout the nation. To share the burden of this costly undertaking, selected libraries were granted the privilege of contributing certain categories of headings to LC for inclusion in the LC authority file.

Although LC is no longer the sole contributor of authority data to the file, it assumes responsibility for the validation function that takes place before the data are amalgamated into the file and distributed through the MARC Distribution Service to subscribers. Decentralization of responsibilities for the project while maintaining high standards has been possible because of effective planning, training, and advanced computer technology.

The initial agreement that led to the formation of NACO was between LC and the Library of the U.S. Government Printing Office (GPO). The GPO was responsible for cataloging government documents for inclusion in its *Monthly Catalog* while LC cataloged those it acquired for its collection. The result was that many of the same government publications were being cataloged by both agencies. Early in 1977 the two agencies began negotiating a cooperative cataloging venture to eliminate this duplication of effort. It was agreed that GPO would prepare bibliographic records and do the authority work for all government publications it catalogs and share that authority data with LC for inclusion into the automated authority database. In 1981, LC agreed that the GPO would assume responsibility for cataloging all U.S. federal government monographic publications added to the permanent collection. These data would be added to the LC database.[6]

As the result of a meeting of the Government Documents Round Table (GODORT) at an American Library Association conference, state libraries were considered for inclusion in the cooperative venture primarily to supply LC with authority file data for names of state corporate bodies. Some state libraries also supply corporate and personal name headings. Texas State Library was the first of this group and the second agency to join the project.

The next group to be invited to participate in the cooperative venture included the major libraries of the National Program for Acquisitions and Cataloging (NPAC), selected in consultation with the Research Libraries Group (RLG). Northwestern University submitted headings from its Africana Collection. The Northwestern Africana Project proved the feasibility of having quality authority data created and input from remote sites provided proper guidance is given and a mode of rapid communication established between LC and the site.

A third major group to join the project was the Cooperative Conversion of Serials (CONSER) libraries. They assume responsibility for headings for CONSER materials.

There are some unusual contributors in NACO such as University Microfilms International (UMI), whose special contribution is from its retrospective Canadian project and its Wing microform collection. The Wing microform collection project is part of the OCLC Major Microforms Project aimed at encouraging institutions to catalog the individual titles of major microform sets and to add the records to the OCLC database. The authority records generated

6."NACO Celebrates Tenth Anniversary," *Library of Congress Information Bulletin* 47 (January 25, 1988): 28.

become a part of the LC authority file. UMI is committed to the retrospective input of records from units 33–51 of *Early English Books, 1641–1700*, compiled by Donald Wing. Indiana University is responsible for the authority work from units 1–32.

Another unique group is Retrospective Music (REMUS), a consortium of eleven libraries with a strong interest in music. REMUS is considered a single contributor in NACO since all member libraries work under the coordination of the University of Wisconsin, Milwaukee. REMUS could serve as a prototype for other groups of libraries that may wish to participate in NACO but may not qualify individually because of size, uniqueness of collections, and supporting resources.

In addition to providing unique entry headings, some NACO participants are engaged in special projects or have special responsibilities. The Eighteenth-Century Short Title Catalog/North America (ESTC/NA) project is a NACO member comprising approximately 350 libraries in the United States coordinated in an effort to identify and catalog all eighteenth-century non-United States English-language imprints in the United States. The project is based at the University of California, Riverside. The British Library coordinates a British eighteenth-century short title catalog project in which it catalogs the remaining eighteenth-century English-language imprints that it locates. The two projects combined constitute the *Eighteenth-Century Short Title Catalogue* Project, funded entirely by the National Endowment for the Humanities.

The authority records produced from the efforts of the *Eighteenth-Century Short Title Catalogue* Project are added to the LC authorities database. The headings produced by the British Library are added to the LC file through RLIN. The British Library is linked to RLIN through a leased telecommunication line for the purpose of unifying the North American and the United Kingdom versions of the *Eighteenth-Century Short Title Catalogue* on the RLIN bibliographic record system.[7]

The American Antiquarian Society is heading the North American Imprints Program (NAIP), a project to identify and create up-to-date catalog records for United States imprints up to 1875. The headings from these records are being added to the *Eighteenth-Century Short Title Catalogue* file and to the LC authorities database through RLIN.

In addition to its regular name authority responsibilities, the National Library of Medicine (NLM) catalogs all medical CIP (cataloging in publication) materials received by LC.[8] With few exceptions, NLM is responsible for creating authority records for all medical materials, not just those it acquires. Its series authorities reflect LC policies and practices to ensure uniformity in treatment.

NACO remains a project for cooperative authority work with name headings except for the libraries at Harvard, the University of Chicago, the University of Illinois at Urbana-Champaign, GPO, and NLM. These libraries provide series authorities as a part of their work of creating full bibliographic records. The many problems in the production of series authority records have not been sufficiently resolved to extend the privilege to all NACO participants.

7. "British Library and RLG to Cooperate," *American Libraries* 16 (February 1985): 83.
8. "NACO Celebrates Tenth Anniversary," p. 28.

Series are closely akin to serials, a relationship that blurs the distinction between the two. The potential exists for libraries to interchange the identity between them even with carefully worded definitions. A distinction is important since serials and series are cataloged according to totally different principles resulting in totally different records for the same item. The lack of agreement among libraries on exactly which publications are serials and which are series could cause serious problems in an authority file with a nationwide context created cooperatively as is the LC file. It would be difficult for a computer to ferret out duplicate records for a single work when the records do not share common data elements.

Once the identity of a work has been declared a series, there are no nationally accepted principles that ensure uniformity of treatment. In the absence of such principles, local handling decisions prevail and these vary from library to library. Most such decisions are based on local needs, which, in turn, are based on a particular collection and a specific clientele.

Variations in treatment decisions could have a variety of origins. They may result from the natural characteristics of series themselves, such as the instability of their titles, the peculiarities of their sequencing elements, the analyzability of their contents, the elusiveness of their various parts, and their often non-descript titles. Variations in treatment may also result from cataloging options such as the option regarding tracing patterns or the option to collocate the work in the collection or its surrogate in the catalog.

Limiting the number of libraries to do series authority work for the nationwide authority file is a workable solution to the problems inherent in cooperatively building a series authority file. It is hoped that series authority control will be less problematic as libraries begin to adopt the policies of the nationwide authority system.

More than forty libraries—principally federal, state, university, and special—have come into the NACO project since its beginning in 1977. Their participation has greatly increased the number and variety of records in the nationwide authority file system and has given it a truly national character. The contributions of these libraries have enabled the Library of Congress to offer to the library community the largest database of quality authority records ever assembled in one system.

The procedures for a participating member of NACO to contribute to the authority file vary according to the library's access to computer technology. Some of the libraries rely on LC tools such as the *National Union Catalog* and the *Name Authorities Cumulative Microform Edition* to determine if LC has already established a particular heading. If the heading does not appear in the tools, the library establishes it and mails the data to LC for validation and inclusion into the authority file.

NACO participants with online access to LC's authorities database search it directly to determine if a particular heading has already been established. If it has not been established, the library does so and mails the data to LC for validation and inclusion into the authority file. Some of these libraries use electronic mail service (EMS) to transmit the data to LC.

The University of Chicago, Harvard University, and the University of Illinois at Urbana-Champaign have direct access to the LC bibliographic and authority files through remote terminals. The University of Illinois at Urbana-Champaign inputs authority records for its Slavic collection directly into the database without prior LC validation. The University of Chicago and Harvard University input full bibliographic records for all cataloging and corresponding authorities directly into the LC files without prior LC validation.

Communication between LC and the NACO participants is frequent and effective. They communicate by telephone, conventional or electronic mail, memos, and workshops. Participants also make onsite visits to LC and LC representatives visit the various NACO libraries.

The NACO project is one of the most valuable cooperative ventures initiated since the *National Union Catalog*. Cooperation in authority control has been most beneficial to libraries of all sizes, types, and orientations.

LINKED SYSTEMS PROJECT

The Linked Systems Project (LSP) is a national-level cooperative venture involving LC, OCLC, RLG, and WLN to provide an online communications link between heterogeneous computer systems for intersystem data exchange.[9] Work on the project began early in 1980, and LSP became operational in 1985.

LSP grew out of a need to expand cooperation and sharing among libraries as a response to continually rising costs of library operations and corresponding reductions in library budgets. The advent of *AACR2* provided an added incentive to explore means to reduce the amount of duplication of effort in libraries, especially in current cataloging and retrospective conversion activities.

The major bibliographic utilities were already facilitating cooperation and sharing among thousands of libraries. Each utility had its own operating system, database, and network of libraries. The problem was that each utility was isolated from the others and could cooperate only among its own member libraries. A method was needed to enable the utilities to communicate not just with their member libraries but also with each other. Their inability to communicate with each other was caused primarily by their dissimilar computer operating systems. This lack of communication encouraged duplication of effort and prevented such cooperative activities as data transmission and information sharing across system lines.

In order for communication to occur among dissimilar computer systems, there needed to be a facility that would provide links over which the data could

---

9. Technical aspects of LSP are beyond the scope of this description, which draws heavily on the following sources: Henriette D. Avram, "The Linked Systems Project: Its Implications for Resource Sharing," *Library Resources & Technical Services* 30 (January/March 1986): 36–46; Richard W. Boss, "Interfacing Automated Library Systems," *Library Technology Reports* 20 (September-October 1984): 632; Wayne E. Davison, "The WLN/RLG/LC Linked Systems Project," *Information Technology and Libraries* 2 (March 1983): 34–46; Ray Denenburg and Sally H. McCallum, "RLG/WLN/LC Computers Ready to Talk: Three Disparate Bibliographic Systems Will Link Up This Fall," *American Libraries* 15 (June 1984): 400–404; Sally H. McCallum, "Linked System Project Will Facilitate NACO Procedures," *Library of Congress Information Bulletin* 43 (March 5, 1984): 59–60; Council on Library Resources, *Twenty-fourth Annual Report, 1980* (Washington, D.C.: Council on Library Resources, 1980), pp. 19–25; *The Name Authority Cooperative/Name Authority File Service*, Task Force on a Name Authority File Service Bibliographic Service Development Program (Washington, D.C.: Council on Library Resources, 1984).

be transmitted. The establishment of such a communications facility required the resolution of technical problems relating to the design of message delivery and message processing systems. The result was the development of the Standard Network Interconnect (SNI), a facility that provides telecommunications links between systems to allow library applications programs on one system to exchange data with library applications programs on another system.

Problems relating to standards had to be resolved also. MARC, a standard format for machine-readable cataloging data, was already available. Protocols of application had to be developed to enable application programs running on one computer to communicate with another even when the computers were operating on incompatible system hardware and software. The result was the development of the Open Standards Interconnection (OSI), a set of computer communications standards specifically designed for the exchange of data between and among several dissimilar systems while using the same set of protocols and software for all. New systems may be added at any time without requiring new protocols or software to accommodate them.

Since the ultimate goal of LSP is to exchange bibliographic records and since the major barrier to efficient exchange of bibliographic records in machine-readable form is inconsistency in access points, the most viable solution to the problem relating to standards was to establish a mechanism in LSP to ensure their consistency. The authority application was thus chosen as the first segment to be implemented.

Other factors that supported the implementation of the authority application as the first phase of a decentralized national database were (1) the high cost and time-consuming nature of authority work, (2) the existence of a prototype for a shared authority file already in place at LC in its NACO project, and (3) consideration for the efficiency to be gained from a master authority file used by all members of the linked system without the records first having to be modified at the local level.

The master authority file maintained by NACO is the foundation for the LSP authority file system. It is mounted on the LC LSP link system. NACO participants will continue to create authority records to add to it in accordance with their NACO enlistment agreement. Those who are not members of a bibliographic utility will continue to follow their usual procedures for transmitting their authority data to LC. Since duplicates of the master authority file are loaded on the system of each of the LSP participating bibliographic utilities for use by their network libraries, those libraries that are also NACO participants will continue to create new records, update old ones, and transmit the data via the link to LC to add to the file and redistribute via the link to other LSP participants. An update is made to the master files of LSP participants at least every twenty-four hours.

When fully operational any library affiliated with any of the LSP participating bibliographic utilities will have full online access to the complete master authority records to use in its daily cataloging activities; however, only those network libraries that are also NACO members may modify or add to the file. A searcher on any of the LSP participating utilities may originate a search formulated in the search language of the system. The search is then translated into an intersystem language by the originating system and is sent to a target system. Once there the search is translated by the target system into its own query language, processed, and a response is sent to the originating system. The response may be the number of retrieved records or the actual records in MARC format. Although the response is sent in the language of the target system, it is displayed in the screen format of the user's system. The contents of the master file are also available on magnetic tape and in microform through the MARC Distribution Service.

LSP does not replace NACO but improves on it. The advantages accrued from NACO are still there; however, with LSP those advantages are expanded. The creation of authority records is still controlled by NACO libraries. The master file is immediately available for searching online to a larger number of libraries through the LSP linked bibliographic utilities. New data are transmitted to the LSP participating utilities online rather than on magnetic tape. The data in all LSP files are always current within a twenty-four-hour time frame. It is now possible to do intersystem searching for authority records that may be in an individual system's file but not in the LSP master authority file.

LSP provides a way to carry out the NACO record distribution process in a more streamlined and efficient manner. It reduces the costs in time and human resources of one of the most capital- and labor-intensive aspects of cataloging, that of verifying and establishing entry headings. NACO participants who are members of an LSP participating utility have access to up-to-date authority information before they establish a heading, which eliminates the need for LC catalogers to review for duplicates. The costly duplication of effort in authority work has, thus, been greatly reduced. The records need only to pass through machine validation for matching of headings, be added to the master authority file, and marked for distribution. The originating system is notified of approval.

If a record fails validation, it is returned to the originating library via the LSP link with the reasons for the failure. Such transactions are not documented in the master file.

In summary, LSP has brought speed and efficiency to authority work and has increased the potential for innovation in numerous areas of library work. The problems relating to data distribution between systems are no longer barriers to communication between such systems. This could mean improvements in interlibrary loan activities and union catalog production. Some futurists are even forecasting full-text transmission over computer-to-computer links.

International Level

UNIMARC

The international activity that has had the greatest impact on current trends in authority control has been the development of UNIMARC, an international standard, under the auspices of the International Federation of Library Associations and Institutions (IFLA). UNIMARC is a neutral MARC format for the international exchange of bibliographic data. It does not possess the national or cultural orientation of the various national MARC formats (e.g., CANMARC, UKMARC, USMARC) that emerged from attempts to develop a MARC format compatible with particular national cataloging practices. UNIMARC serves as an interface between dissimilar, incompatible national MARC formats.

The value of machine-readable cataloging has been demonstrated and documented. As a result, a variety of "hybrid" MARC formats has been developed to meet national needs. In the absence of efforts to coordinate international standards, the formats have taken on different national characteristics that have created barriers to the international exchange of bibliographic data.

In 1972 IFLA set up a Working Group in Content Designation to develop a MARC format into which data in the various national MARC formats could be converted. Work was completed in 1976 and the first edition of UNIMARC was published in 1977. Data converted into UNIMARC is transferrable to any other of the various MARC formats.

National libraries in foreign countries have generally assumed responsibility for updating their MARC formats to make them compatible with UNIMARC. In the United States the Library of Congress has undertaken this responsibility. In 1982 it turned its attention to the conversion of USMARC (i.e., LC MARC) into UNIMARC and the reciprocal conversion of UNIMARC into USMARC. Several problems and deficiencies in UNIMARC were identified. These were solved or rectified at LC through several changes in the content designations and other codes.[10] The success of the effort to exchange bibliographic data internationally is evident in the current undertaking at LC to convert current and prospective records for books, serials, films, maps, and music into UNIMARC.

With the major technical problems resolved, the future of UNIMARC looks bright. It could serve as the vehicle for the exchange of authority records. Access to authority records of foreign names created by nationals in the country of origin could be cost-effective in the processing of works containing those names. Thus, instead of aiming for a national authority file service, an international file should be the goal.

INTERNATIONAL FEDERATION OF LIBRARY ASSOCIATIONS AND INSTITUTIONS

Work is moving forward to make authority control an international reality. IFLA has already begun work on an authorities format that is compatible with UNIMARC. The work is being carried out by the IFLA Section on Cataloging and its Section on Technology.[11] The ideal would be a UNIMARC format for authorities complete with standardized content designators and specified data elements, along with consideration for the various scripts.

During the IFLA World Congress held in Brussels in 1977, the Steering Committee of the IFLA International Office for UBC (Universal Bibliographic Control) approved a project to establish principles for the development of authority files and procedures to facilitate the international exchange of authority information. A survey was conducted to collect data on the status, type, size, data content, maintenance, operation, and distribution of authority files kept by various national bibliographic agencies. The survey also looked at the cat-

10. Sally H. McCallum, "Using UNIMARC: Prospects and Problems" (unpublished paper presented at the IFLA General Conference in Nairobi, Kenya, August 1984).
11. Tom Delsey, "IFLA Working Group on an International Authority System: A Progress Report," *International Cataloguing* 9 (January/March 1980): 10–12.

aloging rules used and the sources for subject headings and references used in establishing headings.

From the data gathered in the survey, work proceeded on the formulation of specifications for an international authority system by identifying a set of tasks. Out of this concerted effort has come guidelines for authority control on an international level, *Guidelines for Authority and Reference Entries*.[12]

Early in 1974 at the Unesco Intergovernmental Conference on the Planning of National Overall Documentation, Library and Archives Infrastructures held in Paris, a key recommendation emerged and was confirmed: that each national bibliographic agency should assume responsibility for establishing authoritative forms of names for its country's authors, both personal and corporate.[13]

NATIONAL LIBRARY AGENCIES

The national agencies have fully supported the recommendation of the Unesco Conference. Some are further along in implementation than others. The Shared Cataloging Division at LC regularly receives machine-readable tapes from foreign sources. The United Kingdom is in the process of converting its authority records into machine-readable form acceptable for exchange with LC where the records will be made available in both UNIMARC and USMARC. The Diet Library in Japan has made some of its authority records available through its *National Diet Library Authority File for Japanese Authors, Post-Edo Era*.[14] In the mid-1970s the Canadian National Library began building an authority file by stripping headings from records exchanged from the Bibliothèque Nationale, Paris, the National Library of Australia, and the Library of Congress, and from purchased records from the *British National Bibliography*.[15] Currently, the file is being maintained as a part of the Canadian Shared Authority File (SHARAF), a shared authorities project in which the National Library of Canada sets the standards, authenticates records, and resolves conflicts.[16]

The National Library of Nigeria has succeeded in building up an authority file of Nigerian authors' names,[17] and other national agencies are taking responsibility for authorities in their respective countries.

LINKED SYSTEMS

The capabilities already exist for the creation of an international authority file system with contributions from libraries around the world and retrievable from

12. International Federation of Library Associations and Institutions. Working Group on an International Authority System. *Guidelines for Authority and Reference Entries*. London: IFLA International Programme for UBC, 1984.

13. Dorothy Anderson, *Universal Bibliographic Control: A Long Term Policy—A Plan for Action* (Munich: Verlag Dokumentation, Pullach, 1974), p. 47.

14. "Japan: Authority File for Japanese Authors," *International Cataloguing* 9 (January/March 1980): 2.

15. Edwin J. Buchinski, William L. Newman, and Mary Joan Dunn, "The National Library of Canada Authority Subsystem: Implications," *Journal of Library Automation* 10 (March 1977): 28–40.

16. Helen MacIntosh, "SHARAF: The Canadian Shared Authority File Project," *Library Resources & Technical Services* 26 (October/December 1982): 345–352.

17. Beatrice Bankole, "Problems in Establishing a Name File for Nigerian Authors," *International Cataloguing* 9 (April/June 1980): 19–20.

any library that is linked to the system. The NACO project provides a model for the decentralization of record creation. LSP demonstrates that dissimilar computer systems can be made to communicate with each other to transmit information without regard for the type of hardware or operating software. UNIMARC provides the foundation for a machine-readable record structure for international interface. With the availability of the IFLA *Guidelines* and authority files from national libraries and other agencies with which to work, an international authority control system is possible.

The architects of an international authority control system could conceivably look to national libraries to mount and maintain an LSP-type structure created in their own countries. This notion would somewhat parallel the proposal launched in the early 1970s for an IFLA/Unesco program of Universal Bibliographic Control through national bibliographies compiled and maintained by national libraries.[18] Once a national authority control system is in place, those national libraries with online access to their records could be linked with each other through LSP to form an international online authority file system. National libraries not yet computerized could be encouraged to contract with a linked library to input and maintain their authority records in the system.

Operational logistics would need to be worked out. One national library would have to be selected as the host library for the system. Some measure of consensus would be necessary as to the types of authorities to be included. Financial support would have to be shared. All of the participating national libraries would have to be committed to the success of the venture and operate respectfully as equal partners.

BARRIERS

To be truly international, any system must be prepared to overcome the geographic, language, and cultural biases that may impede its effectiveness. *AACR2* has reduced the likelihood of geographic or language biases in a quality authority control system such as LSP; however, cultural sanctity may be sacrificed in favor of cost and convenience. The work done in developing the UBC program, the International Standard Bibliographic Descriptions (ISBDs), and *AACR2* in the 1970s exposed areas of potential biases that favored Anglo-American norms. As a result there is much greater awareness today of cultural differences than during any previous period.

Purely cultural biases are difficult to overcome because they are not necessarily obvious or deliberate but rather subtle and unconscious reactions to differing patterns of behavior. Among other categories authority records control names, generally characterizing their elements as either forenames or surnames and requiring uniformity in a Western cultural sense. Some cultures do not embrace the concepts of forenames and surnames. In some cultures, names are not as decisively establishable as catalogers may like. Also in some cultures, especially those where extended families are the rule, personal names may have unique significance that defies analysis by Western criteria. To force them into

18. Anderson, *Universal Bibliographic Control*.

a Western mode is to corrupt the role of the name in relation to the person who bears it.

Concepts of titles of honor do not always coincide with Western views. Royalty and the nobility, such as the emirs and the obas of traditional West African societies, may not be recognized as such. *AACR2-88* provides direction for establishing forms of name in some non-Western cultures, but it is silent on many others.

The international considerations in *AACR2-88* came out of an era when the social climate was conducive to looking outward toward a world view. Economies were generally buoyant and resources plentiful. There were conscientious decisions made to embrace non-Western cultures. Special consideration was given to nonroman scripts and to languages with differing grammatical structures and syntax.[19]

LSP was developed to serve American libraries within an American context. It has the potential of being expanded into an international system. In an expanded form its primary goal will probably remain that of serving American libraries while secondarily helping other libraries develop their potential.

The economic environment of the 1980s, and predictably of the 1990s, is less expansive than it was in the 1970s, which reduces the extent of generous planning and sharing for the common good. There is a general tendency during times of economic decline for groups to turn their attention inward and to concern themselves more with localized activities that are convenient and cost effective. They are less inclined to become involved in activities with little or no direct benefit to them, particularly those at an international level that are likely to be one-way propositions. There are fewer incentives to go international simply to make things easier for the broader international community.

It is foreseeable that the extent of the reach of LSP, for some time to come, will be among bibliographically developed countries with similar patterns of development and with approximately the same level of sophistication and exchange compatibility. To extend beyond this range may require additional facilities to increase flexibility and simplification that may be neither cost-effective nor convenient.

In the absence of economic incentives, perhaps future advancements in technology can neutralize any barriers to international expansion and accommodate the needs of a heterogeneous group of users conveniently and at no extra cost. There is no doubt that the UNIMARC authorities format will be the development that will make extended international exchange of authority records a reality.

Summary

Automation has had a tremendous impact on libraries and how they function. The computer has introduced new techniques of accessing information and new

19. Dorothy Anderson, "An International Framework for National Bibliographic Development: Achievement and Challenge," *Library Resources & Technical Services* 30 (January/March 1986): 13–22.

needs for facilitating that access. One of the most revolutionary innovations is the online catalog. Online catalogs have opened up many avenues of access for library patrons but libraries are still seeking ways to make them more effective. With online catalogs has come the need to improve authority control.

The four major bibliographic utilities have done much to improve control over the bibliographic records in their databases. Each of them has developed its own method of authority control to ensure that the entry headings its members contribute and use are compatible with each other and with those in the LC authority file.

LC has set the standard for authority control. Its authority records represent the ideal against which other libraries measure their work. The bibliographic utilities have developed their own methods to capture the essence of LC authority control for the benefit of their members.

There are many libraries that are not members of a bibliographic utility and, therefore, do not have access to the online services available. Many do not have the technical staff to develop online catalogs and authority control systems to improve their services. Commercial vendors have found this group to be a profitable market for automated services. These vendors are learning about authority control and how to meet the needs of libraries. Some libraries find it convenient and cost-effective to contract with commercial vendors for COM catalogs and even online catalogs with authority control components.

Automation has increased the level of cooperation among libraries and library service agencies. LC has initiated some notable cooperative ventures relating to authority control. National Coordinated Cataloging Operations (NACO) is one such activity and involves more than forty libraries of various types in the creation of authority records at remote sites for a central file maintained by LC. These libraries create authority records for works they catalog and submit them to LC for validation and distribution to the general library community.

The NACO authority file serves as an important component of another cooperative venture in which LC is involved. The Linked Systems Project (LSP) involves LC, OCLC, RLIN, and WLN in a successful effort to link dissimilar computer systems, enabling them to communicate with one another. Currently RLIN and OCLC are linked to LC and to each other for the exchange of authority records. Since authority work is the most costly and labor-intensive aspect of the cataloging function, LSP has great potential for revolutionizing authority control in libraries and for developing into an international authority control system.

UNIMARC is an innovation that has increased the potential for advancing authority control in an automated environment. It serves as an interface between disparate national MARC formats and enables the international transfer of data in machine-readable form. When a special UNIMARC for authorities is developed, authority control can be standardized and exchange facilitated on an international level.

Automation has changed and continues to change the nature of library work, especially authority control. It has diminished many of the time-consuming and labor-intensive manual procedures associated with authority control. With it has come an added dimension to library services. It remains the greatest challenge facing librarians today.

Chapter 3

General Principles

This chapter covers the general principles and procedures of authority work for all categories of headings: names, series, and subjects. Specifically, the chapter defines the levels of authority control; describes the authority record, workforms, and temporary records; and discusses the nature of name, series, and subject authority work.

The chapter provides background information for chapters 4 through 8, which offer guidance for creating the physical authority record including headings, references, the sources found area, notes, and special procedures for particular categories of authorities. The MARC format for authorities is also discussed. The arrangement of the presentations follows the logical order of processes associated with authority work. The procedures detailed in chapters 9 through 13 provide guidance for creating the intellectual authority record. The resulting guide has proved satisfactory in libraries with considerable experience in authority work and is compatible with policies at the Library of Congress. These procedures may be considered the state of the art for the moment.

Nonstandard, library-specific situations, or problems unique to a particular library or group of libraries have not been considered. This includes split files and procedures for handling them. Consideration of retrospective conversion procedures is also excluded.

Some libraries organize their authority work around the particular categories of headings, such as names, series, uniform titles, or subjects. This means that work relating to a single category may be the responsibility of a particular individual. If the staff of the library is sufficiently large, an individual working with a particular category may become the expert in that category.

Other libraries organize their authority work around treatment accorded series and other related tasks. A special staff may be responsible for analyzable series only. Other staff may assume responsibility for searching bibliographic tools and documenting their findings on worksheets. Analysis of the collected data for the creation of the actual authority records may be the responsibility of yet another individual or group of individuals.

Some libraries use a combination of these methods, organizing by categories and by treatment. Others make no distinction in types of authority work—individual staff members perform whatever work needs to be done. In some situations, especially in small libraries, catalogers must do all of the authority work for the items they catalog.

Levels of Authority Control

Each library must decide on one of the two levels of authority control it will maintain to meet its needs: full or partial. A library may decide on the ideal of full authority control over every new heading entered in the catalog to ensure the integrity of the catalog and, thus, to facilitate its use; or, it may decide on partial control where a selected group of headings are chosen for control.

Factors that affect a library's decisions on the level of authority control it will maintain include:

1.   the availability of staff and other resources to do the work
2.   access to externally produced authority records
3.   level of control desired
4.   the library's control over the level of control desired
5.   the importance placed on the integrity of the catalog.

The availability of staff and other resources is cited most often as the reason for adopting a policy that calls for less than full authority control. No matter the importance placed on the integrity of the catalog or the level of control desired, adequate staff and other resources must be available to create and maintain the authority control operation. The demand for sufficient resources to support authority work should be made with the same fervor as that for descriptive and subject cataloging, reference, or personnel. Authority work should not be supported as a secondary responsibility after all other needs have been met.

Names

Libraries that decide on full authority control for names (including uniform titles) usually have access to LC name authority records either on magnetic tape, in microform, or online. They rely on the integrity of these records to ensure the integrity of their catalog. They do authority work only for those headings for which no externally produced records are available. Some of these libraries maintain their own locally produced authority records and a subset of records from the LC authority file. The libraries that do not have access to externally produced authority records do their own authority work and maintain their own authority file.

As an alternative to full authority control, a library may decide on partial authority control, which may, in practice, vary from one library to another. Some libraries may maintain an authority file of records of unique local headings that they establish themselves with the belief that LC will eventually establish all others.

The libraries that settle for control over cross references only do not maintain records of headings that do not generate cross references. For them, systematic use of authorized name headings is not a major concern. These libraries must be aware of the potential problems this policy may impose on their catalog users. Systematic use of authorized name headings is vital to the establishment of effective linkages, and ensuring effective linkages in a catalog is the principal function of authority control. Unless authority work is done on all headings, it is difficult to establish the need for linkages between some headings. Without the research that goes into authority work, it is difficult to differentiate between variant names and discrete names, to identify changed names and titles, or otherwise to define particular headings. There can be no assurance that all headings for which cross references are necessary have been identified and that cross references are, thus, under control.

The libraries that subscribe to the policy of controlling only the local name headings that they establish rely heavily on LC for all others. They do no authority work on the headings they add to their catalog if they suspect that LC can provide the heading. Some of them may temporarily establish a heading and update it later as additional information becomes available from LC. Other libraries may withhold the headings from their catalogs until such time as they are established by LC. These libraries must be aware of the immeasurable damage that can follow this level of control. User access to resources cannot be maintained at an optimal level. Also, there are costs involved in updating catalog records and in searching a less than fully controlled catalog.

Libraries that rely on LC name authority records either for full or partial control may have to modify those records for their own local use. LC records may include esoteric cross references that are irrelevant for a particular library collection or clientele. Also, because authority files are dynamic and are constantly changing, libraries must document those records from the LC file that are relevant to their collection and the modifications they have made to them. Otherwise, they may find that in time the usages in their own catalog may not correspond with those in the LC authority file used for control.

Series

A series is a group of works published separately, usually in some sequence, having, in addition to individual titles, a collective series title. It is the series title that requires some measure of authority control. The nature of authority control for series is characteristically different from that for names and uniform titles. Likewise, the nature of full and partial authority control of series is different.

Libraries that decide on full control will create an authority record for every series of which they have at least one part in their collection. To maintain control at this high level requires diligence on the part of the cataloger because of the innumerable problems associated with series, for example, the problems of defining a series and of identifying series titles. The lack of a large database of externally produced series authority records and the lack of nationally accepted guidelines for treatment make series authority control more an institutional effort than a cooperative venture.

To facilitate the maintenance of a full level of control for series, some libraries conscientiously relate the practices of LC, as interpreted from LC cataloging copy, to their own local needs. Other libraries maintaining a full level of control may merely follow the decisions made by LC, as interpreted from LC cataloging copy, without making any attempt to relate those decisions to their own needs. There is no doubt that LC greatly influences the practices of series authority control in most libraries.

Libraries follow a wide variety of practices in maintaining partial series authority control. Some libraries make series authority records only for numbered series or for those with references. Others limit authority records to those series titles that are traced. Still others have policies relating to omissions such as not making authority records for series titles that contain the name of the publisher, the idea being that publishers' series are not generally sought by catalog users and will not be traced in the catalog. Such standing decisions, therefore, need not be documented on an authority record.

All of the above-mentioned practices and other similar ones may save time and effort on the part of a library at the moment but they may hinder its work in the future. Without an authority record for every series title associated with some work in the library collection, there is no way for the library to be sure if a particular series title is in the collection but the library made a conscious decision to disregard it as worthy of an authority record or inclusion as an access point in the public catalog, or if the library has never acquired any part of it. It is as important for the library to keep track of series and their changing titles and relationships as it is to keep track of changes in names.

Subjects

The *Library of Congress Subject Headings*[1] (LCSH) and the *Sears List of Subject Headings*[2] are the prime sources of subject headings used in library catalogs in the United States and in several other parts of the world. These sources are often considered, like the LC name authority file, as national-level subject authority files from which libraries can cull their own local file; however, neither one can be considered the equivalent of the LC name authority file because each of them has major omissions of entire categories of headings.

Libraries follow a variety of practices in attempting to control their subject files. Unfortunately, many other libraries neglect this vital aspect of authority control and make little or no attempt to ensure the integrity of their files.

To maintain the ideal of full control, an authority record must be made for every subject heading entered in the public catalog, whether it is formulated according to guidelines, is the result of a pattern heading, or is a representative of one of the categories omitted from the source list. As old terms and references are changed, deleted, or modified, or as new terms are added, the affected subject headings and references must reflect these changes. Anything less cannot be considered full authority control.

Full authority control is best maintained through eternal vigilance of additions and changes made by the central agency in charge of the source list used. For example, if the LCSH is used, all relevant updates from the *Weekly List*, the quarterly microform version of LCSH, the annual cumulative edition, and

1. Library of Congress. Subject Cataloging Division, *Library of Congress Subject Headings*. 11th (1988)–   ed. (Washington, D.C.: Library of Congress, 1988–   ).
2. *Sears List of Subject Headings*, edited by Barbara Westby. 13th ed. (New York: H. W. Wilson, 1986).

the LCSH in machine-readable form[3] are incorporated in the authority file as evidence of a controlled public catalog. All new subject headings assigned during original cataloging or culled from MARC bibliographic records are validated against these sources and added to the authority file. Those headings that cannot be located in the sources are validated against the appropriate guidelines for the formulation of subject headings and incorporated into the authority file. It is a labor-intensive process but one of vital importance to the maintenance of integrity in the subject catalog.

Many libraries exercise only partial control over their subject catalog. They maintain authority control only over those subject headings that actually appear in the source list used. Most users of the *Sears* list who attempt subject authority control fall in this category. They make check marks in their source list to indicate those subject headings and references that they have used in their catalog. They also may write in the terms that they have added to the list. Some other libraries create authority records for all new headings but fail to make the necessary additions and changes to old records unless a serious conflict is noted in the public catalog at the time a new heading is being entered.

Those libraries exercising either partial or no subject authority control often do so to reduce costs. Authority control is a costly library activity but it is even more costly not to have it. Validation of many new subject headings becomes a professional task instead of one that can be performed by copy catalogers; otherwise, the efficiency of the cataloging process is reduced as well as the integrity of the subject catalog. An unnecessary hardship is placed on every user who attempts to search the subject catalog. The level of authority control maintained for subjects is reflected in the ease with which users are able to exploit the resources of the library through the subject catalog.

The Authority Record

Authority records may be made for name headings (including uniform titles, and personal and corporate names), series, and subjects with each category serving a different function in the bibliographic organization process. Name authorities establish choices and forms of names; series authorities establish the existence of a series, its title, and the treatment of its parts; subject authorities document use of particular subject headings in the public catalog. Each category of authority record requires a different set of information to control the data assigned to it.

There is no widely used set of national standards for format or data contents of authority records. The MARC format is the standard used or emulated most frequently in automated systems. Either these systems use the MARC format or they adopt a format with fields and subfields that are comparable to those in MARC. Although variations do exist in the format for authorities in various automated systems, the MARC authorities format is emerging as the standard

3. These Library of Congress resources are described in detail in "Sources of Subject Headings" in chapter 14.

that eventually may be used in all media. The format or visual physical display of data in manual files still varies widely from library to library. Fortunately, in these files, with their localized restricted use, the format does not affect the quality of the system as the data contents do.

The data contents required by the MARC authorities are the standard against which quality control is measured in most automated systems. Manual systems are yet to display any measure of uniformity in data contents, particularly in regard to extensiveness and formality.

In either an automated or a manual authority control system, the essential components of an authority record include an authorized heading (a name, or uniform title, a series title, or a subject heading), cross references (if the heading has generated cross references), and sources that justify the heading and its corresponding cross references (for names and series authority records). Basic principles relating to these components follow. Other information relevant to a specific category of record will be included in later discussions of the specific category.

Workforms and Temporary Records

Most libraries use some sort of workform for the preliminary authority work. Workforms are useful instruments for collecting data relevant to a particular heading. They provide a systematic procedure for collecting a structured set of data needed for controlling headings. They ensure that all relevant data are researched, collected, or otherwise documented for use in the building of an authority file. In situations where several people share the responsibility for authority work, workforms are an indispensable medium of communication that saves time and prevents duplication of effort.

Some workforms are simple check slips showing tasks performed; others are rather elaborate. Some libraries may not have a need for workforms at all because of the simplicity of data they maintain in their authority file. Others dispense with the use of workforms if they have access to the LC authority file and can locate the desired authority records. They make printouts of the authority records from which to work since the printouts provide the information that would normally be found on a workform. Libraries that have a need for workforms for authority work usually design their own to meet local needs. The source of authority data and the level of control generally determine the type of workform a library uses. New incoming headings that cannot be matched with existing headings already in the file are the ones for which authority work is done. Temporary records are created from a workform for these new headings and placed in the authority file until permanent records are on file. These brief records alert catalogers to the fact that decisions have already been made about a particular entry and what those decisions are. It keeps the authority file current so that work on any entry may proceed uniformly and without delay or duplication.

The basic contents of the temporary records are generally the same for manual and online files with a few exceptions. They all have space for new headings. Temporary records for online files may also have control numbers, MARC tags, indicators, and subfield codes for machine manipulation.

Name Authority Work

An authority record is needed for every name that is used as an access point to a bibliographic record. The bibliographic record may be for any type of material: serials, nonbook materials, or monographs. An authority record for a name is created only once, that is, at the time a name has been identified as new to the public catalog, no matter how frequently the same name reappears as an access point on subsequent bibliographic records. At each subsequent appearance of the name, it is checked against the authority file for verification that the name is new to the catalog. The presence of a record in the authority file negates the name as being new; therefore, no new authority record is created for it. Sometimes, between the first and a subsequent appearance of a name as an access point on a bibliographic record, new information about the name may be discovered. Sometimes the newly cataloged item may be the source of new information that may generate a cross reference to be added to the authority record for the established heading or may even cause a change in the choice or the form of the authorized name.

Name headings established for use in a public catalog may be for personal authors or corporate bodies, which include conferences and geographic entities. The name may appear in the bibliographic record as the main entry or an added entry. The type of access point—whether main entry or added entry—is insignificant in determining whether or not to make an authority record or the extent of the authority work to be done. The only criterion that determines whether to create an authority record is the newness of the name in the public catalog.

If a name appears as an access point on a newly created bibliographic record and it has not appeared previously on any other bibliographic record that is already in the public catalog, then an authority record must be created for the new name. The authority record will include the authorized form of the name, any cross references that the name may have generated, and the sources that justify the authorized name and its corresponding cross references. If a full level of authority control is being maintained, every entry heading in the public catalog must have a corresponding authority record whether the access point generates references or not. There will be many authority records in the authority file without any cross references.

Series Authority Work

Series vary widely in their importance as an intellectual unit. A library may be collecting in the subject of the series and the items in the series together may provide a thorough, unified treatment of that subject. On the other hand, the items in the series may have only slight importance to the library as a unit but individually each work may add significantly to the strength of a collection in a particular subject area. Sometimes a library may wish to retain items in a series together as a unit as well as to relate the individual parts to their specific subject areas.

There are no standard criteria for defining series nor are there national standards for organizing them. The works that some people consider a series, others may consider a set or even a serial. Still, others may consider them distinct, separate monographs. Before attempting to organize series, the cataloger must make some basic decisions.

At best, decisions about how to handle series are educated guesses. Such decisions are usually made from the first number published or the first number received by the library—the issue with the least information about the characteristics of the series as a whole. Because of the ambiguities and uncertainties in working with series, a library must make many decisions about the ones it acquires. The documentation of these decisions constitutes a series authority file. It is the authority file that ensures consistency in the execution of the decisions made and uniform treatment of the various units in the series.

A series authority record is created for every series statement that appears in a bibliographic record. It does not matter whether the series is traced or not traced or whether the items in the series are classified as a collection or as separates.

Each time a series statement is added to a bibliographic record it should be verified in the series authority file to determine if the series is new to the library and, if not, what decisions have already been made about its treatment. During the cataloging process, the cataloger determines the validity of a new series statement and how works in the new series are to be handled. These decisions are binding on all future items published in the series and, therefore, are preserved in the form of an authority record to ensure that all parts of the series receive the same treatment.

If a check of the authority file reveals a record for a given series, then the cataloger does not have to make new decisions but is obligated to follow whatever decisions are documented there. The decision will usually be one of the following:

1. Consider the phrase as a pseudo-series (i.e., a phrase-like series without the full status of a series worthy of appearing in the series area of a bibliographic record).
2. Catalog and classify as a collection and do not analyze.
3. Catalog and classify as a collection and analyze partially.
4. Catalog and classify as a collection and analyze fully.
5. Catalog and classify each item as a separate and do not trace the series.
6. Catalog and classify each item as a separate and trace the series.

If the new series statement is not already in the authority file, then a decision will have to be made and a new authority record created.

It is impossible to predict every possible search a user will make in a catalog; therefore, every identifiable series could possibly be a useful access point. In any case, authority records should be made for every identifiable series title to ensure proper collocation and linkages. In manual files compromises must be made in providing adequate access while controlling the size of the catalog. In online catalogs size is no problem. In some it is possible to search all key words in any field of a bibliographic record, including the series field.

Subject Authority Work

The physical and intellectual processes of subject authority work are completely different from those of names or series. The basic principles of heading and reference formulation are not as well established for subjects as they are for names. There is no code comparable to *AACR2-88* for subject headings. The facts that names have a code of rules rather than guidelines and are frequently established locally as opposed to being predetermined contribute significantly to the extent of familiarity with the principles and the resulting consistency in the processes associated with name headings.

Working with subject headings is principally an intellectual activity. The subject content of the work being cataloged must first be determined. Once the subject concept has been ascertained, it is summarized into a concise subject concept string that is then matched against the vocabulary of a source list of subject headings to attest to its legality and appropriateness. The subject heading is assigned as an access point in the public catalog to that particular work and to all other works in the collection on that particular subject. Most libraries routinely use LCSH or the *Sears List of Subject Headings* as the source of their subject headings.

Subject headings on MARC bibliographic records and from other external sources are validated before the bibliographic records are added to the public catalog. Each subject heading from each bibliographic record is checked in the local subject authority file to determine whether it has already been used. If a matching subject heading appears in the local subject authority file, no further authority work is necessary and the bibliographic record is prepared for the public catalog. If there is no matching subject heading in the local authority file, the subject heading is considered new to the file and authority work must be done before the term is eligible to be added to the files. The term is checked in the source list for a matching heading. An exact match validates the heading and an authority record is created for it for inclusion in the local authority file.

New subject headings that cannot be exactly matched must then be reviewed in consideration of the exclusion policies of the source list. For example, if LCSH is being used, a number of different categories of subject headings may be valid headings but do not appear in the printed list. These include such categories as name headings for persons (unless used as a pattern or unless a subdivision must be printed), corporate bodies and jurisdictions (unless used as a pattern or example, or unless a subdivision must be printed); uniform titles; headings with free-floating single and multiple subdivisions (unless needed for use as a reference to another heading, or followed by a non-free-floating subdivision); free-floating phrase headings; headings formulated from pattern headings; music headings for instrumental chamber music not entered under musical form; and music headings for musical forms that have qualifiers for instrumental medium.[4] It is the responsibility of the local library to keep track of the subject headings and the reference structures used at the local level in order for consistency to prevail in the public catalog.

If the new headings are valid, nonprinted subject headings formulated according to the guidelines of the source list, authority records are created for the local authority file. The goal is to have an *exact* match in the authority file of every subject heading in the public catalog along with its corresponding references.

The authority file, however, does not ensure that the subject headings are appropriately applied. Only the cataloger can do that. If a subject heading misrepresents the subject concept of the work, is applied at an inappropriate level of specificity, or is incorrectly used, subject headings work must be done to correct the errors but the work may not involve subject authority work.

The authority record includes the valid subject headings, the scope note (if it is the policy of the library), and any references. In June 1988, LCSH replaced its former *sa*, *x*, and *xx* reference notations with the more familiar *BT*, *NT*, *RT*, and *UF* notations to display the hierarchical array of broader and narrower terms and the terms that are related but not in a logical context. By knowing the logical relationships between terms, the cataloger can be more precise in collocating materials on the same subjects under a common subject heading. Users can better predict useful search strategies and can browse the public catalog in a given subject area more effectively. It is, therefore, as important for the reference structure to be effectively controlled as it is for the subject heading itself.

Another important aspect of subject authority work involves file maintenance—the activities associated with keeping old headings and their references up-to-date. Users of the *Sears* list update their file whenever there is a new edition. Those who use check marks in their source list must copy the check marks from the old to the new edition. They must then make note of all changes made in the new edition in order to make adjustments in the public catalog.

Users of LCSH have a more formidable task to perform. Their ultimate goal is to create authority records that are up-to-date and compatible with those at LC. The LC *Weekly Lists* and the quarterly microform edition of LCSH are sources of LC subject headings updates. The additions and changes in these sources must be noted, incorporated into the authority file, and reflected in the public catalog.

Sometimes the noted adjustment affects only one authority record. A typographical error may be corrected, the working of a scope note may be modified, or other such details. This type of case-by-case file maintenance is important but does not require as much time or skill as when the adjustment affects groups of records because of changes LC has made in its files. It is important for the local authority file to be current and consistent with the source list of which it is a subset.

Now that the LCSH file is in machine-readable form and available through the bibliographic utilities and on magnetic tape by subscription (MDS—Subject

4. Lois Mai Chan, *Library of Congress Subject Headings: Principles and Application*, 2nd ed. (Littleton, Colo.: Libraries Unlimited, 1986), p. 173.

Authorities)[5], libraries can use it to build their own local online file. Access to a local online authority file linked to the master LC file can greatly facilitate the validation process and simplify file maintenance.

In an online environment where the authority file is linked in a monitoring mode to the bibliographic file, adjustments to groups of records are easy to make. It becomes a simple matter to maintain compatibility between the authority file and the public catalog. A change made to an affected heading or reference in the authority file results in global changes to all affected headings in the bibliographic file.

There are few similarities between name and subject authority files. Subject authority files experience less growth activity than do those for names. Hundreds of books are written on the same subject and, thus, may generate a single subject heading and a single record in the authority file. On the other hand, new names are frequently encountered during the cataloging process since the average author, each generating an authority record, writes approximately two books in a lifetime.

In spite of the slow growth rate, subject authority files are much more dynamic than name files. Their vocabulary is drawn from natural language and language is dynamic. Words take on new meanings. Old terms are deleted. New concepts generated from new knowledge and new discoveries are introduced and get new names. New relationships are forged between existing terms and new ones. Change in the subject file is perennial.

5. For a description of MDS—Subject Authorities, see "Sources of Subject Headings" in chapter 14.

Chapter 4

The Heading

Headings in the catalog are access points to bibliographic information. Authorized headings are determined by the cataloger during the cataloging process and constitute the principal information in the authority record. In manual authority files, the authorized heading occupies the first line of the record and is the element that determines the filing order of entries. In online files the authorized heading is the most important variable field in the record. A heading may be a name, a uniform title, or a subject. Headings perform an assembling function in the catalog by bringing together all the works of an author, all the editions or manifestations of a work, or all the works on a given subject.

Collocation

Collocation is one of the basic functions of a catalog as set forth in Cutter's *Objects*. Authorized headings are the principal mechanism of collocation associated with catalog construction. Collocation is the process of gathering related items together through some natural or controlled mechanism. A natural mechanism is a heading that is structured in the same form as it appears in a work. A controlled mechanism is an artificially structured heading formulated according to prescribed principles to represent precisely the choices and forms of the name of a person, the title of a work, or a subject concept.

Works by an author whose name varies in form or who is known by more than one name can be collocated by using a controlled mechanism to identify and assemble all of the different names and forms of name. Generally, only one of the names that belong to the individual and only one form of that name can be established in an *AACR2-88* catalog. (There are a few exceptions that will be discussed in chapter 10.) In manual catalogs it is important for headings to be authorized (i.e., always transcribed in a uniform manner according to a set of standards such as *AACR2-88* or a subject headings list) so that collocation can take place under one form of one heading.

Authorized headings are also important in online catalogs. Depending on the particular catalog, it may not always be necessary to select one form of the heading as the access point. Variant headings may be linked to each other in such a way that the computer is able to bring them together during the searching process without human intervention. This means that the linkage is transparent to the user. The user does not need to search for a unique access point because

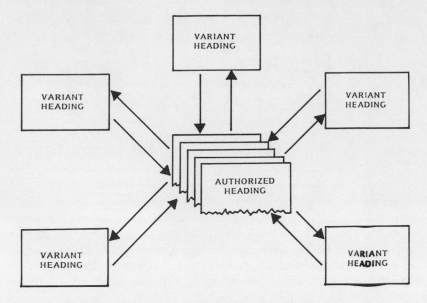

Fig. 1. Uniform and variant headings as access points

the computer makes the linkages. In manual catalogs variant headings must also be linked but the connections are made manually by the user.

Variant headings are all the different names or forms of name that may be used interchangeably. Figures 1 and 2 illustrate the use of various access points in public catalogs. Some catalogs may require one authorized uniform heading as the access point. Variant headings are linked individually to the authorized uniform heading where all bibliographic records reside. At each variant heading there may be an instruction that directs the user to the uniform heading but bibliographic records are retrievable only through the authorized heading. This configuration of authorized uniform headings allows only one choice and one form. Some catalogs require authorized uniform headings as access points but the configuration allows access through each of the variant headings. In figure 1 all records reside with the authorized heading but are retrievable through each of the variant headings. This configuration works well in an online system; however, it would make for a very bulky manual file since all bibliographic records would have to be duplicated at each variant heading.

Figure 2 shows the possibility of searches under a variant heading that retrieves all records. There is no authorized heading for all records. Records are collocated under the term used in the search. This can be done only in an online environment but not all online catalogs have this capability. This configuration is not supported by *AACR2-88* and, therefore, is not widely used.

The procedures discussed in this book require an authorized heading for collocation as is the current practice in most libraries and information centers. Transition to a configuration that does not require an authorized heading is slow in coming because of the changes that must occur in computer programs rather than in the basic principles of authority control.

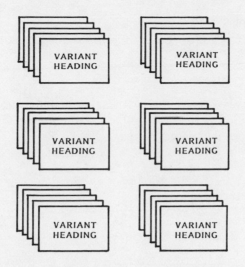

Fig. 2. No uniform heading required as access point

Format

The transcription and display of the authorized heading in the authority record should duplicate the heading exactly as it is used on bibliographic records in the public catalog. This means that capitalization, punctuation, and the content of the heading should be identical wherever the authorized form appears, whether on bibliographic records, in references, or on authority records.

Names

The following prescription is recommended for formatting a name heading of an authority record. If the content of the authorized heading is too long for one line and must be continued onto the next line, every line after the first should follow an inverse paragraph indention for ease of reading. Three spaces (i.e., beginning on the fourth space) are sufficient. For the sake of uniformity a library may wish to use the same spacing that it uses when continuing a main entry heading on a bibliographic record. There is nothing sacred about an inverse indention of three or six spaces. (Of course, catalogers do seem to like the "rule of three.") It is important, however, to be uniform in whatever spacing is chosen as standard for the library. Again, for the sake of uniformity, illustrations in this manual will reflect a three-space inverse indention for name headings. Headings should end with a period unless another mark of punctuation is present.

The examples that follow reflect the format described above.

Manual:

```
    Mount, L.E. (Laurence Edward), 1923-
```

MARC:

```
    100 10 ≠a Mount, L.E. (Laurence Edward), ≠d
       1923-
```

Bibliographic record:

```
Mount, L.E. (Laurence Edward), 1923-
```

Uniform Titles

A uniform title entered under a name heading is transcribed under the name indenting six spaces. Continuations of the title onto succeeding lines should be indented evenly with the preceding line.

Pattern:

```
_____,  _____  _____.

heading


      _____

      uniform title


      _____
```

Example of authority records for uniform titles:

Manual:

```
Dickens, Charles.
      [Martin Chuzzlewit]
```

MARC:

```
100 10  ≠a Dickens, Charles.  ≠t Martin
   Chuzzlewit
```

Bibliographic record:

```
Dickens, Charles.
   [Martin Chuzzlewit]
   The life and adventures of Martin Chuzzlewit
[ ... ]
```

As always, a period ends the name heading. Periods are not placed at the end of the reference unless it ends with an abbreviation. A uniform title on an authority record is not enclosed in brackets. Long uniform titles may be abridged by using ellipsis (...).

Series

Unlike headings for name authority records, authorized headings for series authority records are always titles. Series may be compared to a multivolume set or serial for cataloging purposes in that they all are published in parts. The principal difference lies in the way the item is cataloged. A series statement on a bibliographic record should be conceptualized as representing the title of a multivolume work of which the individual item is a part. The presence of a series statement indicates recognition of the existence of a series for which authority work must be done. Analyzed sets are considered provisional series for authority control purposes.

According to *AACR2-88*, some works will have a personal or corporate author main entry heading while others will be entered directly under title. Series with personal or corporate name headings are rare. When entry is under a name heading, it is described as an indirect entry. The vast majority of series entries are directly under title. When entry is under title, it is described as a direct entry.

Titles in direct entries are always considered as uniform titles. Uniform titles for series are considered for authority control under the guidelines for series because of the additional information required for controlling them. Although the series authority uniform title is different from a name authority uniform title, the rules for uniform titles in *AACR2-88* apply to both when applicable, except that brackets are not used even for an indirect entry under a name heading. With series uniform titles, the initial articles are always omitted in direct entries.

> Examples:
>
> Series statements with initial articles (see figure 3)
>
> Authorized headings:
> ```
> Current research topics publication
> ```
> ```
> Annotated secondary bibliography series on
>     English literature in transition, 1880–1920
> ```
> ```
> Sources of history, studies in the uses of
>     historical evidence
> ```

The name element of a series entry heading, usually in the form of a qualifier, must be established separately and a name authority record created before it can be used as an element of a series entry. If the name has already been established and is already in the authority file, the form established there must be used in the series entry.

Direct entries that are too long for one line are indented three spaces at the next line in an inverse paragraph format.

> Pattern:
>
> ```
> direct entry under title
> ```
> ```
> continuation of the title
> ```
>
> Example:
>
> ```
> Occasional paper series (Research and
>     Management Forum (P.) Ltd.)
> ```

In those rare cases when a series is entered indirectly under the name of a person or a corporate body, the series title is transcribed on the next line folix, 96 p. ; 28 cm. — (A Current research topics publication)

vii, 411 p. ; 24 cm. — (An Annotated secondary bibliography series on English literature in transition, 1880-1920)

xv, 342 p. ; 23 cm. — (The Sources of history, studies in the uses of historical evidence)   GB***

Fig. 3. Series statements with initial articles

lowing the name entry element. An inverse paragraph indention of six spaces is used. If the title is too long for one line, it is continued onto the next line beginning evenly with the preceding line.

Pattern:

```
name entry element
    series title
    continuation of the title
```

Example:

```
Biology Colloquium (Oregon State University)
    Annual Biology Colloquium proceedings
```

PUNCTUATION

A period separates a name element from the series title unless the name ends with another mark of punctuation such as a hyphen or parenthesis. No punctuation is used at the end of the title if it is an indirect entry unless the title ends with an abbreviation. On the other hand, a period is used at the end of the title if it is a direct entry.

Sometimes series titles are exceptionally long. In such cases they may be abridged in the same way titles in bibliographic records are. At least the first five words should be retained and ellipsis, preceded by a space, used.

CAPITALIZATION

The standard rules for capitalization in bibliographic descriptions apply to series authority headings. This means that only first words of titles and proper names are capitalized.

Subjects

Libraries generally use subject headings from a predetermined master subject authority system such as the Library of Congress, *Sears*, or Medical Subject Headings (MeSH). These systems may be accessible in print form, microform, or online. The Library of Congress subject headings are available in all three formats. Libraries seldom, if ever, create original subject headings for their libraries or for the master system of which their subject authority file is a subset.

Libraries can document the format of the subject headings they have used by one of three methods: (1) in the subject headings list itself (book format), (2) on cards, or (3) online. Two frequently used manual authority control systems maintained at the local level as a subset of the LC system are described below: the book format maintained in the subject headings list itself and a file on cards. (For a description of subject authorities in the MARC format, see chapter 8.)

BOOK FORMAT

Some libraries use the subject headings list as their subject authority file. The discussion that follows details the procedure for maintaining an authority file in such a format.

For this illustration it is assumed that the term *beverages* has just been assigned to a bibliographic record for a book about all kinds of beverages. This is the first use of the term in the public catalog. The term has been located in its alphabetical place in the subject headings list (see figure 4). A check mark is placed in front of the term to show that it is now in the public catalog as an established subject heading. Under the heading BEVERAGES is one *use for* reference DRINKS signified by the symbol *UF*. This means that in the subject headings list BEVERAGES and DRINKS are synonyms. With synonyms only one term is permitted in the list as an authorized subject heading. All of the other terms become *use for* references. Here BEVERAGES is the authorized heading and DRINKS is the *use for* reference.

To assist users who may choose *drinks* as a search term, the *use for* reference DRINKS is checked to signify that the following reference has been added to the public catalog:

DRINKS

see

BEVERAGES

The term *drinks* is located in its alphabetical place in the subject headings list and a check mark is placed in front of it to show that it is now in the public catalog.

Beverage processing machinery industry
  (May Subd Geog)
Beverage processing plants
  (May Subd Geog)
  BT Food processing plants
  NT Breweries
      Distilleries
      Milk plants
      Wineries
  — Equipment and supplies
      NT Beverage processing machinery
✓Beverages
      [RM238-RM257 (Therapeutics)]
      [TP500-TP659 (Technology)]
      [TX815-TX817 (Home economics)]
      [TX951 (Bartenders' manuals)]
  UF✓Drinks
  BT✓Diet
      ✓Food
  SA names of beverages, e.g. Cocoa,
      Coffee, Tea
  NT Alcoholic beverages
      Carbonated beverages
      Coasters (for drinks)
      Indians of North America—Beverages
      Lemonade
      Mineral waters
      Soft drink industry
  — Advertising
      USE Advertising—Beverages
  — Law and legislation (May Subd Geog)
      NT Liquor laws
  — Microbiology (May Subd Geog)
  — Packaging
      BT Bottling
  — Taxation (May Subd Geog)
Beveridge family (Not Subd Geog)
Beverley family
  USE Beverly family
Beverly family (Not Subd Geog)
  UF Beaverley family
      Beaverly family
      Bevely family
      Beverley family
      Bevilley family
      Bevilly family

Diesel motor industry (May Subd Geog)
Diesel oil
  USE Diesel fuels
Dieselization of railroads
  USE Railroads—Dieselization
Diess family
  USE Deis family
Diet (May Subd Geog)
      [RA784 (Personal health)]
      [TX551-TX560 (Food values)]
  Here are entered works on the food and drink
  regularly consumed by an individual or group of peo-
  ple. Works on the sum of the physiological processes
  involved in the assimilation and utilization of nutri-
  ents for proper body functioning and health are en-
  tered under Nutrition. The latter heading may be
  subdivided by place to indicate the nutritional status
  of a group of people in the place.
  BT Health
  RT Food
      Food habits
      Nutrition
  NT Animal food
      Astrology and diet
      ✓Beverages
      Black Muslims—Dietary laws
      Fasting
      Food, Dietetic
      Food, Raw
      Gastronomy
      High-carbohydrate diet
      Jains—Dietary laws
      Jews—Dietary laws
      Menus
      Monasticism and religious orders—
        Dietary rules
      Monasticism and religious orders,
        Buddhist—Dietary rules
      Muslims—Dietary laws
      Pork-free diet
      Reducing diets
      Vegetarianism
  — Adverse effects
      USE Nutritionally induced diseases
  — Therapeutic use
      USE Diet therapy
Diet, Chemically defined

Drinking water, Bottled (May Subd Geog)
  UF Bottled drinking water
      Bottled water
      Water, Bottled drinking
  BT Drinking water
  — Law and legislation (May Subd Geog)
      BT Public health laws
Drinking water standards
  USE Drinking water—Standards
✓Drinks
  USE Beverages
      Liquors
Drino
      [QL537.T28]
  BT Tachinidae
  NT Drino lota

Fonts, Romanesque (May Subd Geog)
  UF Romanesque fonts
Fonts baptismaux de Liège
  USE Renier, de Huy, d. 1150. Liège font
Food
      [GT2860 (Manners and customs)]
      [HD9000-HD9490 (Trade)]
      [QH521 (Biology)]
      [RA601-RA602 (Public health)]
      [RM214-RM261 (Diet)]
      [TP370-TP465 (Chemical technology)]
      [TX341-TX641 (Home economics)]
  UF Foods
  BT Digestion
      Dinners and dining
      Home economics
      Table
  RT Cookery
      Diet
      Dietaries
      Gastronomy
      Nutrition
  SA subdivision Food under subjects, e.g.
      Birds—Food; Indians—Food; also
      headings beginning with the word
      Food; and particular foods and
      beverages, e.g. Bread, Milk
  NT Acorns as food
      Agar as food
      Animal food
      Animals—Food
      Aquatic plants as food
      Baby foods
      Bantus—Food
      ✓Beverages
      Cassava as food
      Cereals as food
      Coloring matter in food
      Condiments
      Convenience foods

Fig. 4. The subject heading BEVERAGES from *LCSH*

There are two *broader term* references under the subject heading BEVERAGES:

    DIET

    FOOD

Each one of the terms is an established subject heading in its own right and
each is hierarchically broader in meaning than the term *beverages*. A check mark
is placed in front of the terms *diet* and *food* under BEVERAGES to signify that
the following references appear in the public catalog to assist users who may
search under the broad term:

        DIET

          see also

        BEVERAGES

```
FOOD
        see also
BEVERAGES
```

The terms *diet* and *food* are then located in their alphabetical places in the subject headings list. Under both terms, *beverages* appears in a list of *narrower term* references. A check mark is placed in front of the terms *diet* and *food* at their proper alphabetical places in the list and in front of *beverages* as the *narrower term* under both *diet* and *food* to signify that the references appear in the public catalog.

The procedure described above is repeated for each new term added to the public catalog.

THE CARD FILE FORMAT

In a card file system the subject headings are maintained on three-by-five–inch cards or on a microcomputer. Software programs are available to make the computerized system functional. There is no standard format for the records; however, certain minimum information should be included:

1. the established heading
2. all references
   a. use for
   b. broader terms
   c. narrower terms
   d. related terms
   e. general

Other useful information includes:

1. a symbol to indicate that the heading may be subdivided geographically
2. the cataloger's initials
3. distribution codes if multiple catalogs are involved
4. edition of the subject heading list
5. the date that the record was created

A workable set of format specifications is set forth below. The heading of the record should be typed in lowercase with only the first letter of the heading, an inversion, or a subdivision capitalized. If a second line is needed to complete the heading, it should begin eight spaces under the heading being established. A period is not placed at the end of the heading.

The references (UF, BT, RT, and NT) should be recorded as they appear in the authorized list of subject headings (i.e., in alphabetical order). The designation UF, BT, RT, or NT that begins a reference should be indented two spaces under the subject heading being established. If more than one line is needed for a reference, the second line should be indented two additional spaces so that the beginning and end of each reference is clear. There should be no blank spaces between the lines of reference.

Pattern:

```
Subject heading_____
          _____
   UF _____
          _____
   BT _____
   RT _____
   NT _____
```

Authority record:

```
Beginning
   UF Commencement
   BT Cosmology
   RT Creation
      Space and time
   NT Birth (Philosophy)
      Causation
```

The same punctuation, capitalization, and abbreviation patterns that are used in the list of subject headings should be used in the formatting of authority records for the local library.

The format discussed above is meant not to set a standard but to suggest a possibility. A library generally determines its own design and procedures for dealing with the physical aspects of authority records.

ADVANTAGES AND DISADVANTAGES

There are advantages and disadvantages to both file formats. The major disadvantages of maintaining control of subject headings in the subject headings list itself are:

1. With the supplements and *Weekly Lists*, it is very difficult to view the total file as a unit. With a one-volume list such as *Sears*, this would not be a problem.
2. It is difficult to know in which of the supplements of *LCSH* a particular subject heading is located.
3. It is time consuming to transfer all of the check marks to a new edition when one is published.

The major advantage is that it is easy to check off a subject heading and its references in the subject headings list as they are used.

The book system is workable only in small operations. The *Sears List of Subject Headings* in its one-volume form is better suited for this system than is *LCSH*. Also, with a small collection to control, the number of check marks to be transferred to a new edition would not be such a time-consuming task as it would be for medium-sized or large collections.

When deciding between the two formats, libraries that use *LCSH* probably would benefit more from a subject authority system on cards than from the book system. The major disadvantage of the card file system is the time involved in preparing the cards and filing them to keep the system current. It would be simpler to maintain such data in a computer file. To serve the purpose for which it is designed, an authority file *must* be kept current.

The advantage of having an authority system far outweighs the disadvantage of maintaining one on cards as noted above. Cards are easy to manipulate. Computer databases are easy to access. Information may be changed without difficulty. New headings can be easily inserted, and outdated ones may be removed. New supplements and editions do not create an unusual burden of tranferring data from one source to another.

As in most library operations, the size of the collection and the amount of resources available will affect the type of system a library chooses to maintain. A commitment to effective subject authority control will ensure that the best possible system will be maintained for any given library.

Chapter 5

References

The backbone of authority control is the system of cross references that makes collocation possible. A reference tells the user that the information sought does not reside with the unused heading and directs the user to the authorized, established heading. The reference may also suggest that additional information may be found elsewhere in the catalog. The presence of references is documented on authority records. On the authority record the reference consists of the information from which the searcher will be directed. The reference itself consists of the term *from* which a user is directed, a referral statement, and the heading *to* which the user is directed.

The Referral Statement

Of the three parts of a reference, the referral statement is the most unique. A referral statement is that part of a cross reference that states the action to be taken. It may be a simple, standard text statement or it may be complex and cataloger generated. A standard referral statement consists of the term *see* or *see also*. In a manual authority file the letter *x* signifies a *see* statement and *xx* a *see also* statement. In an online environment field numbers (or tags) and other codes identify cross references and the referral statement. (A detailed discussion of codes in the MARC format appears in chapter 8.)

A reference may be too complex to have a referral statement that can be standardized into a simple *see* or *see also* statement. Subject headings also have a unique reference structure. References that provide additional information or that explain usually fall into this category. The cataloger has to phrase each reference referral statement on a case-by-case basis. The reference may refer to one heading or to several.

Types of References

References fall into four broad categories:

1. see references
2. see also references
3. information references
4. explanatory references

Subject headings require six categories:

1. use
2. use for (UF)
3. see also from broader terms (BT)
4. see also narrower terms (NT)
5. see also related terms (RT)
6. general references (SA)

In subject authority work, references serve different functions from those in other authorities. Because of these differences, references used in subject authorities will be discussed following a general discussion of the four broad categories listed above.

General Categories

SEE REFERENCES
See references direct the user of the catalog from an unauthorized heading to an authorized one. A general principle is to make a *see* reference whenever a heading has a different form.

Examples:

```
Griffith, D.W.
   x Griffith, David Wark


Griffith, David Wark
   see
Griffith, D.W.



Orthodox Eastern Church.
      Akathistos hymnos. Spanish & Greek
   x Orthodox Eastern Church.
         Himno Akathistos


Orthodox Eastern Church.
      Himno Akathistos
      see
Orthodox Eastern Church.
   Akathistos hymnos. Spanish & Greek
```

See references are also made whenever an access point is known by more than one name. A person or a title, for example, may be known by more than one distinct name.

Examples:

```
Orwell, George.
     x Blair, Eric Arthur


Blair, Eric Arthur
     see
Orwell, George




Swift, Jonathan.
       Gulliver's travels
    x Swift, Jonathan.
          Travels into several remote nations
          of the world


Swift, Jonathan.
     Travels into several remote nations of
     the world
     see
Swift, Jonathan.
     Gulliver's travels
```

SEE ALSO REFERENCES

See also references direct the user from one authorized heading to another to show that there is a relationship between them (see figure 5). The type of relationship depends on the type of heading.

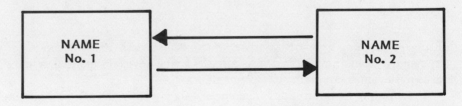

Fig. 5. *See also* references

See also references are used when a heading is known by more than one name. Bibliographic records reside under each name used in the catalog and are linked to each other by *see also* references.

Successive entries are made for series if it is determined that different series titles found in the work or in other sources are the result of a change in title rather than a variation. A *see also* reference is made to link the earlier and the later titles to each other.

Examples:

```
Van Dine, S.
   x Wright, Willard Huntington


   Wright, Willard Huntington
      see also
Van Dine, S.



   British Ornithologists' Union.
   x British Ornithologists' Club


   British Ornithologists' Club
      see also
British Ornithologists' Union
```

INFORMATION REFERENCES

Some headings are so complex that additional information is needed to enable users to maximize their search in the catalog. When more detailed information is needed beyond that provided by *see* and *see also* references, an information reference is created. Some information references provide the history of a corporate name that has undergone several changes; they are the most difficult to create. For reasons of economy LC discontinued making this type of reference in February 1981. Related headings formerly connected by history references are now connected by *see also* references. Examples of this type of reference may be found in the earlier tools published by the Library of Congress, such as the *National Union Catalog* and *Library of Congress Name Headings with References*.

Some information references direct users from one access point to several different ones. These references are the most difficult to use. Both manual and online searches are much more successful when the directions in a reference lead to one heading at a time. Online systems can search separate references very rapidly. Combining references is a space-saving device in manual systems that is irrelevant in an online environment.

The wording of information references varies greatly. Depending on the intent, such references always require more words than *see* or *see also*. Whatever wording is chosen, the reference should be concise, clear, and direct. Examples of information references follow.

Examples:

```
Conference on the Study of the History of
   Canadian Science and Technology
   (1st : 1978 : Kingston, Ont.)
   Publications of this series of meetings are
found under the following headings or titles:
```

```
1st:   Conference on the Study of the History
         of Canadian Science and Technology
         (1st : 1978 : Kingston, Ont.)
2nd:   Conference on the History of Canadian
         Science, Technology and Medicine
         (2nd : 1981 : Kingston, Ont.)

Cliff Brewery.
   For works by this body see also the later
name, Tollemache & Cobbold Breweries Ltd.

Tollemache & Cobbold Breweries Ltd.
   For works by this body see also the early
name, Cliff Brewery.
```

Historical information is being incorporated into the *Sources found* area. (For a discussion of this area, see chapter 6.) As older records are evaluated, information references (Field 665 in MARC) are being eliminated completely from the updated records. To have history information handled with *see also* references that link the various names of an organization in linear order means that a name is linked only to a former name immediately preceding it and to a later name immediately following it. An illustration of this configuration follows (see also figure 6).

The history information:

```
The Westminister Provincial Bank and the
National Provincial Bank merged in 1969 to
form the National Westminister Bank.
```

In an online catalog it is essential to make appropriate references to all previous and subsequent names, whether or not they have been used before in the catalog, in order to prevent "missing links" in the sequence of related names. The links are transparent and cause no problems if a heading to which a reference directs has not been used in the catalog. In a manual catalog care must be taken to withhold the "blind" reference until such time as the library uses the name as a heading. Instead, a *see also from* reference should be made (see figure 7).

A note on the authority record should document the fact that a *see also from* reference was made.

Sometimes an organization will change its name to one that has been used previously. Sometimes titles of series will change. In such cases, the cataloger must be on the alert for redundant references. Figure 8 illustrates the flow of references in such situations.

In the diagram Name 2 needs to be linked to Name 3 and Name 4 only one time.

The extent to which searching should be done for information regarding name changes will depend on the cataloger's judgment and the reference sources available. A library should establish general policies regarding minimum and

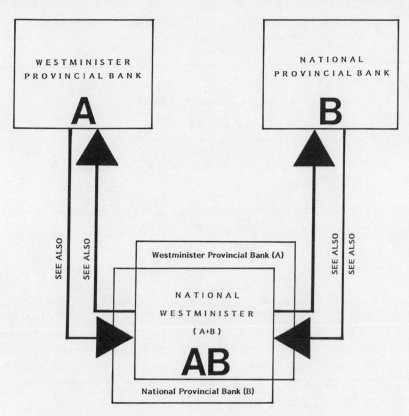

Fig. 6. Explanatory references

maximum searching. A minimum policy should be to identify at least one previous name and one subsequent name if they exist. A maximum policy may be to search a predetermined list of basic tools relevant to the information sought. Once those tools have been exhausted, the search is terminated.

History references are divided into two parts, each serving a separate and distinct function:

1. the information statement of name changes that have occurred over the life of the organization
2. the reference statement

An information statement is created after it has been determined, usually from the item in hand, that some changes have occurred in the name under consideration. If the exact sequence of name changes is not given in the item being cataloged, reference sources must be consulted. The history of the name change is documented in a single paragraph, beginning with the earliest name (and date of the change if known) and ending with the latest name. The information covers mergers, splits, and other meaningful events that resulted in a name change.

In online files the information statement is tagged as a special field of the authority record. In manual files, it may be filed as a separate record, always

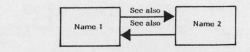

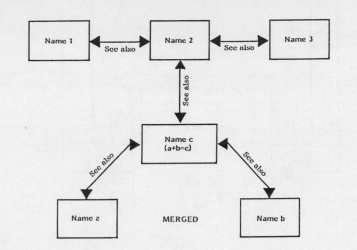

Fig. 7. Name changes linked with *see also* references

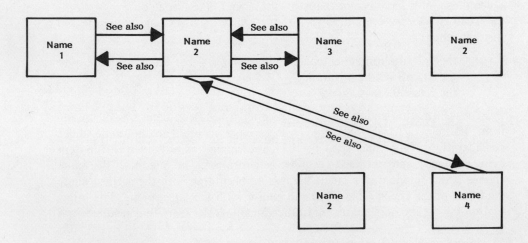

Fig. 8. A potential for redundant references

preceding the authority record for the heading. Some libraries attach the two records to show that combined they constitute a complete authority record.

Instead of placing an information statement with each authority record for a related heading, the phrase "History:——" could be preprinted on the recto of the authority record to show that an information statement exists elsewhere in the file. The heading where the statement resides could be typed in the blank.

Example:

```
History: National Westminister Bank.
```

This procedure saves space in the authority file and reduces the number of copies of a record needed. If space and duplicating records are not problems, it is preferable to have each information statement where one would expect to find it.

EXPLANATORY REFERENCES

An explanatory reference is a scope note that provides the definition and scope of a heading and gives detailed guidance in its use. The reference may explain the use of initials, multiple names, pseudonyms, uniform titles, or subject headings. It has two parts:

1. the authority heading
2. the explanatory statement

The statement is composed by the cataloger. It should be clear, concise, and unambiguous. Depending on the frequency of occurrence of a particular reference, a pattern may be decided on to serve as a guide for the choice of words to use. The pattern should be just that, a pattern, and not a substitute for a potentially unique reference statement.

Sometimes both an explanatory reference and a history reference are needed for the same heading. This could happen in a case in which an organization has undergone a name change and used an initialism or an acronym. In such cases all references that the heading generates should be made. Examples of explanatory references follow.

Initials:

```
H.I.M.A.
    For publications by and about this body, see
Health Industry Manufacturers Association. When
these initials occur in a title or other
headings without spaces or periods, they are
treated as a single word: Hima
```

Multiple names:

```
Iran. Shah (1941-1979 : Mohammed Reza Pahlavi)
    Here are entered works of the Shah acting in
his official capacity. For other works, see
Mohammed Reza Pahlavi, 1919-1980.
```

Subject References

References associated with subject headings[1] are *use*, *use for* (UF), *see also broader terms* (BT), *see also narrower terms* (NT), and *see also related terms* (RT). There are also general references (SA). The *see also narrower terms* reference is normally not added to the catalog at the time the subject heading to which it belongs is assigned to a work. This practice is followed because some of the topics to which the user is directed may not be in the catalog and a basic principle forbids references to unused topics. This type of reference, thus, is not included in the discussions that follow.

USE FOR REFERENCES

Use for references direct a searcher from unused subject headings to used ones. Terms from which *use for* references are made are signified by the symbol *UF* preceding the first term (if there is a list of such references). The term *use* functions as a reciprocal for the *use for* reference.

Example:

```
Artificial corneas
    UF Cornea substitute
```

Reciprocal:

```
Cornea substitute
    USE Artificial corneas
```

The unused term is linked to the used term because they share one of the following general relationships:

1. a synonym

    Example:

    ```
    Civil rights
        UF Human rights
    ```

2. a variant spelling

    Example:

    ```
    Diriku language
        UF Dciriku language
    ```

3. a variant form

    Examples:

---

1. The examples of references used with subject headings are from: Library of Congress. Subject Cataloging Division, *Library of Congress Subject Headings*. 11th ed. (Washington, D.C.: Library of Congress, 1988).

```
Cultural lag
  UF Lag, Cultural

Cuba—History—Invasion, 1961
  UF Cuban invasion, 1961

Germfree life
  UF Germ-free life

Saint Helena Island (S.C.)
  UF St. Helena Island (S.C.)

PACER (Computer program)
  UF Process Assembly Case Evaluator Routine

35mm cameras
  UF 35 mm cameras

Police-fire integration
  UF P.F.I.
```

4. a different language form

   Example:

   ```
   Unborn children (Law)
     UF En ventre sa mere
   ```

5. an antonym

   Examples:

   ```
   Honesty
     UF Dishonesty

   Militarism
     UF Antimilitarism
   ```

6. an unused broader term

   Example:

   ```
   Nuts
     UF Nut culture
   ```

7. an unused narrower term

   Examples:

   ```
   Single parents
     UF Single fathers
        Single mothers

   Hormones, Sex
     UF Female sex hormone
        Male sex hormone
   ```

8. a popular or scientific version of the used term

    Example:

    ```
    Yeast
      UF Nematospora
    ```

9. a cancelled heading

    Examples:

    ```
    Corn
      UF Maize

    Blacks
      UF Negroes
    ```

10. the second term in a conjunctive subject heading relating similar things if the second term is not an authorized subject heading

    Examples:

    ```
    Pride and vanity
      UF Vanity

    Track and field athletes
      UF Field athletes
         Track athletes
    ```

11. the terms in reverse order in a conjunctive subject heading relating different topics

    Example:

    ```
    Traffic safety and children
      UF Children and traffic safety
    ```

12. the vernacular form of a geographic name

    Example:

    ```
    Prince Edward Islands
      UF Iles Froides
    ```

BROADER TERM AND RELATED TERM REFERENCES

In *LCSH*, references to broader terms and to related terms link authorized subject headings to each other and are preceded by BT and RT, respectively.

Example of broader term reference:

```
Internal medicine
  BT Medicine
```

Example of related term reference:

```
Hedges
   RT Fingers
```

GENERAL REFERENCES

Use for, related term, and broader term references link terms on a one-to-one basis, that is, one specific term is linked to another specific term. A general reference (SA) is a space-saving device that directs the user to a group of headings belonging to a particular category or fitting a particular criterion.

Some specific terms have been omitted from *LCSH*. A general reference has been included instead that suggests to the cataloger how to establish the specific subject headings and to the user how to find them in the catalog. In many cases a general reference means that specific references are not made.

Example:

```
Chemical elements
   SA names of elements
```

The number of general references being added to *LCSH* has been greatly reduced in recent years as more and more specific terms are included.

General references are always open-ended (i.e., they do not direct to a single specific term) and always appear at the end of a list of *use for* references under the heading in question.

Examples:

```
Discrimination in employment
   SA subdivision Employment under names of
   racial or social groups, e.g. Afro-Americans—
   Employment; Women—Employment

Devices
   SA individual devices, e.g. Coq gaulois
   (Heraldic device), Eagle (in heraldry),
   Fleur-de-lis, Snake devices (American
   colonies)

Dancing
   SA names of dances, e.g. Quadrille (Dance),
   Waltz

Consulting engineers
   SA particular types of engineers, e.g. Mining
   engineers

Biology
   SA headings beginning with the word
   Biological
```

Format

There is no national standard for the structure of cross references, which has resulted in some innovative and creative displays. Regardless of the choice of format, decisions will need to be made about spacing, indentation, capitalization, punctuation, and wording. Once a decision is made, consistency and uniformity should be maintained. The same format should be used for all *see* and *see also* references whether for names, uniform titles, series, or subjects. Information and explanatory references will require a different format because of the varied wording.

To be compatible with LC, the following format specifications are recommended. The references begin on the second line below the heading two spaces from the left. *See* references precede *see also* references. References should be transcribed each on a separate line in one single-spaced column rather than all in a paragraph. The line-by-line format facilitates ready identification of individual references. There is no ambiguity in determining where one ends and another begins.

If the content of a reference is too long for one line and must be continued onto the next line, every line after the first should follow an inverse indentation in the same style as that used in the heading (i.e., three spaces). In subject authority files, scope notes and general references should be transcribed as separate records, each with the newly established name, uniform title, or subject as the heading. Periods are not used at the end of cross reference headings.

If more than one reference is a name-title reference all with the same name, the name is given for the first reference. In all of the succeeding name-title references, the name may be substituted with one of the following terms: His, Her, Author's, Its.

To avoid confusion an *x* should precede each *see* reference line and *xx* should precede each *see also* reference line. To conserve time some libraries precede only the first *see* and *see also* reference with symbols. Some libraries use the symbols *x*: and *xx*: for *see* and *see also* references.

Some libraries try to maintain long lists of references in alphabetical order. In a manual system an alphabetical arrangement may be difficult to maintain when new references are added later. The original alphabetical order will be disrupted since it is unlikely that the need for new references will occur in alphabetical order. In an online file such a rigid order is not necessary since the computer can display data in any desired order. References should be single-spaced to conserve workspace.

The cataloger may sign and date the authority record and note any localities for proper distribution if applicable. The cataloger may signify that a heading may be subdivided geographically.

In some online catalogs the system does not display the actual reference. It just manipulates the data according to the requirements of reference codes. In other systems the actual references are displayed to prompt further searching under an authorized heading. The following format for references is widely used in libraries of all types.

Pattern:

```
unauthorized heading
(13 spaces)

    referral legend
    (16 spaces)

authorized heading
(9 spaces)
```

Example:

```
Carter, James Earl, 1924-
    see
Carter, Jimmy, 1924-
```

The format of the explanatory reference is similar to that of a bibliographic record. There are as many paragraphs as there are points to be explained. Each explanation constitutes a paragraph and begins at the second indention.

Pattern:

```
authorized heading
    1st explanatory statement



    2nd explanatory statement


```

Example:

```
Pennsylvania State University.
    The Farmers' High School of Pennsylvania was
chartered in 1855. In May 1862 the name was
changed to Agricultural College of
Pennsylvania; in January 1874 to Pennsylvania
State College; and in November 1953 to
Pennsylvania State University.
    Works by these bodies are found under the
name used at the time of publication.
```

The technical aspects of the format illustrated above are:

1. Indentations: The indentations are spaced the same as those used for a bibliographic record, that is, a first, second, and third indentation. The unauthorized heading begins at the second indentation, the referral statement at the third, and the authorized heading at the first. Continuation of data in each field to a succeeding line is indented three spaces (i.e., beginning on the fourth space).
2. Spacing: Each line of data is typed single spaced. There is a single space between adjacent initials in names used in the reference (e.g., cummings, e.e.). All other spacing follows the normal procedure of everyday use.
3. Punctuation: No punctuation follows the unauthorized heading or the referral legend. A period follows the authorized heading unless the heading itself ends with another punctuation mark such as a hyphen or parenthesis.
4. Capitalization: Capitalization follows the prescription of *AACR2-88* (i.e., first words and proper names). The referral legend is not capitalized.

Chapter 6

Sources Found

This chapter discusses the sources found area of name and series authority records. Because libraries generally do not generate original subject headings, there is no need for their subject authority records to have a sources found area. If such an area is required, the principles discussed here are applied.

Sources found is the third principal area in an authority record. It identifies the sources in which data about the established heading and the references were found. It contains citations to the works that the cataloger used to determine the heading and the relationship between the names in the heading and those in the references. The first citation is always for the work being cataloged whether the name in the heading appears in it or not. It also includes a citation to any other sources that contain a variant name or form of name, uniform title, or series.

Sometimes the work being cataloged gives partial, conflicting, or ambiguous information about the authorized heading. The cataloger, then, should search in reference sources to clarify the information and to determine the relationship between the heading and the information found. Any sources that provide any elucidation on the name should be cited in the sources found area to lend authority to the data used in the authority record. Having such information available in the record saves time if, for some reason, the data have to be reverified later. It also provides justification for the use of certain references.

The contents for the sources found area should be concise, clear, and unambiguous. The area contains, minimally, the following information:

1. a citation of the work that generated the heading
2. the location of the data (name or series) in the source
3. the justifying data, including the name in the heading, any variants of the name from any source, and other identifying information about the person or the corporate body. (Variant series titles found in the work being cataloged are not transcribed in sources found although they may appear as references; however, variants found in future publications and in other sources are cited and transcribed as justifying data.)

The information in the sources found area is not an attempt to provide a biographical sketch of an individual or a detailed history of a corporate body. It is merely an attempt to document those facts that contribute to the positive identification of a heading and that clarify the relationship between references and headings. The information should help to distinguish one person, corporate body, or uniform title from another, even when they have the same or similar names.

Pattern:

```
citation:  1st location (data)

     2nd location

succeeding source, date (data)

Main entry heading. Title, imprint date or
     holdings: first location of data found
     (data) other location(s) (data)
Succeeding source, date (data)
```

Examples:

Names:

```
International youth in achievement, c1981: t.p.
     (International Biographical Centre,
     Cambridge, Eng.)

His Evolution of rotogravure, 1957: t.p. (J.S.
     Mertle)
NUC (LC hdg.: Mertle, Joseph Stephen, 1899-  )

Green I. The book of Deal and Walmer, 1983:
     t.p. (Deal)
Barth., 1977 (Deal, Kent)
LC data base, 5-14-84 (hdg.: Deal, Eng.)
Mun. yrbk., 1984 (Deal, England)

His Lecture notes on . . . 1977: t.p. (R.D.T.
     Farmer, sen. lect. in Comm. Med.,
     Westminster Med. Sch., U. of Lond.)
```

Series:

```
Morey, N.M. McEvoy family album, 1977?: p. 2

Michalet, C.A. Le defi du developpement
     independent, c1982: series t.p.

Brown, J.T. Windy city boogie [SR] p1978:
     container

Archaeological investigations of the Mudlane
     . . . 1983: cover
Bayfield, T. Churban, 1981: p. 4 of cover
```

A discussion of each element in the sources found area follows in the order of its appearance in the area.

The Citation

The first source cited should be the work being cataloged for which the heading is being established. The order for all other sources is arbitrary.

The elements that are usually given in the citation are (1) the main entry, (2) the title, and (3) the date of publication.

Main Entry

The information in the main entry should be given in a brief form. Dates and titles in personal names are omitted. Abbreviations are used for forenames and in corporate names. If the main entry is identical to the heading, the following substitutions are used:

For	*Use*
Male authors	His
Female authors	Her
Gender unknown	Author's
Corporate bodies	Its
Conferences	Its (number : date : location)

This procedure is used in name authorities. In series authority records the author's name may not be substituted with *His*, *Her*, *Author's*, or *Its*. If the heading is for an ongoing conference, the qualifier is dropped from the conference heading being established and is transcribed as part of the main entry of the work being cataloged and is cited in the sources found area. The qualifier precedes the title immediately. A conference is considered as ongoing if it is numbered and its name remains the same. If the removal of the qualifier results in a conflict with another heading, the qualifier should remain with the heading instead of being put in the sources found area.

Title

The title proper follows the main entry and is preceded by two spaces. Capitalization and punctuation practices are the same as for transcribing titles in bibliographic records. Long titles may be shortened either by abbreviating words or by using an ellipsis (three dots with a space before and after). Decisions regarding when to shorten titles, which method to use, and how much to shorten are left to the judgment of the individual cataloger. Care must be taken, however, to ensure that the shortened title is intelligible, interpretable, and understandable.

Examples:

```
Sylvester, W.B. A SEASAT SASS simulation . . .
     1984:

Its 1984 International Symposium on . . .
     c1984:
```

```
Her Exercise, the new lang. of love, 1984:

Its (2nd : 1981 : Kingston, Ont.). Crit. issues
    in the hist. of Can. sci., tech., and med.,
    c1983:
```

For series authority records, variations of the series title found in the work are not recorded in the sources found area at all; however, they are still used as *see* references. Earlier and later standard text references should be made to link the titles with each other.

Additional citations may be included if variants of the series title are found in future publications. In the additional citations, the actual series data are transcribed following their appropriate locations.

Changes in the title of the series are treated in the same way as changes in names. Successive entries are made if it is determined that the difference in the titles is, in fact, a change in title rather than a variation. Earlier and later standard text references should be made to link the titles with each other.

Examples:

```
Lloyd, A. Money damages in police misconduct
    cases, c1983: cover

Songs of Nigeria, 1982: cover

Michalet, C.A. Le defi du developpement
    independent, c1982: series t.p.

Mass com periodical literature, Vol. 1., no. 1
    (Jan.-Dec. 1981): t.p.

Folk literature of the Toba Indians, c1982:
    p. i

International and regional conflict, c1983:
    ser. t.p.
```

Uniform titles are transcribed without brackets. If the title ends with a question mark or an exclamation point, no other punctuation is necessary. Otherwise, the title is followed by a comma that separates it from the date of publication.

Examples:

```
1984 courses in analytical techniques, 1984:

''Ach meine lieben Deutschen—,'' 1983:

Its annual report for . . , 1973:
```

It is always appropriate to follow a title (anywhere it is used) with an appropriate general material designation (GMD). Instead of the complete GMD as appears in *AACR2-88*, codes should be used. A workable list of codes appears in *Standards for Cataloging Nonprint Materials* published by the Association for Educational Communications and Technology.[1]

Date of Publication

The last element in the citation is the date of publication (for monographs) and the numeric/chronological designation (for serials and other multipart items). The date here is the same as in the bibliographic description, except that brackets are always excluded. If the date in the bibliographic description is a copyright date (c1985), a range of dates (1983–1985), a probable date (1984?), multiple dates (1985, c1983), or an open date (1985–), transcribe it as such. Sometimes a bibliographic record has multiple dates, each following the name of a different corporate body. The corporate bodies usually are for a publisher followed by a distributor/manufacturer. In such cases, omit the names of the corporate bodies and transcribe the multiple dates, including any word or phrase that clarifies the dates (e.g., 1980, distributed 1982).

A bibliographic description for a serial usually has both a numeric/chronological designation and a publication date. The numeric/chronological designation identifies the sequencing pattern of the individual parts and the date. The sequencing pattern may be by number, volume, part, month, or issue. The date designation represents the currency of the part. In a serial citation, the numeric/chronological designation is used instead of the publication date.

Example:

Syersville Historical Association bulletin,
    spring 1983:

In the absence of a designation date, the publication date is used with the numeric designation. It is enclosed in parenthesis to show that the publication date has been used as a substitute for the designation date.

Examples:

Studies in Confederate history, No. 1 (1966):

Manual medicine, Vol. 1, no. 1 (c1983):

Contemporary writings on long term care
    pharmacy, Vol. 2 (c1980):

Designation data should be transcribed in the language in which it appears in the bibliographic description. The numeric designation should be abbreviated

---

1. Alma T. Tillin and William J. Quinly, *Standards for Cataloging Nonprint Materials*, 4th ed. (Washington, D.C.: Association for Educational Communications and Technology, 1976), pp. 26–28.

according to *AACR2-88*. The first letter of any word or abbreviation used with the numeric designation should be capitalized.

Example:

    Schaumburger Heimat, Hept. 2 (1970):

The citation ends with a colon.

Location

The next element in the sources found area is the location of the data in the source cited. Any relevant information found in the chief source is cited first. Abbreviations to indicate location are used as follows:

t.p.	title page
jkt.	book jacket
label	label pasted in the item
map recto	front of the map [(map] may be substituted for other types of materials
pref.	preface
prelim.	preliminary matter
p. 1 [2, 3, 4, etc.]	page for numbered and unnumbered pages
cover	cover
cover p. 1	recto of front cover
cover p. 2	verso of front cover
cover p. 3	recto of back cover
cover p. 4	verso of back cover
caption t.p.	title at the beginning of the first page of text
verso of t.p.	verso of title page

If the work is a multipart item, the location designation is preceded by the volume number. A comma is used between them. The volume designation is represented by a small *v*.

Example:

    Its Tondokumente in Schallarchiv des
        Norddeutschen Rundfunks, 1973- : v.9, t.p.

If the information appears in more than two different locations within the same work, the first location given is followed by *etc.* A comma is used to separate the two (e.g., p. 3, etc.)

Justifying Data

From Item in Hand

The next element in the sources found area is the documented information from the cited sources that justifies the heading or reference. It always appears within parentheses. Each location should always be followed by information within parentheses except in series authorities. In series authorities the first citation does not include the information following the location. In fact, the citation ends with the location.

Example:

```
Mass com periodical literature, Vol. 1, no. 1
     (Jan.-Dec. 1981): t.p.
```

If variants of the series title are found in future publications or other sources, additional citations are recorded and the actual series data are transcribed following their appropriate locations. Care must be taken to distinguish between a variant series title and a title change. Each unit of information within parentheses should be preceded by a location. All information from the same source should appear together within the same set of parentheses. Each piece of information from different locations within the same item should be preceded by the location from which it came. The different pieces of information within parentheses are separated by a semicolon. No punctuation is used between the location and the data, only single spaces before and after each.

Example:

```
Contemporary writings on long term care
     pharmacy, Vol. 2 (c1980): t.p. (ASCP;
     American Society of Consulting Pharmacists)
     verso of t.p. (Arlington, Va.)
```

If the title is the only place on the chief source of the work being cataloged where the authorized name appears in a recognizable form, the parenthetical statement of the title page data may be omitted.

Examples:

```
Charles, Ray.

Mathis, S.B. Ray Charles, c1973.

X, Malcolm.

His The autobiography of Malcolm X, c1965.
```

If the same form of the name appears in a work in several different locations, the name in the given form should be transcribed only one time. The fact that several locations are involved is indicated by placing *etc.* following the first location, unless the first location is *t.p.*, which is never followed by *etc.*

When transcribing the justifying data, ellipses may only be used to show that surrounding words have been omitted. Names, however, should always be transcribed in full and exactly as found in the source. Names in a nonroman alphabet must be romanized. Other justifying data should always be transcribed in English in a brief, summarizing form. Except in names, abbreviations may be used when possible and comprehensible within the context. No standard pattern has emerged for the use of abbreviations, capitalization, or punctuation in justifying data. The cataloger will have to use judgment in each case.

Different styles have been used successfully for transcribing dates. The cataloger should use judgment to determine which style is appropriate for the context. Possible patterns include 3-24-28; 3/24/28; Mar. 24, 1928; or March 24, 1928.

One pattern should be selected as the standard, particularly for birthdates since they occur so frequently. Care should be taken to remove all ambiguity if the pattern is not appropriate, such as in month-day, month-year, and year dates.

Every line after the first should be transcribed with an inverse paragraph indentation of approximately three spaces.

From External Sources

Sources other than the item being cataloged may be included in the sources found area. Data may come from a variety of other sources such as a database including a bibliographic utility, the public catalog, reference works, or even telephone calls to various sources. Exact forms for the source citations are not prescribed; however, the information should be clear, precise, and intelligible to anyone using the authority file. Only abbreviations that are universally understood should be used. Each source citation should have its own paragraph recognizable by its inverse indentation. Examples of techniques for citing other sources follow.

DATABASES

General pattern:

```
_____, _____ (_____)
 name,    date   (data)
```

Detailed pattern I:

```
_____ _____
name of database, date of search
_____
   (hdg.: heading found in the database)
```

Example:

```
LC in OCLC #123456, 4-22-85 (hdg.: Gastegger,
   Curt Walter, 1929-    )
```

Detailed pattern II:

```
name of database, date of search (hdg.: heading
   found in the database; usage: 1st usage form
   as shown in the description, 2nd usage as
   shown in the description; variant: 1st
   variant form of name found; 2nd variant form
   of name found)
```

Example:

```
Lib. cat., 4-22-85 (hdg.: Anderson, James
   Edward, 1926-    ; usage: James E. Anderson,
   J. E. Anderson; variant: Anderson, James
   Edward)
```

REFERENCE WORKS

Pattern:

```
_____  ____  _____
reference work, date (data)
```

Information found in reference sources can be very helpful in identifying or justifying a heading or a reference. The basic principles of clarity, brevity, and intelligibility must prevail in the same manner as for data from other sources. To shorten the citation, a variety of methods may be employed.

1. Abbreviations may be used in the title indication:

```
Compreh. diss. index
   for
Comprehensive Dissertation Index.
```

2. Some words may be omitted completely:

```
NY times ind.
   for
The New York times index
```

3. The titles of well-known works may be cited by author only:

```
Besterman
   for
Besterman, Theodore. A World Bibliography of
   Bibliographies.
```

4. The titles of well-known works may be cited by initials:

    ```
    NUC
        for
    National Union Catalog
    ```

5. Lesser-known works may be cited by author's surname and a brief
    indication of the title:

    ```
    Farmer. Oxf. dict. saints
        for
    Farmer, David H. The Oxford Dictionary of
        Saints.
    ```

6. Works with distinctive titles that are entered under title may be cited
    by a brief indication of the title:

    ```
    Am. lib. dir.
        for
    American Library Directory.
    ```

TELEPHONE CALLS

Pattern:

```
Phone call to the _____ [date of the call]
    (data)
```

Example:

```
Phone call to the Institute, 7-23-81
    (Minneapolis Institute of Arts, administr.
    by the Minneapolis Society of Fine Arts;
    Minneapolis Institute of Fine Arts is not a
    variant form of name, but a printer's
    error.)
```

Nonunique Names

Sometimes a heading is a nonunique name. This occurs when the name is used
for several different people because no data are available to distinguish between
them. When this situation occurs, the source citations for all works cataloged
under the nonunique heading are listed, single-spaced, on the same authority
record in the order in which the works are cataloged.

Each individual sharing the name is listed in the sources found area by
some unique, informal descriptive term or phrase enclosed in brackets:

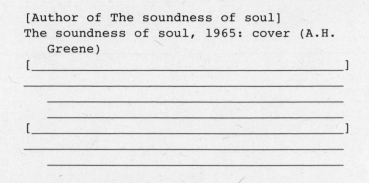

```
[Author of The soundness of soul]
The soundness of soul, 1965: cover (A.H.
   Greene)
```

The same procedure is followed for each individual who is considered to be a different person but who shares the nonunique name.

Whenever dates or other distinguishing terms become available for any of the authors represented on the authority record, the citation and other data relating to that author are removed from the record, a unique heading is established, and a separate authority record is created.

Chapter 7

Other Aspects of the Physical Record

The previous three chapters have covered the mandatory areas that are common to all types of authority records: the heading, references, and sources found. Some libraries may wish to capture additional information for their files. This chapter provides guidance for completing the physical aspects of the authority record with such information. The variety of notes and other special aspects such as data codes and distribution symbols are discussed.

Authority records for series require additional information that is unique to the category. This chapter includes discussions of procedures for displaying those unique data in the physical series authority record. Also included in this chapter are discussions of alternative procedures for controlling subjects.

Libraries with extensive collections to control or libraries with online files will find it useful to document the following data as part of the authority record:

1. control data codes
2. sources not found
3. permanent information
4. notes
5. distribution symbols

The level of control supported and the presence or absence of automated files will determine whether these data should be included in the authority record.

Supplementary Authority Data

Control Data Codes

Control data codes provide MARC content designation conventions and online procedures necessary for the online input/update of machine-readable name authority records. (For further discussion of control data codes, see chapter 8.)

Sources Not Found

Reference works do not always contain the information sought. To alert future searchers to the lack of relevance of certain reference tools to the names in the heading or reference, the reference tools that were used but which yielded no significant information are recorded on the authority record. If these sources are cited, space on the authority record should be designated for them. The types of information that are considered candidates for sources not found are:

1. reference sources in which no information is found and nonunique headings
2. reference sources in which questionable information is found
3. sources that refer to earlier or later names

In series authorities, when a series changes its title, general principles require that a link between the successive titles be provided. Cross references from earlier and later titles are justified by the data recorded in the sources not found area. Not all authority records provide for this area, particularly if data from the Library of Congress are used.

If the decision is to include sources not found information on the authority record, the procedures used for sources found are appropriate, except that all sources should be recorded in one continuous paragraph separated from each other by a semicolon.

Examples:

```
Mun. yrbk., 1984.

Grande Larousse encyc.; Grande encyc.
```

Permanent Information

Some information is important enough to be preserved although it does not exactly qualify as sources found information. A policy decision whether to provide space for this type of information in the authority record is dependent upon the level of control desired and the size of the collection. In transcribing the information, each independent statement should be given as a separate note.

Examples:

```
Not the same as: Presbyterian Church in the
U.S.A.

Reinvestigate before using again.

AACR1 form: Biofeedback Society of America.

Do not confuse with Schmid, Hans Peter;
writes on Swiss commercial laws.
```

Notes

Any important information about the heading, including series title, that is not already provided for in some other area is recorded on the authority record as a note. It is impossible to predict what information may be recorded here. It will vary from library to library, from cataloger to cataloger, and from item to item. Notes information may include the subtitles; the instruction "Give phrase as a quoted note"; the statement "Sometimes published as [variant title]"; state-

ments relating to the relationship between titles, such as "Continued by:——"
and "Continues:——"; and statements that indicate a change from treatment
as an analyzed series to treatment as separates.

Distribution Symbols

Libraries with multiple catalogs to control will need to provide a mechanism
in the authority file to identify a particular record with a particular catalog.
Authority distribution symbols are used for this purpose. Each catalog should
be assigned a set of alphabetic symbols (mnemonic if possible). If the list of
catalogs is not too long, the symbols may be preprinted on the authority record
(or otherwise coded for online catalogs) and appropriately checked or circled to
indicate which catalogs have which headings and references.

Series Treatment Decisions

Treatment decisions convey basic information concerning analysis and tracing
practices. This information is essential to effective bibliographic organization
and information retrieval. It determines where on the shelf an item will be
stored and how it will be searched in the public catalog.

In an online environment, treatment decisions are coded to enable the
computer to manipulate the data and display the decisions made on command.
Numerous coding systems have been developed by various libraries and vendors
for the manipulation of authority data in the systems they have built. The
USMARC authority format provides the coding for the authority records distributed by LC. In the USMARC format, the 640–646 fields contain the series
treatment data. These data include volume designation and numbering pattern,
publishing information, analysis, and tracing and classification practices. Further
discussion of USMARC codes and content designations appears in chapter 8.

In a manual environment, the series authority record should be kept as
brief as possible. Much of the information either can be preprinted on the card
and checked as appropriate or the information may be written in as necessary.

The work being cataloged may be closely associated with the series to which
it belongs either because of its subject, author, or format. On the other hand,
the work may have very little in common with the other items in the series.
Works in the series may be unduly diverse in character, purpose, or content.
To retain the integrity of the library collection and to satisfy the expectations
of users, the cataloger has to make a decision about the classification pattern of
the item. This decision should then be documented on the authority record.
The decision will fall into one of the following categories:

1. Classify each item in the series as a separate bibliographic entity.
2. Classify the items in the series as a collection. Each individual part will
    be assigned the same call number, distinguished only by an appropriate
    sequencing element such as a volume, part, or number. (Subseries nor-
    mally are considered a part of the larger series category.)

Generally, monographic series are classified as separates. Numbered multipart items intended as a unit to cover a particular subject or the works of a particular author are classified and maintained as a collection. Numbered multipart items covering widely diverse subject areas may be classified as separates. Unnumbered multipart items usually must be dealt with on a case-by-case basis. In any situation the decision is that of the cataloger and must be made before an authority record can be created.

The appropriate information relative to the decision, including any variations in practices, should be recorded on the authority record. Some libraries use codes to signify the category for classification, for example, c for collection and s for separate. Others make a brief statement to indicate the decision. Still others let the presence or absence of a call number indicate the classification practice.

Authority systems that are online or that control extensive series holdings cannot operate efficiently without including more than the basic information relating to treatment. Series authority records should include the following information:

1. publisher's information
2. numbering peculiarities
3. numerical/alphabetical/chronological designation data

This information is necessary to identify a particular series and to provide support for decisions relating to the treatment of the series on the bibliographic record and of the item in the collection.

To remove ambiguities and resolve conflicts, a variety of data gathered about a new title must be compared with data already in the file.

For monographic series, the authority record is the only place where bibliographic data about the series can be brought together to form a sort of bibliographic record for the collective work to help distinguish one from another.

Publisher's Information

The place of publication and the name of the publisher recorded on the authority record can be very useful. This information is given only when the publisher of the series is different from the body responsible for it. Since publishers are usually responsible for the series they publish, it is seldom that the publisher and the responsible body are different. When they do differ, a *see* reference should be made for the responsible body. When the publisher's information is recorded, the transcription of the place and the publisher should be identical to that on the bibliographic record for the item being cataloged. On the series authority record the publisher's name should always be explicitly stated and no data should appear in brackets.

Example:

```
Orlando : Academic Press
```

Bibliographically, publishing information is always important. Since most series do not have separate bibliographic records created for them that would give this information, the series authority record is the only place where it is recorded and made readily available.

Numbering Peculiarities

Orderly sequencing of series is very important to maintaining the integrity of the collection. Publishers try to maintain order in their series numbering; however, occasionally, problems do arise. Issues may be misnumbered, unnumbered, or double numbered. Some issues may never get published. A myriad of peculiarities may be identified and recorded on the authority record. Libraries that deal with only a few series may be able to function without providing special space on the authority record for this information. Since time will be spent solving problems of sequencing for cataloging so that an orderly array of records can be displayed in the public catalog, the information should be preserved and the authority file is the place for it.

Numerical/Alphabetical/Chronological Designation Data

Series, like serials, are published in parts over an extended period of time. It is important bibliographically to know the extent or the duration of the item, that is, the beginning and ending volume and date. If a series is unnumbered or if the library does not own the first or the last issue, the information may not be readily available from records of the library's holdings. Although no special effort should be made to secure this information, it should be recorded whenever it does become available.

Examples:

```
Unnumbered

Some vols. unnumbered

Vol. 1 (1975)-
```

Chapter 8

MARC Format for Authorities

A machine-readable cataloging (USMARC) format has been created in the United States for authority records to enable the manipulation of authority data by computer in much the same way as is done for bibliographic data. The format is designed to allow specific data in an authority record to be identified explicitly for machine manipulation. The three elements of the MARC record format are its record structure, the content designation, and the data content.

The previous chapters of this manual dealt with record structure and data content of authority records in general. The purpose of this chapter is to provide explanations of the record structure, data content, and content designation conventions for the USMARC authorities format. The explanations are sufficient to enable the individual to interpret the various tags, values, and codes that appear in a display of a machine-readable record from the Library of Congress online authority file. Clearly, the intent is not to instruct in the application of the MARC content designators. At present, a limited number of persons, including staff at the Library of Congress, is actually applying MARC tags to authority data in order to create new records and modify existing ones residing in the database. Coding authority records is not yet a routine in the average cataloging department. By the time coding authority records becomes a routine function of catalogers, numerous changes to the existing format will make many of the conversion conventions obsolete.

The principal sources of information for this discussion of the USMARC authorities format are three Library of Congress publications:

MARC Conversion Manuals—Authorities (Names). 2nd ed., 1984.
MARC Conversion Manuals—Series Authorities. 2nd ed., 1985.
USMARC Format for Authority Data: Including Guidelines for Content Designation. 1987–

A fourth source is also helpful:

Crawford, Walt. *MARC for Library Use: Understanding Integrated USMARC.* 2nd ed. Boston: G. K. Hall, 1989.

The information in this chapter reflects the current status of the MARC authorities format. (See figure 9 for examples.) Although the USMARC format is subject to change or enhancement sometime in the future, it is fairly certain that the basic structure and content of the MARC format as presented here will be used for a long time.

Enhancements to the USMARC format are continually being made. Later updates, major revisions, and releases are announced periodically in the literature and documentation from the Library of Congress and the bibliographic

utilities, the major suppliers of authority data to the library community. Catalogers and other technical services librarians must be eternally vigilant to keep
up-to-date on all the additions and changes to the formats.

```
ARN: 1070558   Rec stat: n    Entrd: 840829        Used: 840829
Type: z         Geo subd: n    Govt agn: -  Lang:   Source:
Roman: -        Subj: a        Series: n   Ser num: n  Head: aab
Ref Status: a   Upd status: a  Auth status: a        Name: a
Enc lv l: n     Auth/Ref: a    Mod rec:              Rules: c

1 010       n 84092280
2 040       DLC ≠c DLC ≠d   DLC
3 100 10    Paul, Elliot,  ≠d 1891-1958.
4 400 10    Paul, Elliot Harold,  ≠d 1891-  ≠ w nnaa
5 670       His The mysterious Mickey Finn, 1984:  ≠b CIP  t.p. (Elliot Paul)
pub. info   (d. 1958)
6 670       LC data base, 3-27-84 ≠b  (hdg.:  Paul, Elliot Harold, 1891- ; usage:
Elliot Paul)
```

Fig. 9a. LC authority record from OCLC database

```
1 010       n 84229855
2 040       DLC ≠c DLC ≠d DLC
3 100 10    Stevenson, Michael I.
4 670       His Joseph Alois Schumpeter, c1985: ≠b CIP t.p.  (Michael I.
Stevenson) p. 139 (asst. prof. and ref. lib. for business and economics, Univ.
of Nebraska at Omaha)
5 670       Ash, J. Health, 1976: ≠b t.p.  (Michael Stevenson)
```

Fig. 9b. Variable fields for an authority record for a personal name

```
1 010      n 50053964
2 040      DLC ≠c DLC
3 100 10   Rapp, George Robert, ≠d 1930-
4 400 10   Rapp, George Robert, ≠d 1931- ≠w nna
5 400 10   Rapp, George, ≠d 1930-
6 670      Roberts, W. L. ≠b Mineralogy of the Black Hills, 1965.
7 670      Hominid sites, their geologic settings, 1981: ≠b  t.p. (George
Rapp, Jr.)
8 670      Troy, the archaeological geology, 1982: ≠b  t.p.  (George Rapp, Jr.)
publ. info.  (b. 9/19/30)
9 670      AMWS, 12th ed. ≠b  (Rapp, George R(obert); b. 9/19/30)
```

Fig. 9c. Variable fields of an authority record for a personal name

```
1 010      n 50075377
2 040      DLC ≠c DLC ≠d DLC
3 110 20   Planning Executives Institute.
4 410 20   PEI
5 510 20   Budget Executives Institute ≠w  a
6 670      Miley, A. L. ≠b Directory of planning ... 1969.
7 675      Budgeting, Sept. 1963: cover p. 2 (Budget Executives Institute)
```

Source: OCLC

Fig. 9d. Variable fields of an authority record for a corporate name

```
1 010      n 79126981
2 040      DLC ≠c DLC
3 110 20   Mystic Seaport, Inc.
4 410 20   Mystic Seaport, Mystic, Conn. ≠ w  nnaa
5 510 20   Marine Historical Association ≠w a
6 550 0    Whaling ≠z Connecticut ≠w  nb
7 550 0    Historic sites ≠z  Connecticut ≠w  nb
8 551 0    Mystic (Conn) ≠x  Harbors w  nb
9 670      Mallory, P. R. Mystic Seaport, and the origins of freedom, 1954,
10 670     Mystic Seaport, Inc. Annual report, 1973: ≠b  p.21 (By vote of the
trustees, the Marine Historical Association changed its name to Mystic Seaport,
Inc., effectively early in 1974)
```

Fig. 9e. Variable fields of an authority record for a corporate name

```
001        n 42-19782
040        DLC DLC
130        Proceedings (Electrochemical Society) (AACR 2)
646        s: Classified separately  (DLC)
644        f: Analyzed in full  (DLC)
645        t: Traced  (DLC)
642        Form of number in series a.e.:  v. 80-5  (DLC)
643        Pennington, N.J.  :  Electrochemical Society
410        Electrochemical Society.  Proceedings
410        Electrochemical Society.  Proceedings - Electrochemical Society
           [old catalog heading] [do not make]
670        Proceedings of the symposia on Electronic and optical properties
           of polycrystalline or impure semiconductors, c1980.
985        KEY/EKI
```

Fig. 9f. Series authority record

```
001        n 42-2424
040        DLC DLC
130        ASAE  monograph.  [AACR 2]
646        s:  Classified separately (DLC)
644        f:  Analyzed in full (DLC)
645        t:  Traced (DLC)
642        Form of number in series a.e.: no. 3 (DLC)
643        St. Joseph, Mich.:  Amer. Soc. of Agric. Engrs.
410        American Society of Agricultural Engineers.  ASAE monograph
           [old catalog heading]
430        A.S.A.E. monograph
670        Design and operation of farm irrigation systems, 1980.
985        KEY / EKI
```

Fig. 9g. Series authority record

```
001        n  42005430
040        DLC
130        Bulletin (Utah Geological and Mineral Survey) [AACR 2]
646        c: Classified as a collection (DLC)
050        QE169 .A3
644        f: Analyzed in full (DLC)
645        t: Traced  (DLC)
642        Form of number in series a.e.:  116 (DLC)
643        [Salt Lake City]  :  Utah Geological and Mineral Survey
667        Document
410        Utah Geological and Mineral Survey.  Bulletin - Utah Geological and
           Mineral Survey [old catalog heading]  [do not make]
670        Great Salt Lake.  1980.
985        KEY/EKI
```

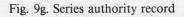

Fig. 9h. Variable fields of LC series authority records from the LC authorities
database

```
ARN: 202384      Rec stat:  c       Entrd: 871218        Used: 871218
Type: z          Geo subd: -        Govt agn: - Lang:    Source:
Roman:-          Subj: a            Series: n  Ser num: n   Head: bab
Ref status: b    Upd status: a      Auth status:  a      Name: n
Enc lvl: n       Auth/Ref: a        Mod rec:             Rules: n

 1 010    sh 85053982
 2 040    DLC ≠c DLC ≠d  DLC
 3 150 0  Geographical perception
 4 360    ≠ i subdivision ≠a Maps, Mental ≠i under the names of cities, countries, etc.
 5 450 0  Cognitive maps
 6 450 0  Environmental perception
 7 450 0  Maps, Mental
 8 450 0  Mental maps
 9 450 0  Perceptual cartography
10 450 0  Perceptual maps
11 550 0  Perception ≠w g
12 550 0  Orientation (Psychology)
13 550 0  Space perception
14 680    ≠i Here are general works on people's mental images of the physical environ-
          ment around them or in distant lands.
```

Fig. 9i. Subject authority record

```
ARN: 2100355     Rec stat: n        Entrd: 871218        Used: 871218
Type: z          Geo subd: -        Govt agn: - Lang:    Source:
Roman:-          Subj: a            Series: n  Ser num: n   Head: bab
Ref status: b    Upd status: a      Auth status: a       Name: n
Enc lvl: n       Auth/Ref: a        Mod rec:             Rules: n


 1 010    sh 85095588
 2 040    DLC ≠c DLC
 3 053    QP88
 4 150 0  Organs, Culture of
 5 450 0  Organ culture
 6 550 0  Cultures (Biology) ≠w g
 7 550 0  Organs (Anatomy) ≠w g
 8 550 0  Tissue culture
```

Fig. 9j. Subject authority record

```
ARN: 2100630   Rec stat: n      Entrd: 871218        Used: 871218
Type: z         Geo subd: -     Govt agn:  Lang:     Source:
Roman: -        Subj: a         Series: n  Ser num: n  Head: bab
Ref status: b   Upd status: a   Auth Status: a       Name: n
Enc lvl: n      Auth/Ref: a     Mod rec:             Rules: n

 1 010     sh 85095634
 2 040     DLC ≠c DLC
 3 053     BF299.07
 4 150  0  Orientation (Psychology)
 5 550  0  Geographical perception
 6 550  0  Instinct ≠w g
 7 550  0  Orientation ≠w g
 8 550  0  Psychology ≠w g
 9 550  0  Senses and sensation ≠w g
10 550  0  Spatial behavior ≠w g
```

Fig. 9k. Subject authority record

Structure of the MARC Record

The data content of a USMARC authority record is divided into two basic categories of fields: variable control fields and variable data fields. The variable control fields (the 00x fields) are structurally different from variable data fields in that they contain a single data element or a series of fixed-length data elements identified by the relative character position, whereas variable data fields are identified in the format by a field tag, two indicator positions at the beginning of each field, and a two-character subfield code preceding each data element within the field. The fixed-length variable control fields contain data elements of predetermined length. These coded data characterize the data elements with sufficient precision to support computer manipulation of the data for a variety of functions. The same categories of data elements are present in each record and the data are supplied as necessary in the form of codes of predetermined length that convey the required information. The size of the field is, thus, constant. Systems vary as to how they display the information, for example, what information is included and where, and how it is displayed.

A variable data field contains data elements that vary in length. For example, the authorized heading of an authority record or a reference tracing may vary in length from record to record. The nature of the data is such that it cannot be reduced to a code of predetermined length. A single authority record will contain several variable data fields.

A USMARC authority record consists of four main sections: the leader, the record directory, fixed-field data elements, and variable field data elements. A description of each section follows.

The Leader

A description of each definable section is given in figure 10. The logical record-length data element gives the length of the entire record including itself and the record terminator. The number is right justified with zero fill. The *record status* data element indicates the relationship of the record to a file for file maintenance purposes. The *type of record* is always coded *z* for authority record. The specific type of authority record is identified by a code in the 008/09 field.

The *indicator count* is always *2* to signify the two-character indicator positions at the beginning of each variable data field. The *subfield count* is always *2* to signify the number of character positions used for a subfield code in each variable data field. Each data element in a variable data field is identified by subfield code consisting of a delimiter *≠* and a lowercase alphabetic or numeric character.

The *base address of data* specifies the first character position of the first variable control field in a record. The number is the base from which the starting position of all of the other fields in the record is addressed. This means that the address identifies the position of the first character in the variable control field rather than the beginning of the record. The number is always justified with right zero fill.

The encoding level indicates whether the authority record is complete or not. In regard to the entry map the length of the length-of-the-field position signifies the number of character positions in each directory entry and is always *4*; the length of the starting character position signifies the number of characters in the starting position and is always *5*; the length of the implementation-defined position of each directory entry is *0* because a directory entry does not contain an implementation-defined position.

The Record Directory

The record directory is the second section of a USMARC record. It contains the field identifiers (*tag*), the starting location and length of each field within the record. Directory entries for variable control fields appear first, in tag order. Entries for variable data fields follow, in the order based on the first character of the tag. The record directory follows the twenty-three-character leader immediately, beginning with the twenty-fourth character position. There is a twelve-character directory entry for each subsequent control or variable field within the record. For example, if there are six fields in the record, the directory will occupy seventy-two character positions.

The content of the twelve-character directory consists of a three-character tag that identifies a field, four numeric characters that indicate the number of characters in the field identified by the tags, and five numeric characters that identify the starting position of the first character of a field. The directory ends with a *field terminator* character.

THE LEADER
(00 - 16: System Supplied)

Character Position	Data Element

00 - 04	Logical Record Length
	Record Status
	   Codes used:
	      n new record
	      c corrected or revised record
	      a increase in encoding level
	      d record deleted
	      s record deleted
	        because heading split into
	        two or more headings.
	      x record deleted
	        because replaced by another
	        heading.

06	Type of Record
	   Code used:
	      z authority data

07-09	Undefined (Blank spaces)
10	Indicator Count
11	Subfield Code Count
12-16	Base Address of Data

17	Encoding Level
	   Codes used:
	      n complete authority record
	      o incomplete authority record

18-19	Undefined (Blank spaces)
20-23	Entry Map
20	Length of the length of field position
21	Length of the starting character position
22	Length of implementation-defined position
23	Undefined (Blank spaces)

Example:

   0 0 2 8 0 N z bbb 2 2 0 0 0 5 4 N bb 4 5 0 0

Explanation of Code:

   Code: 00280 n z bbb 2 2 0 0 0 5 4 n b b 4 5 0 0
   Position: 0——4 5 6 7–9 10 11 12 ——16 17 18-19 20 21 22 23

Fig. 10. The leader

It is not essential for librarians to know the details of the record directory entries since these data are used exclusively for the computer manipulation and processing of the data in the authority records. The data elements in the record directory are displayed in figure 10.

Fixed Field Data Elements

The fixed field is recognized by its structured directory of categories of data elements. Although the coded data included in the fixed field are constant within a system, they often vary from system to system. The variances reflect the system requirements of the organization that creates and maintains the authority file system. Because these data are system-specific equivalents of USMARC fields, a display of specific elements is not given here. Instead, a generalized description of the fixed fields in the USMARC format is given.

In the USMARC format, certain fields of control data convey the general characteristics of the record or of the headings in the record in a fixed field display. The fields consist of data and a field terminator. They do not contain indicators or subfield codes; instead, they contain either a single data element or a series of fixed-length data elements identified by relative character positions. These fields follow the record directory entries immediately. The arrangement is by the order of the tags. They are as follows:

Tag Number	Data Element
001	authority record control number
005	date and time of latest transaction
008	fixed-length data elements

(001) The Authority Record Control Number

The authority record control number (ARCN) is a unique variable-length number assigned to each authority record by the organization creating, using, or distributing the record (see figure 11). This field is system-generated.

(005) Date and Time of Latest Transaction

This field consists of sixteen characters that show the date (eight characters) and time (eight characters) of the latest record transaction (see figure 12). The date and time serve as a version identifier for the record. Once entered on file, this information never changes.

(008) Fixed-Length Data Elements

The fixed-length data element field contains forty character positions that convey coded information about the authority record as a whole (see figure 13). The data elements are positionally defined. If the character position has not been defined, it contains either a blank or a fill character.

Chapter Position	Data Element	Comments
0 - 2	Alphabetic Prefix	The prefix distinguishes an authority record from a bibliographic record.
3 - 4	Year	The data represent the last two digits of the year of creation/input.
5 -10	Serial	The data consist of one to six digits sequentially assigned.
11	Supplement Number	This position is normally blank to be consistent with bibliographic records.
12 +	Alphabetic Identifier and/or Revision Date	Variable in length.

Example:

001 N ƀ ƀ 842341916 ƀ

Explanation of Codes:

```
Code:      N ƀ ƀ 8 4 2 34191 6  ƀ
Position:  0 -2 3-4 5————10 11 12
```

Fig. 11. (001) Authority record control number (ARCN)

005   DATE AND TIME OF LATEST TRANSACTION

Character Position	Data Element
0 - 3	Year
4 - 5	Month
6 - 7	Day
8 - 9	Hour
10 - 11	Minute
12 - 13	Second
14	Decimal Point
15	Decimal Fraction of a Second

Example:

1985 August 19 4:20 .25.8 p.m.
        (4 hours: 20 minutes. 25 seconds
        8 tenths of a second)

005 19850719042025.8

Explanation of Code:

```
Code:      1 9 8 5  07  19  04   2 0  2 5  .  8
Position:  0————3  4-5  6-7  8-9  10-11 12-13 14-15
```

Fig. 12. (005) Date and time of latest transaction

DATA ELEMENT	CHARACTER POSITION	COMMENT
Date Entered on File	00 - 05	Formula (yymmdd)
Direct/Indirect Geographic Subdivision Code	06	Codes Used: b not geographically subdivided i subdivided indirectly n not applicable (heading cannot be subdivided)
Romanization Scheme	07	Codes used: e local a international f of unknown origin b national g conventional c national library n not acceptable association d national library or bibliographic agency
[Blank]	08	Codes Used: a established heading f established b untraced reference heading and c traced reference subdivision d subdivision g reference and e node label subdivision
Authority Reference Record Code	09	d AACR2 compatible n not applicable (i.e., heading is not a name or is a subject heading) z other
Catalog Rules Code (continued)	10	Codes used: d AACR2 compatible a earlier rules n not applicable b AACRI (i.e., heading is not a c AACR2 name or is a subject heading)
Subject Heading System Code	11	a Library of Congress k National Library b LC children's literature of Canada (English) c NLM r Art or Architecture Thesaurus
Type of Series Code	12	Codes used to indicate subject heading system used: Codes used: z other a monographic n not applicable b multipart item (i.e., not a series c series-like phrase heading)
Numbered/Unnumbered Series Code	13	Codes used: a numbered n not applicable b unnumbered (i.e., not a series) c numbering varies (i.e., numbered/ unnumbered)

Heading Use Code—Main or Added Entry	14	Code used: b not appropriate
		a appropriate for use for use as main
		  as main entry or added entry or added
		  entry. entry

Heading Use Code—Subject Added Entry	15	Code used: b not appropriate
		a appropriate for use for use as subject
		  as subject added added entry
		  entry

Heading Use Code—Series Added Entry
 	
Type of Subject
	16	Code used: b not appropriate
		a appropriate for use for use as series
		  as series added added entry
		  entry

Subdivision Code	17	Codes used: a topical d geographic b form e language c chronological n not applicable
[Blank]	18 - 27	Undefined and set to blank
Type of Government Agency	28	Codes used: f federal/national but undeterminable b not a gov. agency l local s state, provincial, etc. a autonomous i international u unknown c multilocal o gov. agency z other
Reference Evaluation Code	29	Codes used: a tracings consistent b value predates b tracings not consistent definiton of code n not applicable
[Blank]	30	Undefined
Record Update in Process Code	31	Codes used: a record can be used b record being updated; do not use
Undifferentiated Personal Name Code	32	Codes used: b undifferentiated a differentiated n not applicable
Status of Authority Heading Code	33	Codes used: a fully established d preliminary b memorandum n not applicable (refers to c provisional status of heading only)
[Blank]	34	Undefined and set to blank
Language code	35 - 37	A 3-character MARC language code is used here.
Modified Record Code	38	Codes used: b not modified X record contains characters that cannot be s shortened input because they are not in the character set.
Cataloging Source Code	39	Codes used: b Library of Congress c LC cooperative programs (i.e., LSP) a NAL d other b NLM u unknown

Fig. 13. (008) Fixed-length data elements

Variable Field Data Elements

The variable fields that follow are the ones that carry information most relevant to the day-to-day practical authority work. The various tags and subfield codes are identified and discussed in detail. This section is not intended to substitute for the authorities manuals themselves. It does, however, provide sufficient information to enable one to interpret LC authority records in MARC format and to work with the data accurately, intelligently, and comfortably.

Three levels of content designation are provided for variable data fields:

1. a three-character tag, stored in the directory entry
2. indicators stored at the beginning of each variable data field
3. subfield codes preceding each data element

The variable fields are recognizable in a USMARC record by a three-character code called a tag. The variable field data may include the following fields in the order of the tags that identify them:

010–090	Identification and classification control numbers and codes
100–151	Heading
260–551	References and tracings
640–646	Series treatment decisions
663–682	Notes

Each variable data field begins with two characters called indicators that relate to the data in the field. They control codes conveying information that interprets or supplements the data found in the field. They also support some machine manipulations such as filing, sorting, search key formation, and data display. Each field also includes a two-character subfield code and a field terminator. There is also a record terminator following the last field in the record.

010–090 Identification and Classification Control Numbers and Codes

Tags in the 0xx block identify the type of variable control field number and codes and are arranged in the order of the tags as displayed in figure 14.

HEADINGS

Authorized headings appear as the 1xx field. The unknown quality (x) of the tag is determined by the type of heading it precedes. The tags and types of headings follow:

100	Personal name heading and personal name/uniform title
110	Corporate name heading and corporate name/uniform title
111	Conference name heading and conference name/uniform title
130	Uniform title heading
150	Topical subject heading
151	Geographical name heading

Tag	Data Element	Indicators	Subfield Codes	Comment
010	Library of Congress Control Number	Blank	a LC authority record control number z cancelled/invalid control number	Same number as carried in field 001
014	Link to Bibliographic Record for Serial or Multipart Item	Blank	a control number for bibliographic record	The number is preceded by the NUC symbol of the institution.
020	ISBN (Series)	Blank	a ISBN b terms of availability z cancelled / invalid	Data serves as a link to the bibliographic record (i.e., multiple item)
022	ISSN (Series)	Blank	a ISSN b incorrect ISSN z cancelled ISSN	Data serves as a link to the bibliographic record (i.e., serial)
035	System Control Number	Blank	a local number z cancelled/invalid	The number is preceded by the NUC symbol of the institution
040	Cataloging Source	Blank	a original cataloging agency b language of cataloging c transcribing agency d notifying agency	Data provides the NUC symbol of the institution that provided input or that modified the record.
042	Authentication Code	Blank	a authentication code	Data represents the code of the authentication center which reviewed/upgraded the authority record.
043	Geographic Area Code	Blank	a geographic area code	The code is made up of 7 characters that provide a hierarchical geographical breakdown associated with the heading.
045	Time Period of Heading	First Indicator b no subfield code b 0 single date 1 multiple date 2 range of dates Second Indicator Blank	a time period b 9999 BC-AD time period c Pre-9999 BC time period	Data are supplied by a special date/time table included in the format.
050	LC Call Number (Series)	First Indicator Blank Second Indicator Source of call number: 0 assigned by LC 4 Assigned by other agency 5 Institution to which field applies	a classification number b item number d volumes/dates	Used for series if all parts of the series are classed as a collection.

Fig. 14. Variable field data elements

Tag	Data Element	Indicators	Subfield Codes	Comment
052	Geographic Classification Code	Blank	a area b subarea	Data taken from LC classification schedule G.
053	LC Classification Number	Blank	a single number or beginning number of a range b end number of a range c explanatory term	Data contains LC classification number associated with an authority heading.
060	NLM Call Number	First Blank Second 0 assigned by NLM 4 not assigned by NLM	a classification number b item number d volume/dates 5 institution to which field applies	Used for series when all parts classed as a set.
070	NAL Call Number	Blank	a classification number b item number d volume/dates	Used for series when all parts classed as a set.
072	Subject Category Code	First Blank Second ⌷ no information 0 NAL subject category code list 7 code source specified	a subject category code x subject category code subdivision 2 code source	
073	Subdivision Usage	Blank	a subdivision z source	Code may relate to all or part of subject category.
082	Dewey Decimal Code Number	First Indicator 0 full edition 1 abridged edition Second Indicator 0 Assigned by LC 4 Not assigned by LC	a classification number b item number d volume/dates 2 edition number to which field applies	Used for series when all classed as a set.
083	Dewey Decimal Classification Number	First Indicator 0 full edition 1 abridged edition Second Indicator Blank	a classification number or beginning number b classification number or ending number c explanatory term 2 source (i.e., edition number)	Data contain the DDC number associated with an authority heading.
090	Local Call Number (Series)	Blank	a class number b item number c volume / date	Data contain a local call number of a series if the series is classified as a collected set.

Fig. 14 (cont.). Variable field data elements

Each type of heading has its own assigned values for indicators and its own list of subfield codes that distinguish data elements in the heading requiring separate manipulation.

INDICATORS
Indicators are independently defined for each field (see figure 15). Parallel meanings are preserved whenever possible. Indicators for personal names are unique whereas those for corporate and conference names are similar. Indicators for uniform titles, topical subject headings, and geographical name headings are identical.

Subfield Codes

Subfield codes distinguish data elements within a field. They are independently defined but parallel meanings are presented when possible. Subfield codes are defined for purposes of identification and the order of subfields is specified by content standards. There are similarities between subfield codes used for personal, corporate, and conference name headings, and uniform titles as reflected in figure 16.

Indicators	Personal (100)	Corporate Names (110)	Conference Names (111)	Uniform Titles (130)	Topical Subjects (150)	Geographical Names (151)
First Indicator						
0 forename only	x					
1 single surname	x					
2 multiple surname	x					
3 name of family	x					
0 surname inverted		x	x			
1 geographic name with subheading		x	x			
2 name in direct order		x	x	x	x	x
ƀ blank						
General Indicator						
0-9 nonfiling character	x	x	x	x	x	x

Fig. 15. Indicators for headings (1xx field)

Subfield Codes	(100) Personal Names	(110) Corporate Names	(111) Conference Names	(130) Uniform Titles	(150) Topical Subject	(151) Geographical Names
a name	x	x	x	x		
a uniform title						
a topical subject or name of place					x	x
b numeration (roman numerals used in entry element)	x					
b each subordinate unit in a hierarchy		x(R)				
b number of conference			x			
b name following place as entry element					x	x
c titles and other words associated with the name	x(R)					
c place where meeting held		x	x			
d dates (of birth, death, etc.; of conference; of signing treaty) as applicable	x	x(R)	x	x(R)		
e relator	x	x				
e subordinate unit			x(R)			
f date of work	x	x	x	x		
g miscellaneous information	x	x	x	x		
h medium	x	x	x	x		
i reference instruction phrase				x		
k form subheading	x	x(R)	x	x(R)		
l language	x	x	x	x		
m medium of performance (for music)	x(R)	x(R)		x(R)		
n number of part/section (for music)	x(R)	x(R)	x(R)	x(R)		
o arranged statement (for music)	x	x				
p name of part/section of work	x(R)	x(R)				
q fuller form	x					
q name of conference following place as entry element			x			

Fig. 16. Subfield codes (1xx field)

Subfield Codes	(100) Personal Names	(110) Corporate Names	(111) Conference Names	(130) Uniform Titles	(150) Topical Subject	(151) Geographical Names
r key (for music)	x	x		x		
s version	x	x	x	x		
t title of a work	x	x	x	x		
w control subfield				x	x	x
x general subject subdivisions	x(R)	x(R)	x(R)	x(R)	x(R)	x(R)
y chronological subject subdivision	x(R)	x(R)	x(R)	x(R)	x(R)	x(R)
z geographical subject subdivision	x(R)	x(R)	x(R)	x(R)	x(R)	x(R)

R= repeatable
(Note: Theoretically, all data elements may be repeated; however, the nature of the data precludes repetition. The repeatability of each subfield code is defined in the USMARC format.

Examples:

Personal name:
100 10 ≠a Clack, Doris H. ≠g (Doris Hargrett)

Corporate name:
110 20 ≠a Florida State University. ≠b School of Library and Infromation Studies

Conference heading:
111 20 ≠a International Conference on AACR2 ≠d (1978 : ≠c Tallahassee, Fla.)

Uniform title:
130 b0 ≠a Chanson de Roland. ≠1 English

Topical subject heading:
150 b0 ≠a Afro-Americans ≠z Florida

Geographic names:
151 b0 ≠a Zimbabwe ≠x History

Fig. 16 (cont.). Subfield codes (1xx field)

References and Tracings

References are not carried explicitly in a USMARC record. Instead, tags are used to indicate the different types of references and subsequently the reference legends. The types of reference tags are:

260	complex *see* reference (subject)
360	complex *see also* reference (subjects)
400	*see from* tracing—personal name
410	*see from* tracing—corporate name
411	*see from* tracing—conference name
430	*see from* tracing—uniform title
450	*see from* tracing—topical subject
451	*see from* tracing—geographic name
500	*see also from* tracing—personal name
510	*see also from* tracing—corporate name
511	*see also from* tracing—conference name
530	*see also from* tracing—uniform title
550	*see also from* tracing—topical subject
551	*see also from* tracing—geographic name
663	complex *see also* reference—name
664	complex *see* reference—name
665	history reference
666	general explanatory reference

COMPLEX REFERENCES

Complex references are of two types: *see from* and *see also from*. They are complex references that cannot be constructed automatically from the tracings by a display program. Instead, the actual text of the reference must be given in a special field: 260 for general explanatory *see* references, 360 for general explanatory *see also* references, or in a 6xx note field.

When the heading referred from is not an authorized heading, the special field containing the text of the reference is combined with a 1xx field containing the referred from heading. The 1xx field is combined with the following fields to create the general explanatory *see* reference as follows:

1. 1xx and a 260 field for *see* references for subjects
2. 1xx and a 666 field for *see* references for names
3. 1xx and a 664 field for cataloger-generated references for names

When the heading referred from is an authorized heading, a general explanatory *see also* reference is created from data in the following fields:

1. 360 for subjects (the reference is not traced)
2. 665 from a reference traced in a 5xx field for an information or history reference
3. 663 from a reference traced in a 5xx field

CONTROL SUBFIELD ≠i

Subfield code ≠i contains a special reference instruction phrase that may be used in a cross reference display. Subfield code ≠i indicates that the generation of a tag-related reference instruction phrase in a cross reference display should be suppressed. The content of the subfield is the reference instruction phrase to be used in the cross reference display.

CONTROL SUBFIELD ≠w

The control subfield ≠w is restricted to the 4xx and 5xx fields only. The control subfield contains a four-position code used to produce reference or print constants to clarify the use of a particular tracing. The codes in ≠w are dependent on the character position in which they occur.

The definitions/values of the position are determined by a one-character alphabetic code for each position that specifies:

1. the relationship between the tracing and the heading
2. the authority reference structure that is appropriate for a given tracing
3. whether a *see from* reference is an earlier form of the authorized heading established under earlier cataloging rules
4. whether a reference is to be displayed

The specific definitions/values of each position code follow.

Position 0: The alphabetic code specifies whether a 4xx tracing is the form of the authorized heading established under the earlier cataloging rules.

a	earlier heading
b	later heading
d	acronym
f	musical composition
g	broader term
h	narrower term
i	reference instruction phrase
n	not applicable

Position 1: The alphabetic code specifies whether the authority reference structure(s) is appropriate for a given tracing.

a	name reference structure only
b	subject reference structure only
c	series reference structure only
d	name and subject reference structure only
e	name and series reference structure only
f	subject and series reference structure only
g	name, subject, and series reference structure only
n	not applicable

Position 2: The alphabetic code specifies whether a 4xx tracing is the form of the heading established under earlier descriptive cataloging rules.

a	earlier rules
n	not applicable

Position 3: The alphabetic code specifies whether a reference is to be displayed from a 4xx or 5xx tracing.

> a   reference not displayed
> b   reference not displayed, Field 664 used
> c   reference not displayed, Field 663 used
> d   reference not displayed, Field 665 used
> n   not applicable

The following control subfield ≠w code values are valid for 4xx fields:

Position 0:   d,n
Position 1:   a,c,d,e,f,g
Position 2:   a,n
Position 3:   a,b,n

The following control subfield ≠w code values are valid for 5xx fields:

Position 0:   a,b,n
Position 1:   n
Position 2:   n
Position 3:   a,c,n

SEE FROM REFERENCE TRACINGS

See from reference tracings are tagged 4xx. They represent the form of name referred from. *See from* reference tracings may be the following types of entry elements as headings:

400   personal name heading
410   corporate name heading
411   conference name heading
430   uniform titles
450   topical subject headings
451   geographic names

Each type of reference tracing has its own assigned values for indicators and its own subfield codes that identify various data elements in the reference tracing. The indicators and subfield codes for the various types of reference tracings are identical to those used for 1xx heading fields with the following exceptions:

w   control subfield
i   text of reference instruction phrase
x, y, and z   subject subdivision

SEE ALSO FROM REFERENCE TRACINGS

See also from reference tracings are tagged 5xx. They represent an established form of a name that is related in some way to the heading in the 1xx field. *See also from* reference tracings may be for the following types of headings:

500   personal name heading
510   corporate name heading
511   conference name heading

530   uniform titles
550   topical subject headings
551   geographic names

Each type of reference has its own assigned values for indicators and its own list of subfield codes that identify various data elements in the reference tracing. The indicators and subfield codes for the various types of reference tracings are identical to those used for 1xx heading fields with the following exceptions:

w   control subfield
i   text of reference instruction phrase
x, y, and z   subject subdivisions

Series Treatment Information

Series treatment decisions vary from institution to institution. In authority records, series treatment information is carried in the 64x fields. The data elements and their appropriate forms are:

640   dates of publication and volume designation
641   numbering peculiarities
642   series numbering example
643   place and publisher/issuing body
644   analysis practice
645   tracing practice
646   classification practice

Each variable field has its own assigned values for indicators and its own list of subfield codes that identify various data elements as is displayed in figure 17.

Notes

Variable fields that contain notes are required under many circumstances. For example, notes are required to provide sufficient facts that contributed to the identification of the authority heading.

Notes are also required whenever there are general explanatory *see also from* references that cannot be constructed solely from the content of the 4xx or 5xx tracing. The different types of notes are:

665   history reference
666   general explanatory reference
667   usage or scope for names
670   source data found
675   source data not found
678   epitome
680   scope note for subject
681   subject example note
682   deleted heading information

TAG	DATA ELEMENT	INDICATORS	SUBFIELD CODES	COMMENTS
640	Date/ Volume Designation	first indicator 0 formatted style 1 unformatted	a dates of publication/ volume designation z source	Containing the beginning/ending date(s) of publication and/or the extent of volumes within the series. Also contains a citation of the source of information.
641	Number Peculiarities	[Blank]	a numbering peculiarities note z source	Indicates such information as suspensions, items not published, double numbering, combined issues, or any other peculiarities that could cause confusion.
642	Series Numbering Example	[Blank]	a series numbering example d volumes/dates to which series numbering applies 5 institution /copy to which field applies	Important in support of consistency in the use of a particular pattern for display.
643	Place and Publisher/ Issuing Body	[Blank]	a place b publisher/issuing body d volumes/date to which place and publisher/issuing body apply	Helpful in determining when new item belongs to a particular series.
644	Analysis Practice	[Blank]	af analyze in full ap analyze in part an not analyzed b exceptions to analysis practice d volume/date to which analysis practice applies 5 institution to which the field applies	
645	Tracing Practice	[Blank]	at series traced an series not traced d volume/date to which tracing practice applies	
646	Classification Practice	[Blank]	ac volumes in series are classified as collections am volumes in series are classified with the main series as volumes in series are classified separately (there is no classification number) d volumes/dates to which classification practice applies 5 institutions to which classification practice applies	

Fig. 17. Series treatment (64x)

Each of the variable data fields has its own assigned values for indicators and its own subfield codes that identify the various data elements as displayed in figure 18.

Summary

The preceding review of the USMARC content designation (e.g., tags, indicators, and subfield codes in the MARC authorities format) is not intended to substitute

Notes	Indicators	Subfield Codes	Comments
665 History Reference	First ϸ Blank Second ϸ Blank	a history reference	Explains the relationship among 3 or more established names. Used when the information cannot be adequately conveyed in a simple see reference.
666 General Explanatory Reference for Names	First ϸ Blank Second ϸ Blank	a general explanatory reference	This field contains information to assist in filing or searching.
667 Usage/Scope (Names)	First ϸ Blank Second ϸ Blank	a usage note	This field gives information about the use or the scope of the heading being established.
670 Source Data Found	First ϸ Blank Second ϸ Blank	a citation b information found	This field contains a citation to a reference source in which significant information relative to the heading was found.
675 Source Data not Found	First ϸ Blank Second ϸ Blank	a source citation	The field contains a citation for reference sources in which no information was found.
678 Epitome	First ϸ Blank Second ϸ Blank	a epitome	This field contains biographical, historical, or other information about the 1xx field.
680 Scope note (Subject)	First ϸ Blank Second ϸ Blank	a subject heading b explanatory text	
681 Subject example/ Tracing Note	First ϸ Blank Second ϸ Blank	a subject heading b explanatory text	This field is intended to serve as an aid in tracing headings used in notes as examples.
682 Deleted Information	First ϸ Blank Second ϸ Blank	a subject heading i explanatory text	The field is used when there is a need to explain why a record was deleted.

Fig. 18. Notes (66x)

for the comprehensive format itself. However, it does provide sufficient information to familiarize a cataloger with the authorities format. The cataloger who has experience with USMARC tagging for books will understand immediately the conversion procedures for delimiting data elements within authority records. As a result of having reviewed the information presented here, any technical services librarian should have a better understanding of the MARC authorities format and an enhanced ability to interpret MARC authority records in terms of their structure and data content.

Chapter 9

Controlling Personal Names

The process of determining the content of authority records is an intellectual one based on the provisions found in the numerous rules in chapters 21–24 of *AACR2-88*. Chapter 26 of *AACR2-88* summarizes the rules in more general terms. The discussions that follow analyze and illustrate the principles for controlling personal names. (For discussions on corporate names, see chapter 10.) Because of the complexity of uniform titles, which are distributed by LC as part of the name authorities service, they are also discussed in a separate chapter (see chapter 11).

Procedures

The work being cataloged is the first source to check for information relating to the established heading. The work should be examined carefully for pertinent information, such as variant forms of names or different names used by the person. Relevant information may be on the chief source of information, in the preface, in the introduction, somewhere in the text, or on accompanying materials. Variant names or forms of names often appear on the packaging, such as the cover, the jacket, a wrapper, or the container. Reference sources should also be consulted for variant names and forms of names. (For a list of reference sources, see chapter 14.)

Once relevant data have been gathered, references must be determined and transcribed in the form that is compatible with the structure of the authorized heading. Since headings are based on the principles in *AACR2-88*, references must be also.

A variant name, particularly a fuller form found on the chief source of information or elsewhere in the work, should be considered for a reference if it differs from that used in the heading. It should be cited in the sources found area and a reference made. If the variant name is taken from a packaging source and is less full than the name on the chief source of information, it should not be used as a reference. Finally, references should not be made from variants of a variant name.

General Principles

See references are generated if any of the following conditions exists:

1. The name is in a form that is significantly different from that used in the heading. *Significant* is defined here as meaning any differences in
    a. any element to the left of the comma in inverted names (i.e., the surname) or the first element to the right of the comma (i.e., the first forename). If the difference appears in the middle name, a reference is not made.
    b. the first five letters in the entry element in noninverted names
    c. fullness
    d. language
    e. spelling
    f. romanization
2. The name is different from that used in the heading. The name may have been identified in reference sources or in the item being cataloged.
3. The name is a compound or a multipart name and the parts are likely access points. The following types of entry elements fall into this category:
    a. compound surnames
    b. names with prefixes
    c. given name entries
    d. names with epithets
    e. saints
    f. family names of rulers
    g. initials
    h. phrase headings

Name-title references are made if any of the following conditions exists:

1. The person produces under several different names and no single one is predominant.
2. The entry heading is represented by a set of initials in direct order.
3. The entry heading is represented by a set of initials that is a pseudonym or that stands for a phrase.
4. Two or more persons use the same pseudonym for some of their works and another name for other works.

See also references are needed if either of the following conditions exists:

1. The works of one person are entered under two or more headings.
2. The name given to an unknown person includes the name of a known person.

Explanatory references are needed if either of the following conditions exists:

1. Detailed guidance is needed to define for the user the scope or nature of the heading, the filing order of a particular heading, or searching strategies.
2. Guidance is needed to explain the use of certain prefixes. (Some libraries, including the Library of Congress, do not follow this option. Instead, they make single references for each heading containing a prefix.)

Specific Principles

AACR2-88 sets forth certain conditions that require references. In this section those conditions are identified and discussed. Examples are given as appropriate to clarify the interpretation. Some of the examples used to illustrate the principles have been taken with permission directly from *AACR2-88* because they are classic examples of the particular situation, because the occurrence of the situation is rare, or because other actual examples were not available. An asterisk (*) preceding the name identifies all such examples.

Official Communications

Communications from heads of state and national governments and international bodies and from high church officials, such as popes, patriarchs, and bishops, may be entered either under a corporate heading representing the office or under a personal heading representing the individual officer. A personal heading is used whenever the work being cataloged is not an official communication (e.g., proclamations, executive orders, messages to legislatures, etc.). Whenever the personal heading is chosen, an explanatory reference should be made from the corporate to the personal heading. Although the Library of Congress no longer makes these references, they can be very useful to a catalog user and a library may establish a policy to make them.

Example:

Authority record:

```
Mohammed Reza Pahlavi, Shah of Iran, 1919-1980.
   xx Iran. Shah (1941-1979 : Mohammed Reza
        Pahlavi)
```

References for the public catalog:

```
Mohammed Reza Pahlavi, Shah of Iran, 1919-1980.
   Here are entered the personal works of the
Shah.
   For works of the Shah acting in an official
capacity, see Iran. Shah (1941-1979 : Mohammed
Reza Pahlavi)
```

```
Iran. Shah (1941-1979 : Mohammed Reza Pahlavi)
   Here are entered works of the Shah acting in
his official capacity.
   For other works, see Mohammed Reza Pahlavi,
Shah of Iran, 1919-1980.
```

Shared Pseudonyms

Whenever two or more persons collaborate and use a single pseudonym as a name for the group, an explanatory reference should be made from the name of each person to the pseudonym. If any member of the group also produces individually under her or his own name and the name is represented in the catalog, an explanatory reference should also be made from the pseudonym to the individual's real name.

Examples:

```
Queen, Ellery.
   xx Dannay, Frederic.
   xx Lee, Manfred.

Queen, Ellery.
   The joint pseudonym of Frederic Dannay and
Manfred Lee.
   For a work written by Dannay under his
earlier name, see Dannay, Frederic.

Dannay, Frederic.
   For works of this author written in
collaboration with Manfred Lee, see Queen,
Ellery.

Lee, Manfred.
   For works of this author written in
collaboration with Frederic Dannay, see Queen,
Ellery.
```

One Pseudonym

Whenever the heading is a pseudonym for a person who always produces under the one pseudonym, a *see* reference should be made from the real name to the pseudonym.

Example:

```
Struther, Jan, 1901-
   x Maxtone Graham, Joyce Anstruther, 1901-

Maxtone Graham, Joyce Anstruther, 1901-
      see
Struther, Jan, 1901-
```

Several Pseudonyms

If the authorized heading is a pseudonym and this pseudonym is the predominant one of several used by the person, a *see* reference should be made from each of the lesser-used names to the one chosen as the heading. The person's real name may be the lesser-used name.

Example:

```
Asimov, Isaac, 1920–
   x French, Paul, 1920–
   x A, Dr., 1920–
```

No Predominant Pseudonym

If different headings have been chosen for different works by the same person because the person has produced under several names and no one of them is predominant, explanatory references should be made to link the various names to one another as appropriate for the catalog.

Example:

```
Creasey, John.
   xx Ashe, Gordon.
   xx Deane, Norman.
   xx Halliday, Michael.
   xx Hunt, Kyle.
   xx Manton, Peter.
   xx Marric, J.J.
   xx Martin, Richard.
   xx Morton, Anthony.
   xx Ranger, Ken.
   xx Reilly, William K.
   xx Riley, Tex.
   xx York, Jeremy.

Creasey, John.
   For works of this author written under
pseudonyms, see
Ashe, Gordon.
Deane, Norman.
Halliday, Michael.
Hunt, Kyle.
Manton, Peter.
Marric, J.J.
Martin, Richard.
Morton, Anthony.
Ranger, Ken.
Reilly, William K.
Riley, Tex.
York, Jeremy.

Ashe, Gordon.
   For works of this author written under his
real name, see Creasey, John.
   For works written under his other
pseudonyms, see
```

```
Deane, Norman.
Halliday, Michael.
Hunt, Kyle.
Manton, Peter.
Marric, J.J.
Martin, Richard.
Morton, Anthony.
Ranger, Ken.
Reilly, William K.
Riley, Tex.
York, Jeremy.

Deane, Norman.
    For works of this author written under his
real name, see Creasey, John.
    For works written under his other
pseudonyms, see
Ashe, Gordon.
Halliday, Michael.
Hunt, Kyle.
Manton, Peter.
Marric, J.J.
Martin, Richard.
Morton, Anthony.
Ranger, Ken.
Reilly, William K.
Riley, Tex.
York, Jeremy.
```

(Only three references are illustrated here to conserve space. References should be made for each of the variant names.)

Different Names in the Same Work

If the name used in the heading is the name most frequently used by a person who produces under several names *and* who uses several different names in the same work, a name-title reference should be made from the less frequently used names to the name used in the heading.

Example:

```
Creasey, John.
    Elope to death / by John Creasey as Gordon
Ashe . . .

    Ashe, Gordon
        Elope to death
        see
Creasey, John
```

If the name used in the heading is the most frequently used name of a person who produces under several names *and* who uses different names in different editions of the same work, a name-title reference should be made from the name(s) used in the earlier edition(s) to the one used in the latest edition of the work.

Example:

1st edition:

```
York, Jeremy.
    The man I killed / by Michael Halliday. --
London : Hodder & Stroughton, 1961.
```

Subsequent edition:

```
York, Jeremy.
    The man I killed / by Jeremy York. -- 1st
American ed. -- New York : Macmillan, 1963,
c1961.

York, Jeremy.
    x Halliday, Michael.
            Man I killed.

Halliday, Michael.
    Man I killed.
    see
York, Jeremy.
```

Fullness of Name

If the name in the heading is the most commonly used name of a person who uses a name in varied fullness, a *see* reference should be made from the other less commonly used form(s).

More searches would be successful in online catalogs if the fullest form of a name were used as the heading at all times when fullness of names varies. Instead, *AACR2-88* requires the most commonly used form of the name, which may or may not be the fullest form. This rule can only be effective in manual catalogs.

Example:

```
Higham, Mary R.
    x M.R.H. (Mary R. Higham)

    M.R.H. (Mary R. Higham)
        see
Higham, Mary R.
```

If the heading contains the fullest form of a name used by a person who produces works under names in varied fullness and who uses no one form more often than the others, a *see* reference should be made from the shorter form(s) to the fullest form. The Library of Congress usually uses the fullest form of a name for living authors rather than the predominant name. This is a good policy since predominant names of living authors could change several times.

Example:

```
Dorfman, Adolfo.
    x Dorfman, A. (Adolfo)

Dorfman, A. (Adolfo)
     see
Dorfman, Adolfo.
```

Romanized Given Name Entries

If the name in the heading is in romanized form from a well-established English-language reference source, *see* references should be made from any variant English-language forms that have also been identified in other well-established English-language sources.

Example:

```
Thucydides.
    x Fukidid.
    x Tucidides.
    x Thukydides.
```

Romanized Surname Entries

If the name in the heading is entered under surname and is in a form romanized by the library, make *see* references from other romanized forms found in reference sources.

Examples:

```
*Dayan, Mosheh.
    x Dayan, Moshe.
```

AACR2-88 permits a library to optionally use the romanized form of name found in well-established English-language sources rather than the romanization adopted by the library, which affects the choice of references. Libraries should take the option since it is more user-oriented than the standard rule. Library users in the United States are likely to be more familiar with the names found in well-established English-language reference sources than with the form of name as romanized by the library.

Example:

```
*Dayan, Moshe.
    x Dayan, Mosheh.
```

Surnames with Prefixes

Because of their derivations, many names include some type of prefix. The prefix generally is derived from a preposition, an article, or a contraction of a preposition and an article in the originating language. The use of prefixes in personal names varies from language to language and, therefore, can pose problems for some users of a catalog. Basic guidelines for transcribing names with prefixes in references follow.

1. If the entry element in the reference is followed immediately by a prefix without any intervening data (i.e., a surname, forename, initials, etc.), place a comma between the entry element and the prefix. The prefix will be considered as an associated word or phrase with the name as the entry element.

    Pattern:

    ```
    _____, _____
    entry element  prefix
    ```

    Example:

    ```
    Sepulveda, Gines de.
        x Gines, de Sepulveda.
    ```

2. If the entry element in the reference is followed immediately by an associated word or phrase rather than by a forename, place the prefix after the associated word or phrase. Place a comma immediately before the associated word or phrase.

    Pattern:

    ```
    _____, _____ _____
    entry element  associated word prefix
    ```

Example:

```
Humboldt, Alexander, Freiherr von, 1767-1835.
    x Humboldt, Freiherr von, 1767-1835.
```

Prefixes as Part of a Surname

If the name in the heading is entered under a prefix and is written sometimes with and sometimes without the prefix hyphenated or attached to the other part of the name, a *see* reference should be made from the part of the name following the prefix to the name in the heading.

Example:

```
DeVille, Philippe.
    x Ville, Philippe de.
```

Titles of Nobility

If the entry element of the name in the heading is a title of nobility that the person uses in place of her or his own surname, a *see* reference should be made from the person's surname to the title.

Example:

```
Clermont-Tonnerre, Aimé-Marie Gaspard, duc de.
    x Gaspard, Aimé-Marie, duc de Clermont-
        Tonnerre.
```

If the title of nobility and the surname are the same, no reference is needed.

Example:

```
Tennyson, Alfred Tennyson, 1st Baron, 1809-
    1892.
```

Given Name Entries

If the entry element in the name in the heading is a given name that is not a title of nobility and if that given name is followed by an associated word or phrase, a *see* reference should be made from the associated word or phrase.

Example:

```
*Leonardo, da Vinci.
    x Vinci, Leonardo da.
```

Sometimes a phrase following a given name is set off from the given name with a comma. In such cases, a *see* reference is made from the form without the comma to the form with the comma. (This reference may not be necessary in catalogs that disregard punctuation in filing. This would include most online and manual catalogs.)

Example:

```
Lawrence, of the Resurrection.
    x Lawrence of the Resurrection.
```

References should also be made from any variant names and any other names by which the person is known.

Example:

```
Bion, of Phlossa near Smyrna.
   x Vieon.
```

Patronymic with Given Name

If the entry element in the heading is a given name followed by a patronymic, a *see* reference should be made from the patronymic to the given name.

Example:

```
Isaac ben Aaron.
   x Aaron, Isaac ben.
```

Initials and Numerals

When the heading consists solely of initials in direct order, a name-title reference should be made from the initials in inverted order form to the direct order form. The Library of Congress prefers to make a simple *see* reference instead of a name-title reference in this situation.

Example of a name-title reference:

```
Y.Z.
   x Z., Y.
           From Moscow to Samarkand.


   Z., Y.
      From Moscow to Samarkand.
      see
Y.Z.
```

In case of numerals used as the heading, a name-title reference should be made from a literal transcription of the numbers written as words to the numeral. The words are treated as a common phrase in regard to capitalization. Another name-title reference should be made from the numerals written as they are spoken. The words are capitalized as in a proper name.

Example:

```
"45562".
   x Four, five, five, six, two.
           London Midland stream on shed.
   x Forty-five Thousand, Five Hundred and
        Sixty-two.
           London Midland stream on shed.
```

Phrases That Are Not Real Names

If the name in the heading is a phrase in direct order and the phrase is not considered a real name, references should be made from the phrase in inverted order and from any other variants of the name.

Example:

```
Tom Thumb.
    x Thumb, Tom.
    x Tom Pouce.
    x Daumesdick.
```

If, however, the phrase can be construed as including a surname and the name appears in the heading in inverted order, a *see* reference should be made from the phrase in direct order to the inverted form.

Example:

```
Mugs, Madame.
    x Madame Mugs.
    x Nees, Sophie.
```

Forenames in Phrases

If the name in the heading consists of a phrase that contains a forename but no surname and if the heading is inverted under the forename, a *see* reference should be made from the phrase in direct order to its inverted form.

Example:

```
Fanny, Aunt.
    x Aunt Fanny.
    x Barrow, Frances Elizabeth Mease.
```

Name of Another Person in Phrase Headings

If the name in the heading is in direct order and consists of a phrase by which the author is known and if the phrase heading contains the name of another person, an explanatory reference is needed to explain the relation between the phrase and the name mentioned.

Example:

```
Pseudo-Jerome.
    x Pseudo-Hieronymus.
    x Pseudo Girolamo.
   xx Jerome, Saint, d. 419 or 20.
```

```
Pseudo-Hieronymus.
    see
Pseudo-Jerome.

    Pseudo Girolamo.
        see
Pseudo-Jerome.

Jerome, Saint, d. 419 or 20.
    For the scriptural interpretations of the
Bible erroneously attributed to this person,
see Pseudo-Jerome.
```

A *see also* reference should also be made from the phrase heading to the name of the person mentioned in the phrase.

Example:

```
Jerome, Saint, d. 419 or 20.
  xx Pseudo-Jerome.

    Pseudo-Jerome.
        see also
Jerome, Saint, d. 419 or 20.
```

Characterizing Words or Phrases

If the name in the heading is a characterizing word or phrase naming another work, a *see* reference should be made from the title of the work named to the heading. The pattern to use for the reference is:

```
_____, Author of
    title of work
```

Example:

```
Author of The peacock at home.
    x Peacock at home, Author of.

    Peacock at home, Author of.
        see
Author of The peacock at home.
```

If the name in the heading is not a characterizing word or phrase but such word or phrase appears on the chief source of information, a *see* reference should be made from the phrase to the name in the heading.

Examples:

Bibliographic data:

```
Arblay, Frances Burney d', 1752-1840.
    Camilla, or, A picture of youth / by the
author of Evelina and Cecilia. — London : T.
Payne, 1796.
```

Authority data:

```
Arblay, Frances Burney d', 1752-1840.
    x Author of Evelina and Cecilia.
```

Reference:

```
Author of Evelina and Cecilia.
    see
Arblay, Frances Burney d', 1752-1840.
```

Surname in Phrase Headings

If the name in the heading consists of a surname followed by an associated word or phrase in inverted order, a *see* reference should be made from the phrase in direct order.

Example:

```
Ray, Madame.
    x Madame Ray.
```

Fuller Forms of Names in Qualifiers

If a part of the name in the heading is represented by initials and the full form is also given as a qualifier, a *see* reference should be made from the full form to the form with the initials.

Example:

```
Harrison, J.F.C. (John Fletcher Clews)
    x Harrison, John Fletcher Clews.
```

Sometimes a variant form of name in a reference requires the fuller form as a qualifier. When this occurs, the qualifier used in the reference should be the same as that part of the name used for the authorized heading. The style of the reference, therefore, should parallel that of the heading.

Example:

```
Miller, John J.H.
    x Miller, J.J.H. (John J.H.)
```

There are some basic principles that should be followed when preparing qualifiers for names with initials.

1. The full form of a name in the qualifier of a reference should never be fuller than the qualifier in the heading. They should match exactly.
2. The qualifier should always follow the forename (including any prefix) immediately and precede any other data such as dates and titles. (Data such as dates, titles, and prefixes are not included in the parentheses of the qualifier.)

The principles listed above do not apply when the initials in the heading do not exactly match the fuller name in the qualifier or when the initials are for a married woman using her husband's name.

Names in the qualifier may represent initials from various parts of the name. Figure 19 explains the contents of qualifiers in various situations.

Royalty

If the heading is for royalty and an epithet that is associated with the name is not included in the heading, a *see* reference should be made from the name with the epithet to the name without it.

Example:

```
Carlos, Prince of Asturias, 1545-1568.
    x Carlos de Austria, Infante of
        Spain, 1545-1568.
```

Nonreigning Royalty

If the name in the heading is for a nonreigning royal person, a *see* reference should be made from the given name of the person to the name in the heading.

Example:

```
Northumberland, John Dudley, Duke of, 1502-
    1553.
    x Dudley, John, Duke of Northumberland,
        1502-1553.
```

	TYPE OF ENTRY					LOCATION OF INITIAL		DATE OF QUALIFIER	
	Surname/ Forename	Surname/ Term of address	Given Name Entry	Initials Only	Surname	Given Name	All Surnames	All Given Names	All Names in Running Order
1	✓				✓		✓		
2	✓				✓	✓		✓	
3	✓					✓			✓
4			✓			✓			✓
5		✓		✓					✓

Fig. 19. Initials and their qualifiers

Chapter 10

Controlling Corporate Names

According to *AACR2-88* and cataloging tradition, geographic entities and conferences are considered corporate bodies. The principles discussed in this chapter relate to all corporate bodies including geographic entities and conferences. Principles that are unique to names of geographic entities and conferences follow the discussions of principles that are relevant to corporate bodies in general.

General Principles for Corporate Names

Different Names

If a name in an authorized heading is significantly different from that found in reference sources or used by the body, a *see* reference should be made from the variant names to the name used as the heading.

Different Forms of Names

Some corporate bodies have used more than one form of their name in their publications. Also different forms of the name may appear in reference sources or in the item being cataloged. The difference in name may be in:

1. language
2. spelling
3. fullness
4. romanization
5. graphemic structure
   a. abbreviations versus spelled-out form
   b. initials versus spelled-out form
   c. acronyms versus spelled-out form
   d. initials with periods versus initials without periods
   e. inverted form versus direct order of words

Only one of the names will be selected as the authorized heading. *See* references should be made from variant forms of the name to the name used as the authorized heading.

Complex Entities

The name in the entry may be a complex one in that it requires more directions for satisfactory use than a simple *see* or *see also* reference. This happens most frequently when a geographic entity changes its name and the library has works entered under each name. An information reference should be made.

Related Names

See also references should be made between headings that are independent but related in some way.

Specific Principles for Corporate Names

Performing Groups

If an authorized heading is the corporate name of a performing group and the name contains the name of one or more members of the group, a *see also* reference should be made for each person named. References are made from the corporate name to the names of the individuals.

Examples:

```
Gladys Knight and the Pips.
   xx Knight, Gladys

Bill Evans Trio.
   xx Evans, Bill
```

Personal Names in Corporate Names

Some corporate names begin with a personal name. The personal name may be a forename and surname or initial(s) and surname. A *see* reference should be made from the shortened form of the corporate name beginning with the surname to the full name. This means that the name in the reference entry will be transcribed without the forename or the initials.

Examples:

```
Gladys Knight and the Pips.
   x Knight and the Pips
  xx Knight, Gladys

Oral Roberts University.
   x Roberts University
```

If the personal name in the corporate name also includes a title for the person, another *see* reference should be made. This reference should begin with the part of the name following the title, usually a forename or initials. This means that the name in the reference entry will be transcribed in its entirety except that the title is omitted.

Example:

```
Doktor Seibold Hoch Conservatium
    (Frankfurt am Main)
    x Seibold Hoch Conservatium
        (Frankfurt am Main)
    x Hoch Conservatium (Frankfurt am Main)
```

Inverted Subheadings

Sometimes a corporate body named in a heading is a subordinate body entered as a subheading directly under a jurisdiction. An inverted *see* reference should be made from the generic term in the subordinate body if such term is preceded by a word that may not be recognized as part of the name of the subordinate body.

Example:

```
Florida. State Dept. of Education.
    x Florida. Dept. of Education, State
```

Also, when a subordinate body appears in a heading as a subheading directly under a jurisdiction, an inverted reference should be made from the first keyword in the name of the subordinate body.

Example:

```
Florida. State Dept. of Education.
    x Florida. Education, State Dept. of
    x Florida. Dept. of Education, State
```

The Word *And*, Ampersands, and Other Symbols

If the name in a heading contains an ampersand or other symbol representing the word *and* and the symbol appears among the first five words of the heading, a *see* reference should be made from the heading with the word *and* (or its equivalent in the language of the heading) to the heading with the symbol.

Example:

```
International Boundary & Water Commission,
    (United States and Mexico)
    x International Boundary and Water
        Commission (United States & Mexico)
```

Abbreviations

If the name in a heading has an abbreviation among the first five words that is not required by *AACR2-88* that represents a proper name, a *see* reference should be made from a heading that includes a spelled-out form to the heading with the abbreviation.

Examples:

```
Mt. Morris Methodist Episcopal Church
    (Barbour County, W. Va.)
    x Mount Morris Methodist Episcopal Church
        (Barbour County, W. Va.)

College of St. Matthias.
    x College of Saint Matthias
```

Initialisms and Acronyms

If an initialism or an acronym appears in the first five words of a heading, an explanatory reference should be made as follows:

1. From all variant forms of the initialism or acronym found in the work that do not appear as the authorized heading.

Example:

```
Credit Union National Association.

    x CUNA
```

```
Comparative digest . . . 1977: t.p. (Credit
    Union National Association, CUNA)
```

2. From the form without periods if the form in the heading has periods. If the only form of the name found is without periods and it is used in the heading without periods, an explanatory reference is *not* made from the form with periods. There is a trend among corporate bodies not to use periods in initialisms and acronyms; therefore, there is little need for a reference from this form of name.

Example:

```
A.A.P.S.O. International Conference in
    Solidarity with Mozambique, Angola, Guinea
    Bissau, Cape Verde, Sao Tome and Principe,
    Lourenco Marques.
    x AAPSO. International Conference in
        Solidarity with Mozambique, Angola,
    Guinea Bissau, Cape Verde, Sao Tome and
    Principe, Lourenco Marques
```

But,

```
USFL (Association)
   x United States Football League
```

If an initialism or an acronym with periods appears in the first five words of a reference, an explanatory reference should be made from the form without periods. If the form in the reference is without periods, a reference should not be made. (The Library of Congress would not make this explanatory reference.)

Example:

```
Automobile Association (Great Britain)
   x A.A.
   x AA
```

Heads of State and High Ecclesiastical Officers

Works by heads of state and high ecclesiastical officers are sometimes entered under the name of the office and sometimes under the personal name of the official, depending on the nature of the document being cataloged. If the name in the heading is a personal name, a *see also* reference should be made from the name of the office to the personal name heading.

Example:

```
Mohammed Reza Pahlavi, Shah of Iran, 1919-1980.
   xx Iran. Shah (1941-1979 : Mohammed Reza
         Pahlavi)
```

If the name in the heading is for the office of a person who is the head of state or a high ecclesiastical officer and the library has materials under the personal name of the individual, an explanatory reference should be made under the heading for the office.

Example:

```
Catholic Church. Pope (1978-   : John Paul II)
   xx Paul II, Pope
```

Reference:

```
Catholic Church. Pope (1978-   : John Paul II)
   Here are entered works of the pope acting in
his official capacity.
   For other works, see John Paul II, Pope.
```

Romanization

If the name in the heading is a romanization done by the library of a work originally in a nonroman script and there are differing romanized forms of the name found in reference sources, *AACR2-88* requires that a *see* reference be made from the romanization found in reference sources to the local romanized form. The value of this rule to the public is questionable. The public may be more familiar with a form of name found in reference sources than with the form created by the library.

Name Changes

If the name of a corporate body changes, a cataloger-generated reference may be made that provides a complete history of all such changes. A library may follow the lead of the Library of Congress and decide not to provide the public with this historical information. Instead, *see also* references may be made to link a name with the ones immediately succeeding and preceding it. (For further details on making references for name changes, see chapter 5.)

Independently Entered Nongovernmental Subordinate and Related Bodies

A subordinate body may be entered independently or it may be entered subordinately. If the name in the heading is for a subordinate body entered independently, a *see* reference should be made from the name as a subheading under its jurisdiction to the name in the heading.

Examples:

```
Center for Learning Skills.
   x Educational Dimensions Group. Center for
      Learning Skills

Political Economy of Women Group.
   x Conference of Socialist Economists.
      Political Economy of Women Group
```

Hierarchical Elements for Nongovernmental Subordinate Bodies

When a subordinate body is entered subordinately, its position in relation to a higher body may be as a direct or an indirect subheading. If the subordinate body in the heading has the form of a direct subheading to a higher body that is not its immediate superordinate body in the hierarchy, a *see* reference should be made from the form with all of the missing superordinate bodies to the form in the heading. An example of hierarchical levels follows.

Hierarchy:

```
Level 1
    Level 2
        Level 3
            Level 4
```

Example 1

Heading:

```
_____.    _____.
Level 1      Level 3
```

Reference from:

```
_____.    _____.    _____.
Level 1      Level 2      Level 3
```

Example 2

Heading:

```
_____.    _____.    _____.
Level 1      Level 3      Level 4
```

Reference from:

```
_____.    _____.    _____.    _____.
Level 1      Level 2      Level 3      Level 4
```

Examples:

```
University of Washington. Center for
    Contemporary Chinese and Soviet Studies.
    x University of Washington. School of
        International Studies. Center for
        Contemporary Chinese and Soviet Studies

Pan American Union. Division of Visual Arts.
    x Pan American Union. Dept. of Cultural
        Affairs. Division of Visual Arts
```

Each element in the hierarchy should be established independently of the principal heading that generated the initial reference.

Independently Entered Governmental Subordinate Bodies

A governmental subordinate body may be entered independently or it may be entered subordinately. If the name in the heading is for a subordinate body entered independently, a *see* reference should be made from the name as a subheading under its jurisdiction to the name in the heading.

Examples:

```
National Cartographic Information Center
     (U.S.)
     x United States. National Cartographic
             Information Center

Library of Congress.
     x United States. Library of Congress
```

Hierarchical Elements for Governmental Subordinate Bodies

When a body is entered subordinately, its position in relation to a higher body may be as a direct or an indirect subheading. If the subordinate body in the heading has the form of a direct subheading to a higher body that is not its immediate superordinate body in the hierarchy, a *see* reference should be made from the form with all of the elements in the hierarchy to the heading without the elements.

Examples:

```
National Cartographic Information Center.
     x United States. Geological Survey. National
             Cartographic Information Center

Library of Congress. Descriptive Cataloging
     Division.
     x Library of Congress. Processing Services.
             Descriptive Cataloging Division
```

Delegations to International and Intergovernmental Bodies

If the name in the heading is that of a delegation, commission, or other international or intergovernmental body entered as a subheading under its jurisdiction, an explanatory reference should be made from the delegation, commission, or other subordinate body as a subheading under the name of the international body.

Example:

```
United States. Delegation to the Meeting of the
     Inter-Parliamentary Union on European
     Cooperation and Security.
     x Inter-Parliamentary Union. Delegations
```

Corporate Name Used as Qualifier for Monographic Series

Sometimes two or more series titles may be identical. In such situations the cataloger will create a uniform title with a qualifier to distinguish them. When the qualifier is the name of a corporate body that has changed its name, a *see also* reference should be made to relate the names in the qualifiers. The same procedure is used as when the corporate body itself is the entry heading.

Pattern:

```
_____  (_____)
      title          qualifier name 1


_____  (_____)
      title          qualifier name 2
```

References:

```
_____  (_____)
      title          qualifier name 1
    see also
_____  (_____)
      title          qualifier name 2


_____  (_____)
      title          qualifier name 2
    see also
_____  (_____)
      title          qualifier name 1
```

Geographic Names

General Principles

Geographic names generate their own authority records. They are an important component of any authority file because they are so widely used in so many different situations. A heading may be a geographic name used alone or the geographic name may be a part of some other type of heading, such as a conference or name of a corporate body. Once established, the form remains the same when used alone or as part of a heading.

References are required for geographic names under certain conditions in the same way that they are required for other types of corporate names. Following are principles unique to the control of geographic names.

Special Treatment for Certain Places

DISTRICT OF COLUMBIA

The name of a place used as a heading should be the form in general use in English language gazetteers and other reference sources. Based on this principle, the name to be used for a heading for Washington, D.C., is *District of Columbia*.

That form, however, may not be used in a reference. Instead, *Washington (D.C.)* should be used both as a qualifier and as the entry element in a reference.

Examples:

```
District of Columbia. Mayor.
    x Washington (D.C.). Office of the Mayor

Forum on Psychiatry and the Humanities.
    x Washington School of Psychiatry
            (Washington, D.C.). Forum on Psychiatry
            and the Humanities
```

LONDON

References for the City of London and Greater London, including its thirty-two boroughs, are handled a bit differently from most other cities. The name *London (England)* is always the entry element in a reference.

Examples:

```
Corporation of London
    x London (England)

Waterloo (London, England)
    x London (England). Waterloo
```

MILITARY INSTALLATIONS

Military installations include forts, bases, camps, airfields, arsenals, and Coast Guard stations (but not shipyards). All military installations are treated as local places in that when a heading is established, a place qualifier is always added. A *see* reference is made from the name of the installation as a subheading of the country that controls it and the military branch to which it belongs.

Examples:

```
Bolling Air Force Base (Washington, D.C.)
    x United States. Air Force. Bolling
        Air Force Base

Eglin Air Force Base (Valparaiso, Fla.)
    x United States. Air Force. Eglin Air Force
        Base
```

Geographic Qualifiers

Sometimes a heading will contain a place name that is qualified by a larger place that has undergone a name change. The smaller place may have existed during the time that the larger place had its earlier name. If the item being cataloged was published during the time of the earlier name, a *see* reference should be made from the current name of the place with a qualifier containing the earlier name of the larger place.

Examples:

```
Salisbury (Zimbabwe)
   x Salisbury (Southern Rhodesia)

Kananga (Zaire)
   x Kananga (Congo)
```

This principle is not used for places in Great Britain.

Places in Cities

When a geographic heading is a place within a city and the name of the city has been added as a qualifier, a *see* reference should be made from the name of the city to the heading.

Examples:

```
Roxbury (Boston, Mass.)
   x Boston (Mass.). Roxbury

Ybo City (Tampa, Fla.)
   x Tampa (Fla.). Ybo City
```

Geographic Names Beginning with an Article

If a geographic name begins a heading and that name begins with an article, a *see* reference should be made from the part of the name following the article to the form of the name in the heading. The article is omitted completely from the reference.

Example:

```
The Hague (Netherlands)
   x Hague (Netherlands)
```

Local Religious Institutions

If the name in the heading is for a local religious institution, a *see* reference should be made from the name of the place where the institution is located with the full name of the institution as a subheading under it.

Example:

```
Bethel Baptist Church (Tallahassee, Fla.)
   x Tallahassee (Fla.). Bethel Baptist Church
```

Chambers of Commerce

If the name in the heading is a chamber of commerce, a reference should be made from the name of the place where it is located with *Chamber of Commerce* as a subheading under it.

Examples:

```
Tallahassee Chamber of Commerce.
    x Tallahassee (Fla.). Chamber of
        Commerce

Chamber of Commerce (Prince George's County,
    Md.)
    x Prince George's County (Md.).
        Chamber of Commerce
```

Governmental Bodies Entered Independently

The name of a jurisdiction in the heading for a governmental body is the same as the geographic name of the place being governed. If a governmental body is entered independently, a *see* reference should be made from the name as a subheading under the controlling jurisdiction.

Examples:

```
Veterans Administration Hospital (Sepulveda,
    Calif.)
    x United States. Veterans Administration
        Hospital

Grey Art Gallery and Study Center.
    x New York (N.Y.). Grey Art Gallery and
        Study Center

National Arts Foundation (Zimbabwe)
    x Zimbabwe. National Arts Foundation
```

Jurisdiction in the Name

If the name of an independently entered governmental body begins with the name or the abbreviation of the jurisdiction, a *see* reference should be made from the body. The name of the body should be shortened to exclude the jurisdiction or the abbreviation and then transcribed as a subheading under the name of the jurisdiction.

Examples:

```
Florida Energy Data Center.
    x Florida. Energy Data Center

Frankfurter Museum.
    x Frankfurt am Main (Germany). Museum

Simpson County Bicentennial Commission.
    x Simpson County (Ky.). Bicentennial
        Commission
```

Changes in Name

Whenever a geographic entity undergoes a change in name, an attempt should be made to relate the earlier and the later names to the current name in the heading with *see also* references. The sources found area should cite sources that justify the references; however, no justification is required if the change is because of a change in the official language.

Examples:

```
Zambia.
   xx Northern Rhodesia

Northern Rhodesia.
   xx Zambia
   xx Federation of Rhodesia and Nyasaland
```

Conference Names

General Principles

The term *conference* is the generic term for any type of meeting. The meeting may be the convening of the members of a particular organization or the gathering of a group whose only commonality is an interest in a particular subject. Neither the structure of the group nor its common interest qualifies a conference to be an authorized heading. The only criterion that qualifies it for main entry is the presence of its name prominently displayed on the chief source of information of the item being cataloged. This means that a conference must have a name and that name must appear on the chief source. The name may be an added entry without being on the chief source. An authority record should be made for the authorized name of the meeting in either case.

Conference names present some of the same general problems that are found in other corporate names, such as the presence of acronyms and initials, different language forms, and variant names. Principles for other corporate bodies should be applied to conference headings as appropriate.

Specific Principles

NAMES OF CONFERENCES

If a conference is known by both a general and a specific name and if the name in the heading is the specific name, a *see* reference should be made from the general name to the specific name.

Example:

```
International Conference on AACR2
   (1978 : Tallahassee, Fla.)
   x Cataloging Conference (1978 : Tallahassee,
      Fla.)
```

INVERTED NAMES OF CONFERENCES

If the heading is for a conference, a *see* reference should be made from the inverted forms of the name. In the references the qualifier should be omitted. The following inversions should be made:

1. from the first word following the name or abbreviation of a sponsor if the name of the sponsor is the first element

Example:

```
University of Wisconsin Symposium on Human
     Services in the Rural Environment.
     x Symposium on Human Services in the Rural
          Environment, University of Wisconsin
```

2. from the generic term in the name that signifies a meeting of some sort provided that the term is preceded by a word that does not signify a meeting

Example:

```
International Symposium on Logic Programming
     (1984: Atlantic City, N.J.)
     x Symposium on Logic Programming,
          International
```

In September 1984 the Library of Congress discontinued the practice of inverting at the first subject word when it is not the entry element.

SERIES OF MEETINGS

Sometimes a conference heading represents a series of meetings. In such cases, an explanatory reference should be used. The same explanatory reference should be made under each of the conference headings involved. (Note: The Library of Congress does not make the type of explanatory reference that follows.)

Example:

```
Conference on the History of Canadian Science,
     Technology, and Medicine (2nd : 1981 :
     Kingston, Ont.)
     xx Conference on the Study of the History of
          Canadian Science and Technology
          (1st : 1978 : Kingston, Ont.)

Conference on the Study of the History of
     Canadian Science and Technology (1st :
     1978 : Kingston, Ont.)
     xx Conference on the History of Canadian
          Science, Technology, and Medicine
          (2nd : 1981 : Kingston, Ont.)
```

Explanatory reference:

```
Conference on the History of Canadian Science,
    Technology, and Medicine (2nd : 1981 :
    Kingston, Ont.)
    Publications of this series of meetings are
found under the following headings:
1st:   Conference on the Study of the History of
           Canadian Science and Technology
           (1st : 1978 : Kingston, Ont.)
2nd:   Conference on the History of Canadian
           Science, Technology, and Medicine
           (2nd : 1981 : Kingston, Ont.)
```

Chapter 11

Controlling Uniform Title

Uniform titles have always been a part of name authority files even though titles instead of names are involved. Because of the tasks titles are expected to perform, they require some sort of control in the same manner as names.

Uniform titles control the collocating function by bringing together various manifestations of a work in a catalog regardless of its title. More recently, uniform titles have also served to distinguish one nondistinctive title from another when they conflict.

This chapter covers all types of uniform titles for the variety of materials normally found in libraries. Manuscripts, incunabula, and certain sacred scriptures are not found in all libraries; therefore, they are excluded.

General Principles

Uniform titles may be necessary whenever a single work has been published under different titles. The variant titles may be identified by browsing through the work being cataloged or by searching in reference tools. *See* references are used to control this category of uniform title.

Sometimes individual parts of a work are published separately. When they are cataloged and the bibliographic records are entered into the public catalog, they could be scattered throughout the catalog because of their varying titles. A uniform title or a *see* reference may be used to bring them together in the catalog. The publishers' titles should be linked to the uniform title in many cases. In such cases *see* references are used.

Sometimes a catalog may contain different works that are related to each other in some way. To facilitate searching, a *see also* reference is used to link the related works to each other and to show that the works have something in common. If the relationship is complex, an explanatory reference may be necessary to assist the user in understanding the relationship. The Library of Congress and a growing number of other libraries prefer separate *see* or *see also* references instead of explanatory references.

Specific Principles

Sometimes a work that requires a uniform title will have a known author. In such cases the author and the uniform title become the heading. Sometimes the author of the work is not known, as in the case of anonymous classics and some musical works. In such cases the uniform title is without an accompanying known author and stands alone as the heading. If the heading is a uniform title without an author, a *see* reference is made from any variants of the title that may have been identified in the work being cataloged or in reference sources.

Example:

```
Talmud.
    x Babylon Talmud
    x Talmud, Babylon
```

Variant Titles for Works Entered under Personal or Corporate Heading

Sometimes the work being cataloged has a known author and a uniform title as the heading. If variants of the title of the work have been identified either in the work itself or in reference sources, a *see* reference should be made from each variant title to the heading. The date of publication is added to *Selections* and *Works*. The date of publication, preceded by a period and enclosed in parentheses, is added to the uniform title as the last element in the heading. It does not appear in references. Also, in transcribing the title, the initial article is always omitted even when the title is preceded by a name heading.

Examples:

Bibliographic data:

```
Chaucer, Geoffrey, d. 1400.
    [Canterbury tales. (1847)]
    Canterbury tales of Geoffrey Chaucer . . .
1842-1851.
```

```
Chaucer, Geoffrey, d. 1400.
    [Canterbury tales. (1972)]
    The Canterbury tales of Chaucer . . . 1972.
```

Authority data:

```
Chaucer, Geoffrey, d. 1400.
     Canterbury tales. (1847)
   x Chaucer, Geoffrey, d. 1400.
         Canterbury tales of Geoffrey Chaucer
```

```
Chaucer, Geoffrey, d. 1400.
     Canterbury tales. (1972)
   x Chaucer, Geoffrey, d. 1400.
         Canterbury tales of Chaucer
```

References:

```
        Chaucer, Geoffrey, d. 1400.
           Canterbury tales of Chaucer
           see
        Chaucer, Geoffrey, d. 1400.
           Canterbury tales. (1847)


        Chaucer, Geoffrey, d. 1400.
           Canterbury tales of Chaucer
           see
        Chaucer, Geoffrey, d. 1400.
           Canterbury tales (1972)
```

Bibliographic data:

```
     Chaucer, Geoffrey, d. 1400.
        [Canterbury tales. Prologue. (1899)]
        Prologue from Chaucer's Canterbury tales
     . . . 1899.


     Chaucer, Geoffrey, d. 1400.
        [Canterbury tales. Prologue. (1954)]
        The Canterbury pilgrims . . . 1954.


     Chaucer, Geoffrey, d. 1400.
        [Canterbury tales. Prologue. (1978)]
        The prologue of the Canterbury tales . . .
     1978.
```

Authority data:

```
     Chaucer, Geoffrey, d. 1400.
           Canterbury tales. Prologue. (1899)
        x Chaucer, Geoffrey, d. 1400.
              Prologue from Chaucer's Canterbury
              tales


     Chaucer, Geoffrey, d. 1400.
           Canterbury tales. Prologue. (1954)
        x Chaucer, Geoffrey, d. 1400.
              Canterbury pilgrims


     Chaucer, Geoffrey, d. 1400.
           Canterbury tales. Prologue. (1978)
        x Chaucer, Geoffrey, d. 1400.
              Prologue of the Canterbury tales
```

Bibliographic data:

```
Chaucer, Geoffrey, d. 1400.
   [Works. 1895]
   The students' Chaucer . . . 1895.

Chaucer, Geoffrey, d. 1400.
   [Works. 1901]
   The complete works of Geoffrey Chaucer . . .
1901.

Chaucer, Geoffrey, d. 1400.
   [Works. 1977]
   Chaucer . . . 1977.
```

Authority data:

```
Chaucer, Geoffrey, d. 1400.
      Works. 1895.
   x Chaucer, Geoffrey, d. 1400.
         Students' Chaucer. 1895

Chaucer, Geoffrey, d. 1400.
      Works. 1901.
   x Chaucer, Geoffrey, d. 1400.
         Complete works of Geoffrey Chaucer.
         1901

Chaucer, Geoffrey, d. 1400.
      Works. 1977.
   x Chaucer, Geoffrey, d. 1400.
         Chaucer. 1977
```

Bibliographic data:

```
Roden, Claudia.
   Picnic : the complete guide to outdoor food
. . . 1981.

Roden, Claudia.
   Picnic : the complete guide to outdoor food
. . . 1982.

Roden, Claudia.
   [Picnic]
   Everything tastes better outdoors . . .
c1984.
                        . . .
NOTE:
   Originally published as: Picnic. 1981.
```

Authority data:

```
Roden, Claudia.
        Picnic.
   x Roden, Claudia.
            Everything tastes better outdoors
```

Reference:

```
    Roden, Claudia.
        Everything tastes better outdoors
        see
    Roden, Claudia.
        Picnic
```

Author's Name in Titles

Frequently the title of a work begins with the author's name. If a uniform heading is created, it consists of the title without the author's name. In such case a reference should be made from the publisher's title, complete with name included, to the uniform title.

Examples:

Bibliographic data:

```
Martin, Phyllis Rodgers.
   [Magic motivation book]
   Martin's Magic motivation book : how to
become an anointed one in your organization
   . . .
```

Authority data:

```
Martin, Phyllis Rodgers.
        Magic motivation book.
   x Martin, Phyllis Rodgers
            Martin's Magic motivation book
```

Reference:

```
    Martin, Phyllis Rodgers.
        Martin's Magic motivation book
        see
    Martin, Phyllis Rodgers.
        Magic motivation book
```

Single Parts of a Work

A work may be made up of several separate, smaller works tied together in some way to constitute a whole. Together they are thought of in terms of the larger work. Separately, each one has its own identity. If a part of the larger work has been published separately under its own title and is cataloged with its own heading, a *see* reference should be made from the heading for the whole with the part as a subheading. A pattern follows that illustrates this principle.

Pattern:

```
      _____
      part

  x _____ . _____
    whole   part
```

Example:

Authority data:

```
Chaucer, Geoffrey, d. 1400.
     Parson's tale.
  x Chaucer, Geoffrey, d. 1400.
         Canterbury tales. Parson's tale
```

Reference:

```
Chaucer, Geoffrey, d. 1400.
     Canterbury tales. Parson's tale
     see
Chaucer, Geoffrey, d. 1400.
     Parson's tale
```

If the work is a monograph and the part has a numeric sequencing element that indicates its place within the whole, the numeric designation should be included as part of the uniform title. It should be transcribed in arabic numerals and without an accompanying item designation such as volume or part.

Examples:

Bibliographic data:

```
Durant, William James.
     The story of civilization . . . 1935-1975.
                    . . .
```

NOTE:
```
     Contents: v. 1. Our oriental heritage—v. 2.
The life of Greece — v. 3. Caesar and Christ — v.
4. The age of faith — v. 5. The Renaissance — v.
6. The Reformation — v. 7. The age of reason
begins — v. 8. The age of Louis XIV, 1643-1715 —
v. 9. The age of Voltaire — v. 10. Rousseau and
revolution — v. 11. The age of Napoleon.
```

Authority data:

```
Durant, William James.
     Caesar and Christ.
  x Durant, William James.
          Story of civilization. 3. Caesar and
          Christ
```

Reference:

```
Durant, William James.
   Story of civilization. 3. Caesar and
   Christ
   see
Durant, William James.
   Caesar and Christ
```

Single Legislative Enactments

If a uniform title is a part of the heading for a single legislative enactment and if the uniform title begins with the name of the jurisdiction, a *see* reference should be made from a form of the title without the jurisdiction to the form in the heading with the jurisdiction.

Example:

```
North Carolina.
     North Carolina Workers' Compensation Act.
  x North Carolina.
        Workers' Compensation Act
```

```
North Carolina.
   Workers' Compensation Act
   see
North Carolina.
   North Carolina Workers' Compensation Act
```

Treaties

If the heading is for a collection of treaties that is identifiable by a distinct name, *see also* references should be made between the heading for the collection and that for the individual treaty.

Example:

```
Operating agreement relating to the
     International Telecommunications Satellite
     Organization "INTERSAT" (1971)
     x Accord d'exploitation relatif a
          l'Organisation internationale de
          telecommunications par satellites
          "INTERSAT" (1971)
     x Agreement relating to the International
          telecommunications Satellite
          Organization "INTERSAT"
  xx United States.
          Treaties, etc. 1971 Aug. 20.
  xx New Zealand.
          Treaties, etc. 1972 Jan. 5.
```

Separate Books of the Bible

If the heading is for a separate book of the Bible that has been published as a separate monograph, a *see* reference should be made from

1. the title of the book with an appropriate qualifier
2. variant titles of the book identified either in the work or in reference sources. Two *see* references should be made from each variant title as follows:
    a. directly from the variant title with an appropriate qualifier
    b. from the variant title as a subheading under the appropriate testament of the Bible
3. the title of the book as a direct subheading under *Bible.*

Example:

```
Bible. O.T. Exodus.
   x Exodus (Book of the Old Testament)
   x Bible. Exodus
```

Single Selections of the Bible

If the uniform title in the heading is for a single selection from the Bible that is known by its own distinctive title, a *see* reference should be made from the selection as a subheading of the appropriate part of the Bible to the distinctive title of the selection.

Examples:

```
Beatitudes.
   x Bible. N.T. Matthew V, 3-12
```

```
23rd Psalm.
   x Bible. O.T. Psalms, XXIII
   x Twenty-third Psalm

Lord's supper.
   x Lord's table
   x Last supper
   x Bible. N.T. Matthew XXVI, 26-29
   x Bible. N.T. Mark XIV, 22-25.
   x Communion
```

Language of the Bible

If the uniform title named in the heading is for a Bible written in both Hebrew and Greek, two *see* references should be made. One of the references should refer from a uniform title for the Bible with Greek as the language and the other one should be from a uniform title with Hebrew as the language.

Example:

```
Bible. Hebrew-Greek.
   x Bible. O.T. Hebrew
   x Bible. N.T. Greek
```

Apocryphal Books

If the uniform title named in the heading is for the apocryphal books that are not a part of the Protestant Apocrypha or the Catholic canon, an explanatory reference should be made that explains how to search for the individual books.

Example of an explanatory reference:

```
Bible. O.T. Apocryphal books.
   For individual apocryphal books of the Old
Testament, see the title of the book, e.g.
Jubilee, Assumption of Moses, Sibylline Oracle,
etc.
```

Talmud Orders and Tractates

The uniform title for an order or a tractate of the Talmud usually is formed with the order or the tractate as a subheading under a higher division. If the heading includes a uniform title for an order or a tractate, a *see* reference should be made from the individual title of the order or tractate to the uniform title. Also an explanatory reference should be made from the order to explain searching procedures for locating other tractates in the particular order.

Pattern:

Authority data:

```
_____.  _____.
Talmud   Tractate
      x _____
         Tractate
```

Reference:

```
 _____
 Tractate
     see

_____.  _____.
Talmud   Tractate
```

Example:

Authority record:

```
Talmud. Yoma.
    x Yoma.
    xx Talmud. Mo'ed.
```

Reference:

```
    Yoma.
        see
Talmud. Yoma.
```

Explanatory reference:

```
Talmud. Mo'ed.
    For separately published tractates belonging
to this order, see Talmud. [name of tractate],
e.g. Talmud. Yoma
```

Specific Liturgical Observances

If the heading is a uniform title for a liturgy of a particular observance in either the Catholic church or in any Protestant denomination, a *see* reference should be made from the specific liturgy as a subheading of a longer work to the uniform title. Uniform titles for such liturgies usually consist of just the liturgy itself without the larger work being included.

Example:

```
Catholic Church.
    Holy Week rite
  x Catholic Church.
        Missal. Holy Week rite
```

```
Catholic Church.
    Missal. Holy Week rite
    see
Catholic Church.
    Holy Week rite
```

Office and Mass as Subheadings

If the heading names a uniform title for an office or a mass for the observance of a particular day, an explanatory reference should be made to explain the procedure for searching for particular offices for special days and occasions.

Explanatory reference:

```
Catholic Church.
    Breviary. Offices for particular days or
occasions
    For offices for particular days or
occasions, see Catholic Church.  Office, [name
of day], e.g. Catholic Church.  Office,
Christmas
```

Separately Published Parts of a Musical Work

If the heading is the name of a composer and the title of a separately published part of a musical work, a name-title reference should be made from the composer and title of the part to the title as a subheading of the whole work. When the reference is a uniform title under a name heading, the name is given in the first reference. If other name-title references include the same name, *His*, *Her*, or *Its* may be substituted for the name.

Example:

```
Handel, George Frideric, 1685-1759.
    Messiah. Hallelujah.
  x Handel, George Frideric, 1685-1759.
        Hallelujah chorus
  x Handel, George Frideric, 1685-1759.
        Hallelujah
  x Handel, George Frideric, 1685-1759.
        Messiah. Hallelujah chorus
```

Relevant Phrases and Titles That Are Not Title Proper

The chief source of information of some works contains information that may easily be construed by some catalogers and users as title proper. The information may in fact be a parallel title, other title information, *At head of title* information, or just a relevant phrase that the publisher added. If such information is not clearly definable as the title proper and if a name heading has been selected for the work, a name-title reference should be made from the name heading and phrase to the name heading selected for the work. Figure 20 and the accompanying examples illustrate this principle.

Bibliographic data:

```
Doyle, Bill.
     Fast way to physical fitness . . .
```

Authority data:

```
Doyle, Bill.
        Fast way to physical fitness
  x Doyle, Bill.
           The "I hate exercise" fast way to
           physical fitness
```

Reference:

```
Doyle, Bill.
     "I hate exercise" fast way to physical
     fitness
     see
Doyle, Bill.
     Fast way to physical fitness
```

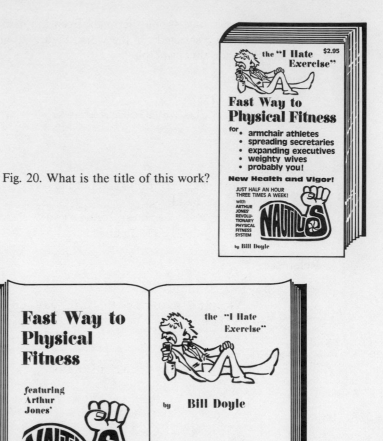

Fig. 20. What is the title of this work?

Title page

Running title

Chapter 12

Controlling Series

This chapter deals with the principles of controlling series in libraries. Although the principles and practices discussed here are compatible with those at the Library of Congress, the underlying philosophy is that control over the intellectual decisions relating to the treatment of series should remain with the individual library. The discussions that follow reflect that philosophy. The general principles and practices discussed in previous chapters that are relevant to series authority control are not repeated here; nevertheless, they must be taken into consideration when reviewing the complete process of creating records for series authority files. Examples of series statements are shown in figure 21.

It is no small task to make effective decisions about the treatment of a work, parts of which have yet to be published. Many libraries have relinquished their responsibilities in this area to the Library of Congress. They trace and analyze series based on decisions implied from cataloging copy. These libraries are less likely to have systematic procedures, authority files, workforms, and essential reference sources with which to work. As online catalogs become more widespread, libraries will assume more responsibility for the integrity of their collections and will resume their control over series authorities.

Types of Series

In dealing with authority control there are different types of series that must be given special attention. This section discusses pseudo-series, subseries and multipart items, including what they are and how they should be handled in the authority control system.

Pseudo-Series

Pseudo-series are series-like constructions that do not fully and clearly fall within the definition of a series. They include sequences of numbers, letters, or both that cannot be associated with a series title, for example, USDA/EIA-0031/2. They also include phrases that do little more than identify the publisher or the issuing body, or a division or an official of the publishing company, for example, Pelican Books (see figure 22). Such phrases generally are not subject specific but rather serve as a control device. These series-like titles create problems for catalogers. They are considered to be genuine series by some libraries and appear in bibliographic records as such. Other libraries consider them to be important but yet do not recognize them as true series. Instead of being placed in the series

> xxiv, 166 p. ; 24 cm. — (A Reference publication in Afro-American studies)
> Includes index.
> ISBN 0-8161-8318-X

> xiv, 607 p. : ill. ; 22 cm. — (A Longman text)
> Includes index.

> iv, 799 p. ; 28 cm. — (Health planning information series)
> Spine title: Health Planning Literature—Title Index.
> "October 1980."
> "HRP-0902592"
> Item 509-A-6
> Supt. of Docs. no.: HE 20.6110/2:T 53

> 9 p. ; 29 cm. — (Architecture series—bibliography, ISSN 0194-1356 ; A-373)
> Cover title.
> $2.00 (pbk.)

> xvi, 365 p. ; 23 cm. — (Garland reference library of the humanities ; v. 162)
> Includes indexes.
> ISBN 0-8240-9777-7 : $35.00

> xiv, 196 p. : ill. ; 26 cm. — (IHRC ethnic bibliography ; no. 3)
> Includes index.

Fig. 21. Examples of series statements

area in the bibliographic record, they become quoted notes or are ignored completely.

There are no firm, well-defined standards or guidelines for determining which phrases are pseudo-series and which are not. Attempts to distinguish between phrases that should be treated as series and those that should not have been a matter of individual judgment on the part of catalogers. In either situation a series authority record is created so that the phrases may be treated consistently.

xii, 245 p. ; 27 cm. — (Publication ; no. E-80-14010)
Edition for 1972 by Karen Bruner.
"A summary of research projects and reports funded by the Office of Educa-
tion, the National Institute of Education, and the Fund for the Educational
Research Information Center."
"Department of Education."
Includes index.
S/N 065-000-00027-0

47 p. ; 28 cm. — (Bibliographic series / Institute of Paper Chemistry ; no. 264.
Supplement ; 1)

Bibliography prepared from the Abstract bulletin of the Institute of Paper
Chemistry, v. 45(6) through v. 51(7).
Includes indexes.

446 p. : ill. ; 18 cm. — (10/18 ; 1065)   F***

Bibliography: p. [411]-412.
Includes index.
ISBN 2-264-00054-6 : 15.00F

195 p. : ill. ; 21 cm. — (Veröffentlichungen der Gesamthochschulbibliothek
Essen, ISSN 0721-0469 ; 6 = Publications of Essen University Library ; 6)

Bibliography: p. 195.
ISBN 3-922602-07-X (pbk.)

ii leaves, 39 p. ; 28 cm. — (Illinois Valley Library System, OCLC Experimen-
tal Project report ; no. 1)

"October 1982."

31 p. ; 27 cm. — (Forest Service research paper SE ; 202)

Cover title.
"March 1980"—Verso t.p.

x, 43 p. ; 21 cm. — (Mousaion ; II. 9)   (Miscellanea ; 26)   SA***
Bibliography: p. 35-36.
ISBN 0-86981-218-1

Fig. 21 (cont.). Examples of series statements

In the Fall 1981 issue of *Cataloging Service Bulletin,*[1] the Library of Congress
provided some guidance in this area.

1. *Cataloging Service Bulletin* (Fall 1981): 9–12.

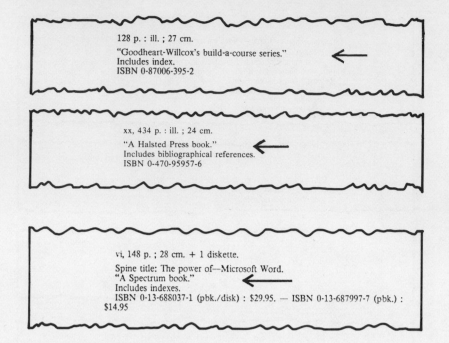

Fig. 22. Examples of pseudo-series

1. Names of corporate bodies as series

   If a statement on an item consists solely of the name of a non-commercial corporate body and a sequencing element such as a volume or part number, the name should be treated as a true series and placed in the series area of the bibliographic record.

   If the name is represented in the statement by initials which have been established as the authorized form of name for the body, the initials also may be considered to be a true series. If, however, the name of the corporate body has been established in its full form, the initials are not treated as a series. Instead they are transcribed as a quoted note. If the series is entered under title, the name or the initials should be followed by the qualifier (Series).

   If, however, the corporate body is a commercial publisher but is not the publisher of the item, the statement is transcribed as a quoted note. If the commercial publisher is also the publisher of the item, the sequencing element is transcribed alone in the notes area.

2. Numbers/letters not associated with a series title

   If numbers, letters, or a combination of letters and numbers appears on an item and there is no evidence that they are associated with a series title, they should be transcribed as a quoted note. (If the item is a serial, they should be ignored completely.)

3. Phrases

    If the phrase is essentially a statement of the name of the issuing body, it should not be treated as a series. It should be transcribed as a quoted note if the name of the body is not also recorded in the publishing area of the item. If the corporate body is also the publisher, the phrase should be ignored.

    If the phrase includes the name of a subsidiary or division of a publisher and appears on all of the publications issued by that subsidiary or division, the phrase should be transcribed as a quoted note. If the subsidiary or division named in the phrase is also recorded in the publishing area, the phrase should be ignored.

    If the phrase includes the name of an official of the publishing firm, it should be transcribed as a quoted note.

Subseries

Subseries can present problems in somewhat the same manner as pseudo-series. Often it is a cataloger's judgment that determines what a subseries is and how it should be treated. The decisions made relative to subseries in bibliographic records also affect the authority file.

    If the cataloger finds two series titles in a work and one is construed to be a component of the other, the larger one is termed the main series and the smaller one a subseries. It is not always easy, however, to understand the relationship between the larger and the smaller statements found in a work. The following guidelines offered by the Library of Congress[2] may produce more consistency among catalogers than has been possible in the past.

1. Numbered series

    If the main series and a subseries appear together in any one source within the preliminaries of the same publication and if they are both numbered, separate authority records should be created for each of them. If the main series lacks its own numbering, it should not be established as a separate series. Instead it would be established as a part of the heading for the subseries.

2. Multiple subseries

    If a main series has multiple subseries, some of which are numbered and some are not, separate authority records should be created for those that are numbered. Those that are unnumbered should be established as one entry consisting of the main series and the unnumbered subseries. The main series should end with a period. The first word of the subseries is *always* capitalized.

3. Source of the series

    If a main series and a subseries do not appear together in the same source in the preliminaries, they should be considered as two separate

2. Ibid., pp. 11–12.

series. Two separate authority records should be created, one for each series.

Multipart Items

A multipart item is a monograph that is complete in a definite number of finite separate parts. Considered together the parts constitute a single work. The work may be cataloged and classified as a finite unit, a set. Sometimes the parts are considered separately as individual works. Whenever the parts are cataloged separately (not necessarily classified) as individual works, the composite title becomes the series title for the parts. Series headings for multipart items usually have personal name entries established according to *AACR2-88*. Authority records are created for all analyzable multipart items. The same procedures used for monographic series should be used for multipart items, including full sets of references.

Special practices that refer to multipart items only must be taken into consideration. When the title proper of a multipart item changes or if there is a change in responsibility, the concept of successive entry used for serials does not apply. Only one authority record should be created and maintained. Sometimes when a multipart item is considered for analysis, not all of the parts are analyzable. An authority record should be created and a record of the parts that have been analyzed should be documented. The series title should always be traced.

Analysis

A library may decide that each item in a series is important enough to warrant its own bibliographic record, complete with coextensive subject headings to indicate what the work is about, bibliographic added entries to show who is responsible for its intellectual or artistic content, and title access.

Full analysis of a series offers users the best opportunity to exploit fully its contents. To be compatible with Library of Congress practice regarding analysis, a library would have to analyze the following categories:

1. all monographic series
2. all analyzable multipart items
3. special issues of serials the whole of which constitutes a monographic-like work. (These works include festschriften and conference proceedings that make up the issue. Technical reports are excluded.)
4. issues of serials that constitute or have the characteristics of a monographic work such as yearbooks.

Depending on the nature of the particular series, a library may decide

1. to analyze in full
2. to analyze in part
3. not to analyze

The analysis decision, including any variations in practice, should be recorded on the authority record. Some libraries use codes to signify the decision, such as *f* for full analysis, *p* for partial analysis, and *n* for not analyzed. Other libraries simply make a brief statement to indicate the decision, such as *Analyzed, Not analyzed, Partially analyzed.*

Tracing Decisions

Once part of a series, an item will always be a part of that series. Neither the classification policy nor the policy regarding analysis can change that fact, but the library can control the use of the series as an access point in the public catalog. If the series is considered sufficiently important and possibly recognizable by some library users or if the library wishes to collocate items in the catalog that have been scattered on the shelves, the series should be traced. Otherwise, it will be untraced and, thus, unsearchable by title unless the catalog is online with key word search capabilities.

Many online catalogs have the capability of permitting searching by fields. The mere presence of a series on a bibliographic record, though untraced, can still be searched and all records containing the series can be brought together. Future online catalogs surely will make many of the traditional practices of bibliographic organization obsolete.

Libraries that wish to be compatible with the Library of Congress will need to establish policies to trace the following:

1.   all titles entered indirectly under a name entry element
2.   series titles published by a noncommercial publisher
3.   series titles published by small or alternative presses
4.   series titles for works published earlier than the twentieth century
5.   titles of multipart items

The Library of Congress does not trace a title if:

1.   the titles in the series have only physical attributes in common
2.   the series has nonessential sequencing elements such as stock control numbers
3.   the series was published by commercial publishers and the title simply has the name of a literary genre. (LC would trace the title if words are included that narrow the scope, such as subject words or audience level.)

Whenever there is doubt about tracing a series, it is best to trace it. Also, if there is a conflict in the criteria for tracing and those for not tracing, again it is best to trace it.

The tracing decisions, including any variations in practices, should be recorded on the authority record. Some libraries use codes to signify whether the series is to be traced or not, such as *t* for traced and *nt* for not traced. Others simply make a brief statement, such as *Traced*, or *Not traced.*

Call Numbers

If the treatment decision for a series is to catalog it or any part of it as a collection, the authority record should display the call number that is assigned to it. As each new part of the series is received and verified in the authority file, the call number is immediately available. Only the numeration will need to be added to distinguish the new item from the others in the series.

Some series can be quite complicated. Some of the individual items may be a part of other series. The multiple series to which the individual part belongs may each be cataloged as a collection. The part can only be classified with one of the series. A record should be maintained of all call numbers that affect any part of the series resulting from variations in practice. The call number supplies information about the physical location of each unit of the series.

The call number for a subseries should be the same as that for the main series. Some distinguishing designation should be added to the call number to identify it as a subseries.

Pattern of Numeration Designation

The form of numeration used in the series statement or the series tracing to identify the individual parts of the series must be documented on the authority record so that it can be consistently used in bibliographic records for the other items in the series received at a later date. Some libraries with manual authority files add the numeration as it would appear in the public catalog to the series title. The example then serves as a pattern for future use. Other authority files have special areas for this information. Some libraries carefully monitor and document significant changes in numeration as they occur in the various issues of the series. The first item cataloged sets the pattern for all succeeding issues. (See figure 23 for examples of series numeration.)

Specific Principles

Authority records are created for all types of multipart works as long as they are analyzable and are not considered serials. Basic principles for series authorities follow.

Variant Titles

If a variant series title is found in the item being cataloged and it is significantly different from the one chosen as the authorized title, a *see* reference should be made from the variant title to the authorized title.

Example:

```
A V A-Manifest.
    x AVA-Manifest
```

xiv, 224 p. ; 23 cm. — (St. Paul's bibliographies ; 8)

v. <1   > ; 28 cm. — (Occasional publication / Boreal Institute for
Northern Studies, ISSN 0068-0303 ; no. 8-5)   C***

13 p. ; 28 cm. — (Public administration series—bibliography, ISSN 0193-
970X ; P-783)

46 p. : ill. ; 23 cm. — (Occasional papers / University of Illinois Graduate
School of Library and Information Science, ISSN 0276-1769 ; no. 160 (July
1983))

36 p. ; 23 cm. — (The Emporia State research studies ; v. 31, no. 1)

viii, 311 p. : ill. ; 28 cm. — (Open-file report / U.S. Geological Survey ; 83-
540)

53 p. ; 29 cm. — (Cadernos dos SIP ; 2/1983)

41 p. ; 22 cm. — (Mideast directions, ISSN 0731-8944 ; MED 83-1)

iv, 41 p. ; 28 cm. — (Staff technical report / State Council of Higher Education for Virginia ; STR 83-03)

147 p. : ill. ; 30 cm. — (INIS reference series ; IAEA-INIS-17 (Rev. 2))

Fig. 23. Examples of series numeration

Acronyms and Initialisms

If the authorized title includes an acronym or an initialism with periods or spaces in the first five filing words, a *see* reference should be made from the acronym or initialism without periods to the form with periods.

Example:

```
B.B.A. Library.
   x BBA Library
```

Title Changes

If the series is for a numbered multipart item that is cataloged as a set and the item has had a title change, the title of all parts should be changed on the bibliographic record to match the title of the predominant parts. A *see* reference should be made for the series authority record from the earlier title to the later predominant title.

Abbreviations

If an abbreviation appears in the first five filing words of the heading, a *see* reference should be made from the spelled-out form to the form with the abbreviation.

Example:

```
Dr. John Matthai memorial lectures.
   x Doctor John Matthai memorial lectures
```

Ampersands

If the authorized heading contains an ampersand or other symbol that represents the word *and* in the first five filing words, a *see* reference should be made from the spelled-out form to the form with the symbol.

Examples:

```
A&R poetry classics.
   x A and R poetry classics

Punt, pass, & kick library.
   x Punt, pass, and kick library
```

This principle also applies to other signs and symbols that appear in the first five words of a series heading.

Dates in Roman Numeral Form

If the authorized heading contains dates in roman numeral form in the first five filing words, two *see* references are needed: one from the spelled-out form of the date (as spoken) and the other from the arabic numeral form. If, however, the date represents a single year or a range of dates, a reference should *not* be made from the spelled-out form.

Example:

```
Documents of XXth century art.
    x Documents of 20th century art
    x Documents of twentieth century art
```

Numbers in Roman Numeral Form

If the authorized heading contains numbers other than dates in roman numeral form in the first five filing words, two *see* references are needed: one from the spelled-out form (as spoken) and the other from the arabic numeral form.

Example:

```
Poesie I.
    x Poesie 1
    x Poesie one
```

Numbers in Their Arabic Numeral Form

If the authorized heading contains arabic numerals in the first five filing words, a *see* reference should be made from the spelled-out form (as spoken) to the form in the heading.

Fractions and decimals are excluded. Numerals that do not have standard spoken forms are referenced from a spelled-out form.

Examples:

```
10/18.
    x Dix/dix huit

Poesie 74 Seghers.
    x Poesie soixante-quatorze Seghers
```

Parallel Titles

If the series has a parallel title, a *see* reference should be made from the parallel title to the authorized series title. The following examples are based on the series parallel titles shown in figure 24.

Authority data:

```
Bibliographien zur regionalen Geographie und
    Landeskunde.
    x Bibliographies on regional geography and
        area studies
```

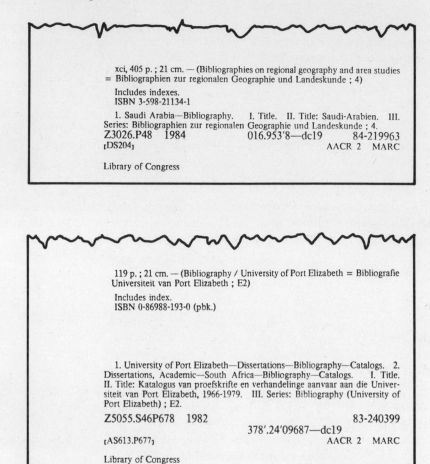

xci, 405 p. ; 21 cm. — (Bibliographies on regional geography and area studies = Bibliographien zur regionalen Geographie und Landeskunde ; 4)

Includes indexes.
ISBN 3-598-21134-1

1. Saudi Arabia—Bibliography.   I. Title.   II. Title: Saudi-Arabien.   III. Series: Bibliographien zur regionalen Geographie und Landeskunde ; 4.

Z3026.P48   1984   016.953'8—dc19   84-219963
ₜDS204ₗ   AACR 2   MARC

Library of Congress

119 p. ; 21 cm. — (Bibliography / University of Port Elizabeth = Bibliografie Universiteit van Port Elizabeth ; E2)

Includes index.
ISBN 0-86988-193-0 (pbk.)

1. University of Port Elizabeth—Dissertations—Bibliography—Catalogs.   2. Dissertations, Academic—South Africa—Bibliography—Catalogs.   I. Title. II. Title: Katalogus van proefskrifte en verhandelinge aanvaar aan die Universiteit van Port Elizabeth, 1966-1979.   III. Series: Bibliography (University of Port Elizabeth) ; E2.

Z5055.S46P678   1982   83-240399
                          378'.24'09687—dc19
ₜAS613.P677ₗ   AACR 2   MARC

Library of Congress

Fig. 24. Examples of series parallel titles

```
Bibliography (University of Port Elizabeth)
    x Bibliografie (Universiteit van Port
            Elizabeth)
```

Publisher's Title versus Uniform Title

If the publisher's title is different from the authorized uniform title in the heading, a *see* reference should be made from the publisher's title to the uniform title. (The addition of a language or a parenthetical qualifier is not considered in determining that titles are different.)

If the heading is in name-title form, a name-title reference should be made from the name-publisher's title to the authorized heading.

Indirect Entries

If the authorized series title is an indirect entry under a personal or corporate name, a *see* reference should be made from the title as a direct entry to the indirect title entry.

Example:

```
International Working Conference on Violence
    and Non-violent Action in Industrialized
    Societies. Proceedings of the . . .
    International Working Conference on Violence
    and Non-Violent Action in Industrialized
    Societies.
x Proceedings of the . . . International
        Working Conference on Violence and Non-
        Violent Action in Industrialized
        Societies
```

This principle does not apply to multipart items with an indistinctive title under a personal name.

At Head of Title Phrases

If the chief source contains a phrase at the head of the title that may be construed as the series title proper but was not selected as the series title proper, a *see* reference should be made from the phrase to the chosen series title proper.

Partial Titles

TYPOGRAPHY

If part of a series title is given prominence by typography but was not chosen as the series title proper, a *see* reference should be made from the partial title to the series title proper.

AMBIGUOUS TITLES

If the wording of the series title is ambiguous and can be construed in more than one way, a *see* reference should be made from the partial title not chosen as the series title proper to the series title proper.

GENERIC TERMS

If the series title begins with a noun or a noun phrase that includes as its first word a generic term such as *Series* or *Collection*, followed by a noun, a *see* reference should be made from a partial title that excludes the generic term to the series title proper. This type of reference will usually occur with series in Romance languages.

Examples:

```
Collection Sports pour tous.
    x Sports pour tous
```

```
    Serie Lettres, langues vivantes et sciences
       humaines.
    x Lettres, langues vivantes et sciences
          humaines
```

EMBEDDED STATEMENTS OF RESPONSIBILITY

If the series title includes a statement of responsibility embedded in the title, a *see* reference should be made from a partial title that begins with the statement of responsibility to the series title proper. This reference should be made even if the name does not appear in its full or authoritative form. If the resulting title consists solely of the statement of responsibility, then an inverted reference should be substituted for the partial title.

OTHER TITLE INFORMATION

If the series other title information is ambiguous by wording or typography and may be construed as being the series title proper, a *see* reference should be made from the other title information as a partial series title to the chosen series title proper.

Surnames

If the series title begins with a forename or initials and surname, a *see* reference should be made from the surname and the remainder of the title to the series title.

Examples

```
    C.R. Gibson gift books.
    x Gibson gift books


    Louis Charles Elson memorial lectures.
    x Elson memorial lectures


    Doctor Rajendra Prasad memorial lecture series.
    x Prasad memorial lecture series
```

Titles of Honor or Address

If the series title begins with a person's title and forename or initials, a *see* reference should be made from the forename or initials and the remainder of the title to the series title.

If the person's title appears in the series title in an abbreviated form, a second *see* reference should be made from the spelled-out form of the title to the abbreviated form.

Example

```
    Dr. John Matthai memorial lectures.
      x John Matthai memorial lectures
      x Doctor John Matthai memorial lectures
      x Matthai memorial lectures
```

Subseries

If the authorized series heading contains a subseries with a distinctive title and a main series and if the subseries is independent of the main series, a *see* reference should be made from the title of the subseries to the main series through the subseries.

Example:

```
Monographs in international studies. African
    series.
    x African series
```

If the subseries is preceded by a numeric or alphabetic designation, the designation should be omitted from the reference.

Pattern:

```
_____. _____, _____.
main series   designation  subseries
              Part A
```

Authority data:

```
_____. _____, _____.
main series   designation  subseries
    x _____
        subseries
```

Reference:

```
_____
subseries
    see
_____. _____, _____.
main series   designation  subseries
```

If the subseries is entered directly, a *see* reference should be made from the title of the main series through the subseries to the subseries.

Pattern:

```
_____
subseries
    x _____. _____.
        main series  subseries
```

Reference:

```
_____.  _____.
main series   subseries
    see

_____
subseries
```

Publishers and Responsible Bodies (Noncommercial)

Consider a corporate body as responsible for a series if it is a noncommercial firm and its name appears in the publication/distribution area of the bibliographic record that generated the authority record. University presses as well as commercial publishers are excluded from being responsible for series. In all name-title references, the name of the corporate body should be in main entry form according to *AACR2-88*. (See figure 25 for examples of responsible corporate bodies.)

If the publisher of a series or the corporate body responsible for it is a noncommercial firm and is not a university press, a name-title reference should be made from the name of the corporate body and publisher's series title to the series title (see figure 26). If more than one corporate body is the publisher or is responsible for the series, up to three name-title references may be made.

Pattern:

```
_____
series title
   x _____.  _____.
     publisher   publisher's series title
```

Reference:

```
_____.  _____.
publisher   publisher's series title
   see

_____
series title
```

Example:

```
1981 bibliography of cases.
   x Harvard University. Graduate School of
       Business Administration. Division of
       Research.
          1981 bibliography of cases
```

If the name or the initials of the responsible body appear in the series title, a name-title reference should be made from the name of the body to the series heading.

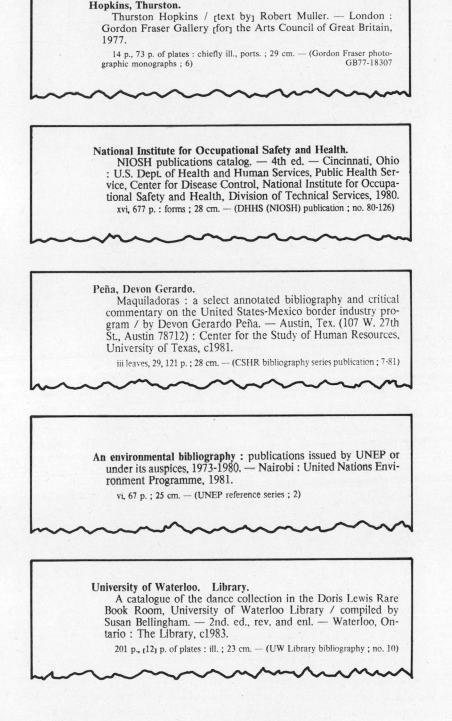

Hopkins, Thurston.
Thurston Hopkins / [text by] Robert Muller. — London : Gordon Fraser Gallery [for] the Arts Council of Great Britain, 1977.

14 p., 73 p. of plates : chiefly ill., ports. ; 29 cm. — (Gordon Fraser photographic monographs ; 6)   GB77-18307

National Institute for Occupational Safety and Health.
NIOSH publications catalog. — 4th ed. — Cincinnati, Ohio : U.S. Dept. of Health and Human Services, Public Health Service, Center for Disease Control, National Institute for Occupational Safety and Health, Division of Technical Services, 1980.
xvi, 677 p. : forms ; 28 cm. — (DHHS (NIOSH) publication ; no. 80-126)

Peña, Devon Gerardo.
Maquiladoras : a select annotated bibliography and critical commentary on the United States-Mexico border industry program / by Devon Gerardo Peña. — Austin, Tex. (107 W. 27th St., Austin 78712) : Center for the Study of Human Resources, University of Texas, c1981.

iii leaves, 29, 121 p. ; 28 cm. — (CSHR bibliography series publication ; 7-81)

An environmental bibliography : publications issued by UNEP or under its auspices, 1973-1980. — Nairobi : United Nations Environment Programme, 1981.

vi, 67 p. ; 25 cm. — (UNEP reference series ; 2)

University of Waterloo.   Library.
A catalogue of the dance collection in the Doris Lewis Rare Book Room, University of Waterloo Library / compiled by Susan Bellingham. — 2nd. ed., rev. and enl. — Waterloo, Ontario : The Library, c1983.

201 p., [12] p. of plates : ill. ; 23 cm. — (UW Library bibliography ; no. 10)

Fig. 25. Examples of responsible corporate bodies

Marketing : including cases in agribusiness : new cases, best selling cases. — Boston, MA : Division of Research, Harvard Business School : Distribution, HBS Case Services, Harvard Business School, c1981.

vii, 216 p. ; 22 x 28 cm. — (1981 bibliography of cases ; v. 5)

Includes indexes.
$5.00 (pbk.)

1. Marketing—Case studies—Bibliography.   I. Harvard University. Graduate School of Business Administration.   Division of Research.   II. Series.

Z7164.M18M27   81-202900
                                        016.6588′00722—dc19
₁HF5415₁   AACR 2   MARC

Library of Congress

Fig. 26. Example of reference from publisher

Pattern:

```
_____
series title
    x  _____
       responsible body
```

Reference:

```
_____
responsible body
    see

_____
series title
```

Example:

```
SSA publication.
    x United States. Social Security
        Administration.
            SSA publication
```

Statements of Responsibility in Series

If the name of a corporate body appears as a statement of responsibility in the series area of a bibliographic record, a name-title *see* reference should be made from the corporate body named and series title to the authorized heading. The following examples are based on figure 27.

9 leaves, [1] leaf of plates : 1 map ; 28 cm. — (Research pamphlet / Genealogy/Local History Department, Springfield City Library)

viii, 69 p. ; 24 cm. — (Resources series / Industrial Relations Research Centre, ISSN 0705-310X)

ii, 46 p. ; 28 cm. — (Special paper / State of Oregon, Department of Geology and Mineral Industries ; 16)

297 p. ; 28 cm. — (Research report / Canadian Institute of Ukrainian Studies ; no. 4)

26 p. ; 19 cm. — (Readers' guide / Library Association, Public Libraries Group ; no. 29)   GB***

51 p. ; 21 cm. — (Bibliographical bulletin / Auckland University Library, ISSN 0067-0499 ; 11)   NZ***

23 p. ; 23 cm. — (Research report / New Jersey State Museum ; no. 4)

Beauregard, Jean-Marie Dufour, François Vaillancourt. — Montréal : Département de science économique et Centre de recherche en développement économique, Université de Montréal, [1981?]

43 p. ; 28 cm. — (Cahier / Département de science économique et Centre de recherche en développement économique, ISSN 0709-9231 ; 8044)   C***

iii, 83 p. : 14 maps (some col.) ; 28 cm. — (Information circular / State of Washington, Department of Natural Resources, Division of Geology and Earth Resources ; 77)

Fig. 27. Statement of responsibility in series

Authority records:

Research pamphlet (Springfield City Library.
    Genealogy/Local History Dept.)
    x Springfield City Library. Genealogy/Local
        History Dept.
            Research pamphlet

Resources series (University of New South
    Wales. Industrial Relations Research Centre)
    x University of New South Wales. Industrial
        Relations Research Centre.
            Resources series

Special paper (Oregon. Dept. of Geology and
    Mineral Industries)
    x Oregon. Dept. of Geology and Mineral
        Industries.
            Special paper

Research report (Canadian Institute of
    Ukrainian Studies)
    x Canadian Institute of Ukrainian Studies.
        Research report

Readers' guide (Library Association. Public
    Libraries Group)
    x Library Association. Public Libraries
        Group.
            Readers' guide

Cahier (Université de Montréal. Centre de
    recherche en développement économique)
    x Université de Montréal. Centre de
        recherche en développement économique

Bibliographical bulletin (University of
    Auckland. Library)
    x University of Auckland. Library.
        Bibliographical bulletin

Research report (New Jersey State Museum)
    x New Jersey State Museum.
        Research report

```
Information circular (Washington (State).
   Division of Geology and Earth Resources)
   x Washington (State). Division of Geology
      and Earth Resources.
            Information circular
```

Corporate Name as Title

If the series title consists solely of the name of a corporate body but the name is not in *AACR2-88* catalog entry form (excluding qualifiers), a *see* reference should be made from the catalog entry form of the name to the series title.

Variant Forms

If the series contains data in the first five words that are searchable in another form, a *see* reference should be made from the alternate form to the authorized form.

Example:

```
Uni Pax.
   x UniPax
```

Different Languages

If the series title appears in the item in different languages, a *see also* reference should be made to connect the multilingual titles.

Some of these references are relevant only in an online environment and may not be appropriate in manual files. Also, the filing system used will influence the cross references needed.

Chapter 13

Controlling Subjects

Subject headings work requires a clear understanding of the subject matter, knowledge of subject cataloging principles, and a thorough familiarity with the list of subject headings used as the basic authority file. In the absence of national standards for establishing subject authority records, libraries have proceeded on an individual basis and have organized authority files based on their own perceived needs. Most libraries need to (1) determine what subject headings are in the public catalog, (2) determine the established form for the various components of the subject heading, and (3) know what references are in the public catalog. To fill these needs an authority record must contain (1) an authorized heading in the same form as it appears in the public catalog, and (2) a record of all cross references that are displayed with the subject heading in the list used.

Policies concerning references in the public catalog vary from library to library. Some libraries with manual catalogs do not put *broader term* (BT) and *related term* (RT) references in the catalog and, therefore, do not include them in the authority file. Instead, they make the basic list of subject headings and the supplements available to the public. This procedure saves library time since hundreds of reference cards do not have to be prepared, typed, filed, and maintained. Time saved at one point, however, is lost at another. Consideration of the users' time, expertise, and skill should be an important factor in deciding whether to include or to omit BT and RT references.

Controlling Subject Headings Printed in the List

The illustrations and examples that follow explain graphically the procedure for selecting authority data for subject authority records for subject headings printed in an authorized list. The examples below include a variety of data elements that must be considered when creating an authority record for the various structures that subject headings may have. Although the record format displayed in this discussion reflects a manual authority file, the data elements are the same in an online system. An online authority system would have data displayed in the MARC format. (For a discussion of the MARC format for subjects, see chapter 8.)

Topical Subject Headings

From bibliographic record (single word heading):

1. Calligraphy.   2. Writing, Italic.   I. Title.

Z43.T15   1983   745.6'1977—dc19   83-60047
                                                        AACR 2   MARC

Library of Congress

From LCSH:

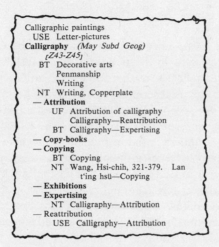

Calligraphic paintings
    USE Letter-pictures
Calligraphy   *(May Subd Geog)*
        ₍Z43-Z45₎
    BT Decorative arts
          Penmanship
          Writing
    NT Writing, Copperplate
    — Attribution
        UF Attribution of calligraphy
              Calligraphy—Reattribution
        BT Calligraphy—Expertising
    — Copy-books
    — Copying
        BT Copying
        NT Wang, Hsi-chih, 321-379.   Lan
              t'ing hsü—Copying
    — Exhibitions
    — Expertising
        NT Calligraphy—Attribution
    — Reattribution
        USE Calligraphy—Attribution

Authority data:

        Calligraphy
            BT Penmanship
                Writing

From bibliographic record (adjectival heading):

1. Technical publishing.   I. Firman Technical Publications.   II. Title.

Z286.T4F57   1983   070.5—dc19   83-189113
                                                      AACR 2   MARC

Library of Congress

From LCSH:

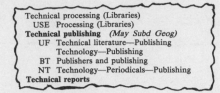

Technical processing (Libraries)
  USE Processing (Libraries)
Technical publishing *(May Subd Geog)*
  UF Technical literature—Publishing
       Technology—Publishing
  BT Publishers and publishing
  NT Technology—Periodicals—Publishing
Technical reports

Authority data:

> **Technical publishing**
>   UF Technical literature—Publishing
>   Technology—Publishing
>   BT Publishers and publishing

To create and maintain a local subject authority file as a subset of an authorized list, every subject heading used in the public catalog must have an authority record made for it. UF references made for the public catalog to direct the user from the unused term to the used term must be recorded.

BT references from broader terms to the newly established heading must also be noted. If the broader term has not yet been established in the authority file, it must be established and enclosed in brackets to signify that the heading has not been used. When the term is finally used as a subject heading, the authority work on the term must be completed and the brackets removed.

NT references to narrower terms are not recorded for such headings unless the narrower terms have already been established in the authority file, thus signifying that the subject heading has been used and appears in the public catalog. To include such NT references when the narrower terms have not been established would generate blind references to headings that do not exist in the public catalog.

Topical Subdivisions

From bibliographic record:

1. Economics—Mathematical models.   I. Title.   II. Series.

Z7164.E2V343   1983   83-195284
                              016.33'00724—dc19
[HB141]   AACR 2   MARC

Library of Congress

From LCSH:

Economic zoology
  USE Zoology, Economic
Economics *(May Subd Geog)*
  ₍HB₎
    Here and with local subdivision are entered works
  on the discipline of economics. Works on the eco-
  nomic conditions of particular countries, regions, cit-
  ies, etc., are entered under the name of the place
  subdivided by Economic conditions.
  UF Economic theory
      Political economy
  RT Economic man
  SA *subdivision* Economic aspects *under*
          special subjects, e.g. Agriculture—
          Economic aspects
  NT Austrian school of economists
      Balance of trade
      Barter
      Business
      Capital
      Capitalism
      Chicago school of economics
      Classical school of economics
      Commerce
      Comparative economics
      Competition
      Consumption (Economics)
      Cooperation
      Cost
      Demography
      Depressions
      Diminishing returns
      Division of labor
      Economic anthropology
      Economic development
      Economic forecasting
      Economic history
      Economic lag
      Economic policy
      Economics, Prehistoric
      Economists
      Elasticity (Economics)
      Employment (Economic theory)
      Equilibrium (Economics)
      Exchange
      Externalities (Economics)
      Factory system
      Fascist economics
      Finance
      Forensic economics

      Urban economics
      Value
      Waste (Economics)
      Wealth
      Welfare economics
— **Bibliography**
    RT Economics literature
— **Computer programs**
      NT SMS (Computer program)
— **History**
    ₍HB75-125₎
      Here are entered works on the history of eco-
    nomics as a discipline. Works on economic histo-
    ry or conditions are entered under the heading
    Economic history or the subdivision Economic
    conditions under names of countries, regions, cit-
    ies, etc.
      NT Historical school of economics
— — **To 1800**
      ₍HB77-83₎
— — **19th century**
      ₍HB85₎
— — **20th century**
      ₍HB87₎
— **Mathematical models**
      BT Economics, Mathematical
      SA *subdivision* Economic conditions—
            Mathematical models *under*
            names of countries, regions,
            cities, etc., e.g. United States—
            Economic conditions—
            Mathematical models
      NT Agriculture—Economic aspects—
            Mathematical models
          Demand functions (Economic
            theory)
— **Mathematics**
      USE Economics, Mathematical
— **Methodology**
      ₍HB71₎
      NT Economics, Mathematical
— **Psychological aspects**
— **Religious aspects**

The subject heading is ECONOMICS—MATHEMATICAL MODELS, which has its own references. Users who decide to search under *economic theory* or *political economy* must be directed to the chosen term in order to execute a successful search for information collocated in the catalog under the heading ECONOMICS—MATHEMATICAL MODELS.

If the subject heading ECONOMICS has not been used already, the UF references under ECONOMICS must be entered in the catalog to direct the user from the unused term *economic theory* or *political economy* to the chosen heading. An authority record should be made for the heading ECONOMICS. It should be bracketed to signify that the references are in the catalog but that the heading itself has not yet been used.

Only the UF references that direct the user to the chosen term should be included on the authority record. When the library acquires materials on *economics* and assigns the subject heading to a work, the brackets must be removed and the authority work for the term completed. It is the cataloger's responsibility to ensure that searchers in the public catalog get all of the help possible with their subject searches.

Authority data:

```
[Economics]
   UF Economic theory
      Political economy


Economics—Mathematical models
   BT Economics, Mathematical
```

Free-Floating Subdivisions under Topical Headings

From bibliographic record:

1. Church decoration and ornament—Bibliography.   I. Title.   II. Series.
Z5956.D3V35   1984   016.726′52—dc19   84-165706
[NK2190]   AACR 2   MARC

Library of Congress

From LCSH:

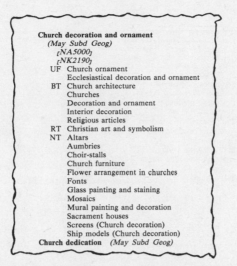

```
Church decoration and ornament
    (May Subd Geog)
    [NA5000]
    [NK2190]
    UF  Church ornament
        Ecclesiastical decoration and ornament
    BT  Church architecture
        Churches
        Decoration and ornament
        Interior decoration
        Religious articles
    RT  Christian art and symbolism
    NT  Altars
        Aumbries
        Choir-stalls
        Church furniture
        Flower arrangement in churches
        Fonts
        Glass painting and staining
        Mosaics
        Mural painting and decoration
        Sacrament houses
        Screens (Church decoration)
        Ship models (Church decoration)
Church dedication    (May Subd Geog)
```

The subject heading is CHURCH DECORATION AND ORNAMENT—BIBLIOG-RAPHY. A free-floating subdivision —BIBLIOGRAPHY has been added to the subject heading CHURCH DECORATION AND ORNAMENT. Before a free-floating subdivision can be added to a subject heading that has not been established in the authority file, the heading must be established along with its UF references.

The heading CHURCH DECORATION AND ORNAMENT must be established and placed in brackets to show that it has not yet been used. It is recommended, however, that only the UF references be made at this time. The UF references assist users in finding the lead term in the public catalog. When the library finally acquires materials on *church decoration and ornament* and assigns the subject heading to the work, the brackets should be removed and the authority work completed.

Authority data:

Church decoration and ornament
    UF Church ornament
        Ecclesiastical decoration and ornament

Church decoration and ornament—Bibliography

Subject Headings with Geographic Subdivisions

From bibliographic record:

```
    1. Type and type-founding—United States—Wood type—History.  2. Amp-
ersand.    I. Smith, Edward O.  II. Title.
Z250.5.W65E28   1984                                    84-159403
                            686.2'24'0973—dc19
                                        AACR 2   MARC
    Library of Congress
```

From LCSH:

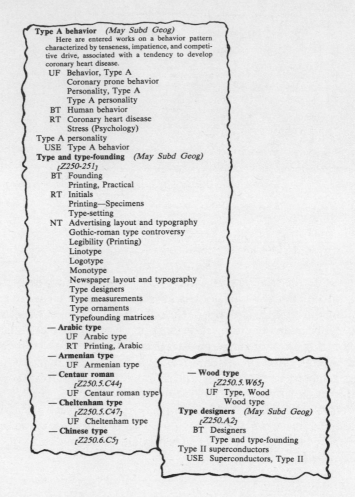

Type A behavior *(May Subd Geog)*
 Here are entered works on a behavior pattern
characterized by tenseness, impatience, and competi-
tive drive, associated with a tendency to develop
coronary heart disease.
 UF Behavior, Type A
   Coronary prone behavior
   Personality, Type A
   Type A personality
 BT Human behavior
 RT Coronary heart disease
   Stress (Psychology)
Type A personality
 USE Type A behavior
Type and type-founding *(May Subd Geog)*
  [Z250-251]
 BT Founding
   Printing, Practical
 RT Initials
   Printing—Specimens
   Type-setting
 NT Advertising layout and typography
   Gothic-roman type controversy
   Legibility (Printing)
   Linotype
   Logotype
   Monotype
   Newspaper layout and typography
   Type designers
   Type measurements
   Type ornaments
   Typefounding matrices
 — Arabic type
   UF Arabic type
   RT Printing, Arabic
 — Armenian type
   UF Armenian type
 — Centaur roman
    [Z250.5.C44]
   UF Centaur roman type
 — Cheltenham type
    [Z250.5.C47]
   UF Cheltenham type
 — Chinese type
    [Z250.6.C5]

 — Wood type
    [Z250.5.W65]
   UF Type, Wood
    Wood type
Type designers *(May Subd Geog)*
  [Z250.A2]
 BT Designers
   Type and type-founding
Type II superconductors
 USE Superconductors, Type II

This heading has an interposed geographic subdivision. Earlier policy would have required two subject headings to cover the subject instead of one. One subject heading would have had a topical subdivision (e.g., TYPE AND TYPE-FOUNDING—WOOD TYPE) and the other a geographical subdivision (e.g., TYPE AND TYPE-FOUNDING—UNITED STATES). The policy was discontinued in the 1960s.

There are no UF references under the main heading TYPE AND TYPE-FOUND-ING; therefore, it does not have to be established as the main subject heading. The topical subdivision —WOOD TYPE has its own reference structure to help the user locate the subject heading.

The subject heading TYPE AND TYPE-FOUNDING—WOOD TYPE must be established and enclosed in brackets to signify that the term has not yet been used in the catalog. When the heading is assigned to a work, the brackets should be removed to signify that the term is in the public catalog.

Authority data:

```
[Type and type-founding—Wood type]
   UF Type, Wood
      Wood Type


Type and type-founding—United States—Wood type
```

Scope Notes

From bibliographic record:

> 1. Shorthand—Forkner.   I. Weber, Edwin J.   II. Forkner, Hamden Landon, 1918-   III. Title.
>
> Z56.2.F67W42   1982   653'.2—dc19   81-67853
>   AACR 2   MARC
>
> Library of Congress

From LCSH:

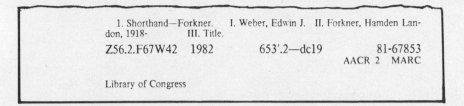

Shorthand
  [Z53-Z100]
  [Z54-Z57 (English)]
  Here are entered general works on shorthand and shorthand for the English language.
  Subdivided by system, e.g. Shorthand—Gregg.
  UF Brachygraphy
     Briefhand
     Phonography
     Shorthand, English
     Stenography
     Tachygraphy
  BT Business education
     Office practice
     Writing
  RT Abbreviations
     Dictation (Office practice)
     Stenographers
  NT Medical shorthand
     Musical shorthand
     Stenotypy
     Technical shorthand
     Tironian notes
  — **Alpha hand**
     UF Alpha hand shorthand
  — **Alphabet**
     UF Alphabet shorthand
  — American
     USE Shorthand—Benn Pitman
  — **Avancena American language**
     [Z56.2.A]
     UF Avancena American language
        shorthand
  — **Barnes**
     UF Barnes shorthand
     BT Shorthand—Pitman
  — **Benn Pitman**
     UF American shorthand
        Benn Pitman shorthand
        Shorthand—American
     BT Shorthand—Pitman
  — **Carter**
     UF Carter shorthand

Shorthand *(Continued)*
  — **Century 21**
     UF Century 21 shorthand
  — **Chartier**
     UF Chartier shorthand
        Shorthand—Spencer
        Spencer shorthand
  — **Dacomb**
     UF Dacomb shorthand
  — **Dement**
     UF Dement shorthand
     BT Shorthand—Pitman
  — **Dewey**
     UF Dewey shorthand
  — **Duployé-Institut**
     UF Duployé-Institut shorthand
     NT Shorthand, French—Duployé-
        Institut
        Shorthand, Greek (Modern)—
        Duployé-Institut
  — **Eclectic**
     UF Eclectic shorthand
  — **Exercises for dictation**
  — **Forkner**
     UF Forkner shorthand
  — **Gabelsberger**
     UF Gabelsberger shorthand
     NT Shorthand, Armenian—
        Gabelsberger
        Shorthand, German—Gabelsberger
        Shorthand, Italian—Gabelsberger-
        Noë
        Shorthand, Polish—Gabelsberger-

Authority data:

[Shorthand]
Subdivided by system, e.g. **Shorthand—Forkner**
UF Brachygraphy
   Briefhand
   Phonography
   Shorthand, English
   Stenography
   Tachygraphy
   Transcription (Shorthand)
BT Abbreviations
   Business education
   Dictation (Office practice)
   Office practice
   Writing

Shorthand—Forkner
UF Forkner shorthand

The subject heading to be established is SHORTHAND—FORKNER. The scope note under SHORTHAND directs the user to a potentially long list of shorthand systems that are relevant to the subject heading under consideration. The heading SHORTHAND must be established but, because it has not been used in the catalog, it must be enclosed in brackets. The UF references under it are recorded in the authority record and placed in the public catalog to assist users in getting to the proper heading.

From bibliographic record:

1. Arms and armor—Exhibitions. 2. Firearms—Exhibitions. 3.
Opočno, Czechoslovak Republic—Antiquities.   I. Title. II. Title:
Illustrated guide to the collection of arms. III. Title: Illustrierter
Katalog der Waffensammlung.

U803.C96O662   75-573153

Library of Congress   75

From LCSH:

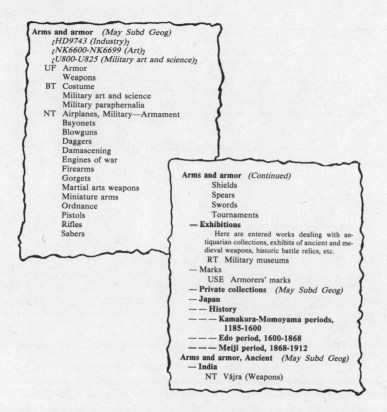

Scope notes can provide useful information to catalog users as well as to catalogers. ARMS AND ARMOR—EXHIBITIONS is an example of the subject heading with a subdivision and a scope note. Some libraries include scope notes in their public catalogs to assist their users in enhancing search strategies.

The subject heading also has its own reference structure. Under the general heading ARMS AND ARMOR there are UF references that should be made to assist the user in finding the chosen term. The subject heading ARMS AND ARMOR must be established, its UF references documented, and the heading enclosed in brackets to signify that it has not yet been used and, therefore, does not appear in the public catalog.

Authority data:

> **Arms and armor—Exhibitions**
>   Here are entered works dealing with antiquarian collections, exhibits of ancient and medieval weapons, historic battle relics, etc.
>
> **[Arms and armor]**
>   UF Armor
>   Weapons

Personal Names

From bibliographic record:

1. Lawrence, D. H. (David Herbert), 1885-1930—Bibliography—Catalogs.
2. Nottinghamshire County Library—Catalogs. 3. University of Nottingham.
University Library—Catalogs.   I. Nottinghamshire County Library.   II. University of Nottingham.   University Library.   III. Title.

Z8490.5.C66   1980   016.823'912—dc19   81-127270
₍PR6023.A93₎   AACR 2   MARC

Library of Congress

From LCSH:

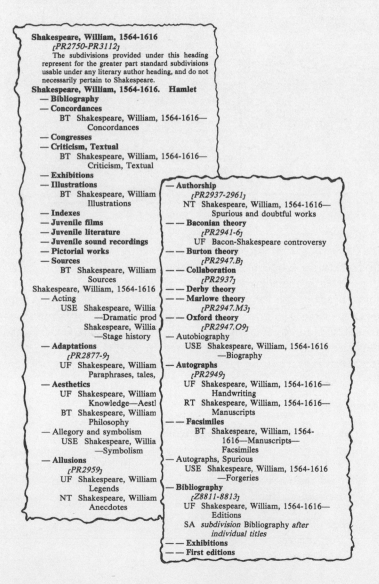

Shakespeare, William, 1564-1616
  ₍PR2750-PR3112₎
    The subdivisions provided under this heading
  represent for the greater part standard subdivisions
  usable under any literary author heading, and do not
  necessarily pertain to Shakespeare.
Shakespeare, William, 1564-1616.   Hamlet
— **Bibliography**
— **Concordances**
      BT Shakespeare, William, 1564-1616—
            Concordances
— **Congresses**
— **Criticism, Textual**
      BT Shakespeare, William, 1564-1616—
            Criticism, Textual
— **Exhibitions**
— **Illustrations**
      BT Shakespeare, William
            Illustrations
— **Indexes**
— **Juvenile films**
— **Juvenile literature**
— **Juvenile sound recordings**
— **Pictorial works**
— **Sources**
      BT Shakespeare, William
            Sources
Shakespeare, William, 1564-1616
  — Acting
      USE Shakespeare, Willia
            —Dramatic prod
      Shakespeare, Willia
            —Stage history
— **Adaptations**
      ₍PR2877-9₎
      UF Shakespeare, William
            Paraphrases, tales,
— **Aesthetics**
      UF Shakespeare, William
            Knowledge—Aestl
      BT Shakespeare, William
            Philosophy
— Allegory and symbolism
      USE Shakespeare, Willia
            —Symbolism
— **Allusions**
      ₍PR2959₎
      UF Shakespeare, William
            Legends
      NT Shakespeare, William
            Anecdotes

— **Authorship**
      ₍PR2937-2961₎
      NT Shakespeare, William, 1564-1616—
            Spurious and doubtful works
— — **Baconian theory**
      ₍PR2941-6₎
      UF Bacon-Shakespeare controversy
— — **Burton theory**
      ₍PR2947.B₎
— — **Collaboration**
      ₍PR2937₎
— — **Derby theory**
— — **Marlowe theory**
      ₍PR2947.M3₎
— — **Oxford theory**
      ₍PR2947.O9₎
— Autobiography
      USE Shakespeare, William, 1564-1616
            —Biography
— **Autographs**
      ₍PR2949₎
      UF Shakespeare, William, 1564-1616—
            Handwriting
      RT Shakespeare, William, 1564-1616—
            Manuscripts
— — **Facsimiles**
      BT Shakespeare, William, 1564-
            1616—Manuscripts—
            Facsimiles
— Autographs, Spurious
      USE Shakespeare, William, 1564-1616
            —Forgeries
— **Bibliography**
      ₍Z8811-8813₎
      UF Shakespeare, William, 1564-1616—
            Editions
      SA *subdivision* Bibliography *after*
            individual titles
— — **Exhibitions**
— — **First editions**

LC omits some categories of subject heading from its subject headings list as a space-saving device. Names of persons, corporate bodies, and jurisdictions are usually omitted but they still may be used as subject headings. They are established according to name authorities principles.

When such terms are needed as subject headings, the forms established in the name authority file are used. A few proper names are printed in *LCSH* as patterns for subdivisions and references. The subject heading SHAKESPEARE, WILLIAM, 1564–1616 is the pattern for literary authors. Any references or subdivisions that are listed under his name may be used with any other literary author. There are no subject-related references under SHAKESPEARE, WILLIAM, 1564–1616–BIBLIOGRAPHY–CATALOGS; therefore, the only references that are required for this heading are those established for name authority control.

Authority data:

```
Lawrence, D.H. (David Herbert), 1885-1930.
    x Lawrence, David Herbert, 1885-1930

Lawrence, D.H. (David Herbert), 1885-1938—
    Bibliography—Catalogs
```

Print Pattern Headings

From bibliographic record:

1. Harari language. 2. Gurage language.   I. Title.

PJ9293.M6   74–194040
                                             MARC

Library of Congress   75 [4]

From LCSH:

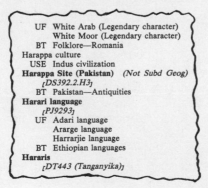

```
    UF   White Arab (Legendary character)
         White Moor (Legendary character)
    BT   Folklore—Romania
Harappa culture
    USE  Indus civilization
Harappa Site (Pakistan)   (Not Subd Geog)
      [DS392.2.H3]
    BT   Pakistan—Antiquities
Harari language
      [PJ9293]
    UF   Adari language
         Ararge language
         Harrarjie language
    BT   Ethiopian languages
Hararis
      [DT443 (Tanganyika)]
```

There are several subject headings printed in the list that may be used as patterns in the creation of other subject headings in the same category. The subdivisions under a pattern heading may be used under other subject headings of the same category. The English language is the pattern for all languages; therefore, the subdivisions listed under ENGLISH LANGUAGE may be used under any other language, if appropriate. Since the subject heading under consideration does not have a subdivision, there is no need to consider further the list of subdivisions under the pattern heading. The subject heading is established and controlled by its own UF and BT references.

Authority data:

```
Harari language
    UF Adari language
       Ararge language
       Harrarjie language
    BT Ethiopian languages
```

Controlling Nonprint Subject Headings with Patterns

Before 1976 proper names were omitted from the subject headings list primarily because of space considerations. In 1976 the decision was made by the Library of Congress to print the following types of formerly omitted headings: names of sacred books; names of families, dynasties, and royal houses; gods; legendary and fictitious characters; works of art; biological names; and chemicals. Also in 1976 the Library began to print several other categories of former nonprint headings: geographic regions and features; city sections; archaeological sites; ancient cities; empires; structures; buildings; roads; parks and reserves; plazas; streets; and other proper names not usually capable of authorship. These headings, however, were all affected by the adoption of *AACR2* in 1981. Those headings that did not conform to *AACR2* were removed from the subject headings list. The current edition of *LCSH* contains headings in the above categories only if they have been established since 1981.

Since 1981, all subject headings (except free-floaters) established by the Subject Cataloging Division at the Library of Congress and usable for *AACR2-88* cataloging are listed in *LCSH*. They comprise the following types:

1. Topical subject headings and subdivisions
    Includes types of objects and concepts; disciplines; methods and procedures; activities; industries; classes of people.
2. Nonjurisdictional geographic names
    Includes geographic features; areas and regions (unless free-floating); trails, parks, and reserves; city sections; early cities, empires, kingdoms.
3. Names of persons incapable of authorship; families
    Includes legendary, mythological, and fictitious characters; gods; dynasties; royal houses.
4. Names of artworks

5. Names of chemicals, drugs, and minerals; biological names
6. Other proper names
    Includes languages; computer languages and systems; ethnic groups; roads; structures and buildings; railroads and other engineering systems; tests; projects; programs; movements; events; trade names; games.

Name headings are usually controlled by name authorities and are listed in *LCSH* only if they fall in one of the following categories:

1. Personal names
    If the names of important personages require special topical subdivisions, for example, MARY, BLESSED VIRGIN, SAINT; or the name of a person serves as the pattern heading in subdivision practice, for example, LINCOLN, ABRAHAM, 1809–1865.
2. Jurisdictional names
    If provided with special topical or period subdivisions.
3. Corporate body names (other than jurisdictional)
    If they are to be provided with special subject cataloging treatment, including provision for local subdivision, topical subdivisions, and scope notes; if they are used in examples; or if they serve as pattern headings in subdivision practice.
4. Uniform titles
    Many uniform titles are listed in *LCSH* because they are commonly used as topics. This category includes sacred works, prayers, declarations, proclamations, commandments, and so forth. Concordats, treaties, charters, and constitutions, however, are now being deleted from *LCSH*.

Patterns for constructing references and, thus, controlling headings for the variety of categories of proper names that may not appear in the subject headings list follow. In the examples, the word [country] in a pattern refers not only to countries but also to states in the United States, provinces in Canada, republics in the Soviet Union, and constituent countries in Great Britain as first-level political jurisdictions.

Pattern headings are useful when establishing subject headings that are not printed in the list. The cataloger must follow a set of instructions to create the headings. Knowledge of the patterns described below will facilitate the creation of legitimate but unprinted subject headings as needed in local library catalogs.

Archaeological Sites

Pattern:

```
[site name] Site ([geographic qualifier])
   UF [alternate name(s)] ([geographic
      qualifier])
   BT [modern country]—Antiquities
      If applicable, one of the following:
```

```
          Caves—[modern country]
          Kitchen-middens—[modern country]
```

Authority data:

```
    Bird Hammock Site (Fla.)
      BT Florida—Antiquities

    Boca Site (N.M.)
      UF Boca Pueblo Ruins (N.M.)
      BT New Mexico—Antiquities
```

Artworks (Artist Known)

Pattern:

```
    [name of artist]. [title of work in English]
      UF [title of work in English] ([art form or
          medium])
         if appropriate:
         [title of work in vernacular] ([art form
             or medium])
      BT [art form or medium], [nationality]
```

Authority data:

```
    Velazquez, Diego, 1599-1660. Maids of honor
      UF Cuadro de Familia (Painting)
         Familia (Painting)
         Maids of honor (Painting)
         Meninas (Painting)
         Royal family (Painting)
      BT Painting, Spanish
```

Artworks (Artist Unknown)

Pattern:

```
    [title of work in vernacular] ([art form or
        medium])
      UF [title in English] ([art form or medium])
      BT [art form or medium], [nationality]
```

Authority data:

```
    Mumuye (Sculpture)
      UF Ancestor figure (Sculpture)
      BT Sculpture, Nigerian
```

Bridges

Pattern:

```
[name of bridge] ([geographic qualifier])
    UF [alternate name of bridge, if any]
        ([geographic qualifier])
    BT [river or water body]—Bridges
        Bridges—[country or 1st order division]
```

Authority data:

```
Natural Bridge (Newport, Fla.)
    BT Bridges—Florida
        Saint Marks River (Fla.)—Bridges


Pont-Neuf (Paris, France)
    BT Bridges—France
        Seine River (France)—Bridges
```

Buildings, Houses, and Other Structures

Additional structures governed by this pattern are forts, gates, plazas, tunnels, and walls in cities.

Pattern:

```
[name of structure] ([geographic qualifier])
    UF [alternate name of structure]
        ([geographic qualifier])
    BT [type of structure]—[country or 1st order
        division]
```

Authority data:

```
John G. Riley House (Tallahassee, Fla.)
    UF Riley House (Tallahassee, Fla.)
    BT Dwellings—Florida
```

If the heading is established in English and there is a name in the vernacular, a UF reference should be made from the vernacular. If, however, the heading is established in the vernacular, a UF reference should be made from the English form of name if one has been well established. If the name begins with a generic term, the words should be manipulated in such a way that the proper name is placed in the lead position. If, however, the proper name appears in the lead position in another reference, the inverted reference is not necessary and may be omitted.

Building Details

Pattern:

```
[name of detail] ([name of structure]
   [geographic qualifier])
   UF [alternate name(s)], ([name of structure]
      [geographic qualifier])
   BT [name of structure] ([geographic
      qualifier])
      [type of detail]—[country or 1st order
      division]
```

Authority data:

```
C.K. Steele Baptistery (Bethel Baptist Church,
   Tallahassee, Fla.)
   UF Steele Baptistery (Bethel Baptist Church,
      Tallahassee, Fla.)
   BT Baptisteries—Florida

Brandenburg Gate (Berlin, Germany)
   BT Gates—Germany (West)
```

Areas Associated with Cities

The environs of a city may be known as the metropolitan area, the suburban area, or the city region. City regions usually are not well defined and, therefore, do not have an exact size or boundaries as would be the case with metropolitan and suburban areas. Subject headings for these categories of areas associated with cities are free-floating phrases constructed by inserting the appropriate word or phrase (i.e., *Region*, *Metropolitan Area*, or *Suburban Area*) between an established city name and its geographic qualifier. Because these subject headings are free-floating, they do not have references to control them.

Patterns:

```
[city] Region ([geographic qualifier])

[city] Metropolitan Area ([geographic
   qualifier])

[city] Suburban Area ([geographic qualifier])
```

The geographic qualifier used with the free-floating construction should be the same as that used with the city proper. If the city is established in the authority file without a qualifier, then the area should, likewise, be unqualified. New York (N.Y.) and Washington (D.C.) are exceptions.

Authority data:

> **Tallahassee Region (Fla.)**
>
> **Orlando Metropolitan Area (Fla.)**
>
> **Detroit Suburban Area (Mich.)**

Forks in Rivers

If the name of the fork is directional, such as East Fork or West Fork, the pattern that follows should be used. Forks with nondirectional names are treated as any other individually named river.

Pattern:

> **[name of main river], [name] Fork ([geographic qualifier])**
> UF [name] Fork, [name of main river]
>   ([geographic qualifier])
> BT Rivers—[geographic subdivision]

Authority data:

> **Salmon River, Middle Fork (Idaho)**
> UF Middle Fork, Salmon River (Idaho)
> BT Rivers—Idaho

> **Solomon River, North Fork (Kan.)**
> UF North Fork, Solomon River (Kan.)
> BT Rivers—Kansas

Gods of Greek and Roman Mythology

The name of each god of Greek and Roman mythology should be qualified by either *Greek deity* or *Roman deity* in parentheses. The term *Gods* refers to male deities and *Goddesses* to female.

Pattern:

> **[name of god] (_____ deity)**
> RT [equivalent god]
> BT Gods, [Greek or Roman]
>   Mythology, [Greek or Roman]
>   or where appropriate:
>   Goddesses, [qualified to designate
>   religion]

Authority data:

Artemis (Greek deity)
  RT Diana (Roman deity)
  BT Goddesses, Greek

Pluto (Greek deity)
  UF Hades (Greek deity)
  BT Gods, Greek

Islands

Pattern:

[name of island or island group] ([geographic
   qualifier])
  UF [alternate name(s)] ([geographic
    qualifier])
   [name in vernacular] ([geographic
    qualifier])
   [uninverted form of name] ([geographic
    qualifier]) (Make this reference if the
    heading is inverted)
  BT [name of island group] ([geographic
    qualifier]) (Omit this reference if the
    name of the group is the same as the
    jurisdiction used in the next BT)
   Islands—[geographic subdivision]
     or
   [specific type of island, if established]—
    [geographic subdivision]
     or
   Islands of the [surrounding body of water]
    (Make this reference if the island does
    not lie near its controlling
    jurisdiction)

The BT reference from ISLANDS—[geographic subdivision] or [specific type of island]—[geographic subdivision] is made if the island is close to its controlling jurisdiction. If the island is a distance away, the following reference is made:

    BT Islands of the [surrounding body of water]

Authority data:

Amelia Island (Fla.)
  UF Islands—Florida
   Sea Islands

Florida Keys (Fla.)
  UF Islands—Florida

Easter Island
  UF Isla de Pascua
     Pascua Island
     Rapa Nui
     Rapanui
  BT Islands of the Pacific

National Parks, Including Wild and Scenic Rivers

Pattern:

[name of park] ([country])
  BT National parks and reserves—[country]

Authority data:

Klondike Gold Rush National Historical Park
  (Alaska and Wash.)
  BT National parks and reserves—Alaska
     National parks and reserves—Washington

Zion National Park (Utah)
  BT National parks and reserves—Utah

Railroad Lines

Pattern:

[name of railroad]
  UF [alternate name of railroad, if any]
  BT Railroads—[country]
     [type of railroad, if appropriate]

Authority data:

New York Central Railroad
  BT Railroads—United States

Royal Houses and Dynasties

Patterns:

[name], House of
  UF [variant names]
     House of [name]
  BT [country]—Kings and rulers

```
[name] dynasty
  UF [variant names]
  BT [country]—History—[period subdivision]
```

Authority data:

```
Habsburg, House of
  UF Austria, House of
     Hapsburg, House of
     House of Austria
     House of Habsburg
     House of Hapsburg
  BT Austria—Kings and rulers
```

```
Achaemenid dynasty
  UF Achaemenians
     Achaemenidae
     Achaemenids
     Hakhamanishiya
  BT Iran—History—To 640
```

River Valleys

Pattern:

```
[name of river] Valley ([geographic qualifier])
```

Authority data:

```
Shenandoah River Valley (Va.)
```

If the qualifier contains two geographic areas, a BT reference should be made from each one as a subdivision. Valleys other than river valleys are not free-floating and are established and printed in *LCSH*.

Example:

```
Ojai Valley (Calif.)
  BT Valley—California
```

Rivers

The term *rivers* is used generically to include all types of surface water, such as ponds, lakes, streams, and so forth. References are not made for large streams of which the river is a tributary.

Pattern:

```
[name of river] ([geographic qualifier])
   UF [variant name] ([geographic qualifier])
   BT [name of river]—[geographic subdivision]
      Rivers—[geographic subdivision]
```

If the river is located in two or three countries (or first-level jurisdictions of Canada, Great Britain, the Soviet Union, or the United States), a BT reference should be made from each of them whether named in the qualifier or not. If the qualifier is for a region that represents more than three countries (*not* first-level jurisdictions), the BT reference should be made from the next largest region that encompasses all of the jurisdictions in which the river is located. If the qualifier contains the name of a region that represents more than three first-order political divisions of Canada, Great Britain, the Soviet Union, or the United States, the BT reference should be made from the name of the country as the geographic subdivision.

Authority data:

```
Apalachicola River (Fla.)
   BT Rivers—Florida
```

Trials with Names

Pattern:

```
[name of trial, city, larger geographic entity,
   dates]
   UF [alternate name, city, dates]
   BT Trials ([type of crime])—[geographic
      subdivision]
```

Authority data:

```
Scottsboro Case, Scottsboro, Ala., 1931-1937
   BT Trials (Rape)—Alabama

Watergate Trial, Washington, D.C., 1973
   BT Trials (Burglary)—Washington (D.C.)
      Trials (Conspiracy)—Washington (D.C.)
      Watergate affair, 1972-1974
```

Chapter 14

Reference Sources

Good authority work is supported by an extensive collection of good reference tools. When creating original authority records, a thorough search of the appropriate reference tools is essential to identify names or forms of names by which the individual or corporate body may be known. This is the most labor-intensive part of authority work and, thus, the most expensive. The time spent in researching names, however, is time well spent. It can save considerable time and disappointment in the future. Reference tools that are considered essential to authority work are listed below. The list includes a brief description of tools relating to names, series, and subject authorities.

The reference sources listed represent an ideal core collection that would support the needs of most libraries involved in authority work. A majority of libraries, however, will not have a need for all of these resources to support their work in technical services. It is essential, nevertheless, for each library to have access to at least some of the works from each category. The choices should be determined by the acquisitions policy of the library. For example, a library that seldom collects materials on a given country (e.g., Africa, Latin America, etc.) would have less need for tools that specialize in that area.

Library of Congress Sources

There are several sources from which authority information generated by the Library of Congress may be secured. The machine-readable Library of Congress name authority file is available through the various bibliographic utilities, such as OCLC, RLIN, WLN, and UTLAS. A library must be a member of one of the utilities to have direct access to the online authority file. Presently, the capability is for searching only. All records in the file have been established and authenticated either by the Library of Congress or under its supervision.

Reference cards are a by-product generated from the Library of Congress authority system and are available for purchase from the Library of Congress. The Library of Congress authority tapes are also available through subscription; however, libraries not holding membership in a bibliographic utility usually do not have the resources to subscribe to and use the tapes independently.

Library of Congress Name Headings with References. Compiled and edited by the Catalog Management and Publication Division, Library of Congress, 1974–1980. Ceased publication. (Superseded by *Name Authorities Cumulative Microform Edition.*)

The headings included in this publication are limited to those with references. The publication is the only print source of the Library of Congress authority records covering the period 1974–1977 that is available to the general library community. In 1978 the records began to appear in microform in the *Name Authorities Cumulative Microform Edition.* After 1980, they became available in machine-readable form.

Name Authorities Cumulative Microform Edition. Prepared under the editorial coordination of the Catalog Management and Publication Division, Library of Congress, 1977–   . Quarterly with a fifth issue consisting of multiyear cumulations of the entire file. 48x cumulative microfiche.

The publication includes all of the name authority records in the computerized master file at the Library of Congress, including personal and corporate names, conference headings, geographical names of political and civil jurisdictions, uniform titles, and series. Each record contains the established heading, a list of significant sources that contributed to the identification of the heading, the reference tracings, and other relevant codes and control data. Also included are cross references that direct the user from an unused heading to a used one. This publication supersedes the now-ceased publication *Library of Congress Name Headings with References, 1974–1980.*

The National Union Catalog (NUC). Compiled and edited by the Catalog Management and Publication Division, Library of Congress, 1956–   .

The publication ceased as a book-form catalog in 1982 and in January 1983 began publication in computer-output microfiche only. It contains bibliographic records for monographs, pamphlets, maps, atlases, and serial publications cataloged by the Library of Congress and other cooperating libraries. Access is by main entry. All volumes, including the 755-volume pre-1956 imprints, are available in microform. The work is more valuable for the guidance given by the statements of responsibility in the descriptions than for the choice and form of headings. The headings are valuable for dates in personal name. Beginning in 1981 all headings are *AACR2* or *AACR2*-compatible.

The National Union Catalog. Audiovisual Materials. Quarterly. 48x microfiche, 1983–
———. Books. Monthly. 48x microfiche, 1983–
———. Cartographic Materials. Quarterly. 48x microfiche, 1983–   .

These three publications replace the book form that ceased publication in 1982. They feature an additive register of full records and four separate cumulative indexes (name, title, subject, and series). The NUC *Cartographic Materials* also includes a fifth index, the Geographic classification code index, which provides access by the geographic classification code based on the *LC Classification Schedule G.*

Sources of Personal Names

The sources included here primarily support the establishment of contemporary names. Only a few of the tools provide retrospective personal biographies and historical information about corporate bodies.

A majority of libraries collect primarily in English and in the Western European languages. Specialized sources in less common languages have been omitted.

There are numerous specialized "Who's Who" type publications available on a variety of geographic areas; ethnic, national, and religious groups; subject areas; and a combination of the above. These include works such as *Who's Who in America, Who's Who in Library Science, Who's Who in Colored America, Who's Who in Cypriote Archaeology*, and so on. These publications have also been omitted here primarily because of limited space. They may be identified by consulting Sheehy's *Guide to Reference Books*[1] and its supplements.

Atkinson, Frank. *Dictionary of Literary Pseudonyms: A Selection of Popular Modern Writers in English.* 4th ed. London: Library Association, 1987.

> Covers writers of the twentieth century. Information has been verified with the authors.

Contemporary Authors: A Bio-bibliographical Guide to Current Authors and Their Works. 1st revision. Vol. 1 (1967)–   . Detroit: Gale Research.

> Covers current authors in many fields and from many countries with as complete a bibliography as possible, including works in progress, as well as other sources of biographical data.

Current Biography. Vol. 1 (1940)–   . New York: Wilson. Monthly with annual cumulations.

> Covers persons of various nationalities, professions, and occupations who are currently active in their particular fields with references to sources for further information.

International Who's Who. 1935–   . London: Europa Publications and Allen & Unwin. Annual.

> Includes worldwide biographical information.

The New Encyclopaedia Britannica. 15th ed. 32 vols. Chicago: Encyclopaedia Britannica, 1987.

> The twelve-volume *Micropaedia* contains biographies that have useful information for authority work.

New York Times Index. Vol. 1 (1913)–   . New York: New York Times. Semimonthly with annual cumulations.

> Includes numerous references to names.

Pseudonyms and Nicknames Dictionary. 3rd ed. 2 vols. Edited by Jennifer Mossman. Detroit: Gale Research, 1987.
New Pseudonyms and Nicknames: Supplement to the Third Edition of Pseudonyms and Nicknames Dictionary. Edited by Jennifer Mossman. Detroit: Gale Research, 1988.

> The two works listed above include real names, pseudonyms, and nicknames of persons in the twentieth century listed in a single alphabet with cross references to

---

1. Eugene P. Sheehy, *Guide to Reference Books*, 10th ed. (Chicago: American Library Association, 1986).

link them. Full biographical information about the person is found under the real name.

Washington Post. Newspaper Index. 1971–1978. Annual cumulation of the monthly publication. 7 vols. Superseded.
Bell & Howell's Newspaper Index to the Washington Post. 1979–1981.

The two works listed above include numerous references to names.

Webster's New Biographical Dictionary. Springfield, Mass.: Merriam, 1983. Frequently updated and reprinted.

Includes brief biographical information not restricted to period, nationality, race, religion, or occupation.

The Writer's Directory. 4th ed. (1980/82)–   . New York: St. Martin's.

Gives biographical information about fiction and nonfiction writers, poets, and dramatists.

Sources of Corporate Names

Africa South of the Sahara. 1971–   . London: Europa Publications. Annual.

Includes a directory section that gives names of political parties and members of government media, banks, trade unions, shipping companies, and so forth. Complements *Europa Year Book.*

Directory of European Associations. Pt. 1 (1971)–   . Detroit: Gale Research.

Covers industrial, trade, and professional associations in all fields of activity in all countries in Europe.

Encyclopedia of Associations. 1956–   . Detroit: Gale Research. Biennial.

Covers a wide variety of national and international organizations: trade, business, agricultural, governmental, military, legal, scientific and technical, educational and cultural, social welfare, health, fraternal, religious, athletic, and ethnic.

Europa Year Book. 1959–   . London: Europa Publications. Annual.

Covers international organizations including the United Nations and its specialized agencies; contains directories of political, industrial, financial, cultural, and scientific organizations in Africa, the Americas, Asia, Australia, and each European country. Complements *World of Learning.*

Middle East and North Africa. 1948–   . London: Europa Publications. Annual.

Contains a section on regional organizations.

World of Learning. 1947–   . London: Europa Publications. Annual.

Covers institutions of learning in Europe, Africa, Asia, the Americas, and Australia. Institutions include learned societies, research institutions, libraries, museums, universities, and other institutions of higher education. Also covers Unesco and other international councils and organizations.

Yearbook of International Organizations. 1948–   . Brussels: Union of International
Associations. Biennial.

Covers international organizations and associations currently active.

Sources of Geographic Names

Columbia Lippincott Gazetteer of the World. Edited by Leon E. Seltzer with the Geographical Research Staff of Columbia University Press and with the cooperation of
the American Geographical Society. Morningside Heights, N.Y.: Columbia University Press, 1970.

Lists some 130,000 geographic names of places of the world, including both political
subdivisions and geographic features, variant spellings, major politico-geographical
changes, and identifications of new nations.

Political Handbook and Atlas of the World. 1927–   . New York: Harper. Annual.

Covers the governments of the world giving chief government officials, party leaders,
governmental agencies.

Rand McNally Commercial Atlas and Marketing Guide. 1876–   . New York: Rand
McNally. Annual.

Covers countries of the world but is primarily an atlas of America.

Sources for the Fine Arts

American Architects Directory. 1956–   . New York: Bowker. Annual.

Includes the names and brief biographical sketches of members of the American
Institute of Architects and other architects who have established a reputation in the
field.

American Art Directory. 1898–   . New York: Bowker. Triennial.

Covers museums, art organizations, university and college departments of art, art
schools, councils, and exhibitions.

Contemporary Architects. Edited by Ann Lee Morgan. 2nd ed. New York: St. James Press,
1987.

Lists architects and architectural firms with brief biographical sketches. International
in scope. Includes primarily those who are living or recently deceased.

Directory of World Museums. Edited by Kenneth Hudson and Ann Nicholls. 2nd ed.
New York: Facts on File, 1981.

Gives an enormous list of museums with permanent collections. All museum names
are in English.

International Directory of Arts. Frankfurt/Main: Verlag Muker, 1952/1953–   . Annual.

Includes the names of museums, art galleries, libraries, associations, and artists. Text in English, French, and German.

Official Museum Directory of the United States and Canada. 1971–   . New York: American Association of Museums and Crowell-Collier Educational Corporation.

Contains information on museums in the United States and Canada accredited by the American Association of Museums. Includes also museum associations, both foreign and domestic.

Sources for the Performing and Visual Arts

Baker, Theodore. *Biographical Dictionary of Musicians.* 7th ed. New York: Schirmer, 1984.

Includes musicians of all eras and nations.

Feather, Leonard G. *The Encyclopedia of Jazz in the United States in the Sixties.* New York: Horizon Press, 1966.
———. *The Encyclopedia of Jazz in the United States in the Seventies.* New York: Horizon Press, 1976.

The two works above are exhaustive surveys of principal personalities in the field of jazz music. Include biographies of working jazz artists and lists of jazz record companies.

International Motion Picture and Television Almanac. 1929–   . New York: Quigley. Annual.

Includes a section on who's who in motion pictures, corporations, and motion picture and television organizations.

International Television Almanac. 1956–   . New York: Quigley. Annual.

Includes information on performers, producers, distributors, television stations, and agencies.

The New Grove Dictionary of Music and Musicians. 2 vols. Edited by Stanley Sadie. London: Macmillan, 1985.

Covers the whole field of music from the earliest time to the present with emphasis on English subjects. Includes biographies of composers, performers, scholars, theorists, patrons, publishers, and people in other arts.

The New York Times: Film Reviews. New York: New York Times and Arno Press, 1913–   .

Includes a personal name and corporate index section.

Sources for Religion

American Jewish Year Book. 1899–   . Philadelphia: Jewish Publishing Society. Annual.

Includes biographies, necrologies, and directory information relating to Jewish matters in America and in other countries.

Annvario Pontifico. 1716–   . Roma: Tipografia Poliglotta Vaticana. Annual.

Contains list of popes, the Roman Catholic hierarchy in Rome and throughout the world, Catholic institutions and offices, lists of religious orders, index of personal names.

The Book of Saints; A Dictionary of Persons Canonized or Beatified by the Catholic Church. Compiled by the Benedictine Monks of St. Augustine's Abbey, Ramsgate. 5th ed. New York: Crowell, 1966.

Lists names of saints in alphabetical order. When names have variant forms, they are included also. Gives descriptive appellation, hagiological rank, death dates, and the liturgical group to which the saint belongs.

Crockford's Clerical Directory. 1858–   . Oxford: University Press. Annual.

Covers the clergy of the provinces of Canterbury and York and other Anglican provinces and dioceses. Includes biographical sketches of Church of England clergy.

Farmer, David Hugh. *The Oxford Dictionary of Saints.* 2nd ed. Oxford: Oxford University Press, 1987.

Includes saints venerated in the Christian church and all English saints of whom there is a notable cult in England. Byzantine saints are omitted. Listed in alphabetical order up to the end of the fifteenth century under their Christian names. Later ones are entered under surnames.

Yearbook of American and Canadian Churches. 1916–   . New York: National Council of Churches of Christ in the U.S.A. Annual.

Includes names of organizations and activities of all faiths.

Other Important Sources for Names

American Dental Directory. 1947–   . Chicago: American Dental Association. Annual.

Lists dentists in the United States who hold membership in the American Dental Association.

American Library Directory. 1923–   . New York: Bowker. Biennial.

A classified list of libraries in the United States and Canada with personnel and statistical data.

American Men and Women of Science. 1917–   . New York: Jacques Cattell Press. Irregular.

Covers the biological and physical sciences and the social and behavioral sciences.

American Universities and Colleges. 1st (1928)–   edition. Washington: American Council on Education. Quadrennial.

A current list of names of American universities and colleges accredited by a regional accrediting association or a professional agency. The index includes named associations and research facilities.

Directory of American Scholars: A Biographical Directory. 1942–   . New York: Bowker. Irregular.

Includes persons in the areas of English, speech and drama, foreign languages, linguistics, philology, philosophy, religion, and law. Complements *American Men and Women of Science.*

Federal/State and Municipal/County Executive Directory. 1985–   . Washington, D.C.: Carroll Publishing Company. Annual.

Covers federal government officials in the executive and legislative branches, including the White House staff, Cabinet, and top- and mid-level branch officials in 87 departments and agencies, plus all members of Congress and their staffs. Covers staff officials in all 50 states and the District of Columbia from the governor and staff to top- and mid-level executives in all functions, departments, and agencies. Covers county and city officials in 750 counties and 1,200 cities and towns, including chief executives, commission chairpersons, and administrators of key departments and agencies.

Moody's Municipal and Government Manual. Vol. 1 (1979)–   . New York: Moody's Investor's Service. Updated semiweekly.

Describes state agencies, including educational institutions, authorities, commissions, housing and redevelopment agencies.

Municipal Year Book. G, Directories (Agencies, Organizations, City Officials). Vol. 1 (1934)–   . Chicago: International City Managers' Association. Annual.

Contains data about American cities. A useful tool for determining if a place bears the name of a jurisdiction that has ceased to exist.

Official Catholic Directory. 1886–   . New York: Kennedy. Annual.

Covers Catholic organizations, clergy, churches, missions, schools, and religious orders in the United States, Great Britain, and other parts of the world where the Catholic church exists.

Official Congressional Directory for Use of the U.S. Congress. 1809–   . Washington, D.C.: Government Printing Office. Irregular.

Includes biographical information on members of Congress, state delegations, committee members, commissions, and other governmental officials.

United States Government Manual. 1935–   . Washington, D.C.: Government Printing Office. Annual.

Includes information about the organization of the federal government, current officials, abolished and transferred agencies.

Sources for Series

Unlike name authority work, only a fraction of the recognized series must be verified in reference sources. A series title printed in the item is generally used as is. There is no need to establish a predominant title or to identify variant titles in other languages or forms.

Series titles, however, do change. Sometimes titles must be distinguished or made unique. Also, when a title is nondistinct, a responsible body must be identified. A list of essential tools to facilitate series authority work follows. Citations are in alphabetical order.

Baer, Eleanora A. *Titles in Series: A Handbook for Librarians and Students.* 3rd ed. 4 vols. New York: Scarecrow Press, 1978.

Lists titles published in series and their sequence within the series. Arranged in numerical, chronological, or alphabetical order as appropriate. Gives the official Library of Congress entry. Explains oddities and irregularities in publishing. Excludes publishers' series, government publications, yearbooks, and reprints.

Books in Series in the United States. 1st-   ed. New York: R.R. Bowker. Irregular.

Original, reprinted, in-print, and out-of-print books published or distributed in the United States in popular, scholarly, and professional series.

Catalog of Reprints in Series. Edited by Robert M. Orton. 1st (1940)–   ed. New York: Scarecrow Press. Irregular.

An author-title dictionary catalog of reprints in series. Gives full bibliographic information in each entry. Also includes different editions of the same book listed in alphabetical order by publisher, followed by series name in parentheses. Includes anthologies and omnibus volumes. Contains a list of series titles and the works in the series and a list of publishers of series titles.

Library of Congress Monographic Series. 1974–   . Washington, D.C.: Library of Congress. Quarterly and annual cumulations.

Reproduces bibliographic records printed by the Library of Congress during the period of the issue. Represents all monographs cataloged by the Library of Congress as parts of series. Excludes nonbook materials and series of a single personal authority.

MDS—Name Authorities [The machine-readable Library of Congress authority file].

On January 14, 1983, OCLC received and loaded the first Library of Congress Name-Authority tapes containing series records. These first records were created as the result of a retrospective series authority project at the Library of Congress. The records are recognizable by the beginning digits (42) in the control number.

Name Authorities Cumulative Microform Edition. Prepared under the editorial coordination of the Catalog Management and Publication Division, Library of Congress, 1977–   . Quarterly with a fifth issue consisting of multiyear cumulations of the entire file. 48x cumulative microfiche.

The publication includes all of the name authority records in the computerized master file at the Library of Congress, including personal and corporate names, conference headings, geographical names of political and civil jurisdictions, uniform titles, and series. Each record contains the established heading, a list of significant sources that contributed to the identification of the heading, the reference tracings, and other relevant codes and control data. Also included are cross references that direct the user from an unused heading to a used one. This publication supersedes the now-ceased publication, *Library of Congress Name Headings with References, 1974–1980.*

Publishers' Trade List Annual. 1874–   . New York: R.R. Bowker.

Lists series offered for sale by publishers. Arranged by publishers.

Rosenberg, Judith K. *Young people's literature in series: publishers' and non-fiction series: an annotated bibliographical guide.* Littleton, Colo.: Libraries Unlimited, 1973.
———. *Young People's Literature in Series: Fiction, Non-fiction, and Publishers' Series, 1973–1975: An Annotated Bibliographical Guide.* Littleton, Colo.: Libraries Unlimited, 1977.

These two works list all individual volumes of a given series. Include annotations. Arrangement is alphabetical by series title. Individual titles within each series arranged first by author then by title.

Sources for Subjects

The contents of a subject authority file are basically ready-made by a central agency such as the Library of Congress; therefore, the tools that are recommended here are not the type that would be useful in determining new terminology. The majority of the listed tools are resources that a cataloging department needs in order to improve the precision of application at the local level and to assist in the interpretation of policies of application at the Library of Congress.

Cataloging Service Bulletin. No. 1 (1945)–   . Washington, D.C.: Processing Services, Library of Congress. Quarterly.

Formerly *Cataloging Service.* Includes information about current Library of Congress cataloging practices. Each issue has a section on current practices and policies regarding subject headings. An indispensable source of information.

Chan, Lois Mai. *Library of Congress Subject Headings: Principles and Application.* 2nd ed. Littleton, Colo.: Libraries Unlimited, 1986.

Updates the basic principles and application described in the 1978 first edition. Based on practices and application of the Library of Congress subject headings. It is the only work on the practical aspects of subject headings published outside of the Library of Congress. Provides an excellent review of the principles of subject headings work.

L.C. Subject Headings Weekly Lists. Prepared by the Subject Cataloging Division, Processing Services, Library of Congress. 1984–   . Washington, D.C.: Library of Congress. Monthly.

Contains groups of weekly lists (working documents) of subject heading changes and additions that have been approved by the Subject Cataloging Division. Represents the most current source of information concerning additions and changes in subject headings and references.

Library of Congress Subject Headings. Prepared by the Subject Cataloging Division, Library of Congress. 11th–   ed. Washington, D.C.: Library of Congress, 1988–   .
———. *Quarterly Supplements.* 1988–   . Washington, D.C.: Library of Congress.
Library of Congress Subject Headings in Microform. Prepared by the Subject Cataloging Division, Library of Congress. 1983–   . Washington, D.C.: Library of Congress. 48x microfiche. Issued cumulatively on a quarterly basis.

These three publications contain subject headings established by the Library of Congress, including subject headings for children's literature. Beginning with the eleventh edition, *LCSH* is an annual cumulation of all subject heading changes and additions that have been approved by the Subject Cataloging Division. The quarterly supplements include all additions and changes that have been made to the subject headings since the previous annual edition. The children's literature subject headings list is published in full in every quarterly supplement as well as in the annual cumulative edition. The microform edition cumulates with each issue and reflects all changes that have been made since the last issue. It is equivalent to a new edition each quarter. Cumulative children's literature subject headings are published as a separate fiche. The introduction is not included in the microform edition.

MDS—Subject Authorities [The machine-readable Library of Congress subject authority file].

This is the newest of the MARC subscription services offered by the Cataloging Distribution Service of the Library of Congress. Although both name-series and subject authorities are accommodated in the same USMARC authorities format, subject authorities are distributed in the *MDS—Subject Authorities* while the name-series authorities continue to be distributed via *MDA—Name Authorities.*

This file contains all machine-readable subject authority records available at the time of production. The regular weekly distribution service consists of current authority work completed by the Subject Cataloging Division. New, changed, and deleted records are distributed as full records according to the usual pattern for other CDS distribution services.

The Library of Congress control number in this cumulative master file is permanently assigned to each record. These control numbers carry the prefix *sh.*

Authority records are created only for those heading and heading-subdivision combinations that are printed in *Library of Congress Subject Headings.* Categories that currently are not printed and for which no MARC subject authority records are created are (1) names of persons, unless used as a pattern or example, or unless a subdivision must be printed; (2) names of corporate bodies and jurisdictions, unless used as a pattern or example, or unless a subdivision must be printed; (3) headings incorporating free-floating subdivisions; (4) phrase headings created by incorporating free-floating terms (e.g., —— Region, —— Valley, —— in art, —— in literature). The file does not contain records for subdivisions because the USMARC authorities format does not allow encoding of records for subdivisions. Neither are authority records for Library of Congress juvenile headings included.[2]

2. "Authority Research for Subject Heading Proposals." *Cataloging Service Bulletin* 16 (Spring 1982): 52–55.

Subject Cataloging Manual: Subject Headings. Prepared by the Subject Cataloging Division, Processing Services, Library of Congress. 3rd. ed. Washington, D.C.: Library of Congress, 1989. 2 v. (loose-leaf).

Includes guidelines for cataloging library materials in the Subject Cataloging Division of the Library of Congress. Comprises Section H, Subject headings, of the staff manual used at the Library of Congress for all subject cataloging. Emphasizes practices and procedures.

Glossary

Access point—any data element or heading (including a name, title, subject, or reference) in a public catalog that directs the user to a particular bibliographic record in the catalog. The access point, therefore, enables the user to determine if a library owns a particular work.

Authority control—a bibliographic organization function that ensures the establishment of logical links between authority records and access points to bibliographic records.

Authority file—a set of records maintained that documents the established forms of entries used in public catalogs, including the references that support them.

Authority work—the process of checking headings against an authority file and verifying that the form of entry matches the form already in use in the catalog and that linking references are made for headings requiring them.

Authorized heading—the form of an access point that is used to point to a bibliographic record established according to a particular set of criteria or standards.

Bibliographic record—a unique description of a specific physical item in a library collection.

Bibliographic utility—an organization that maintains large online bibliographic databases enabling it to provide services and products to libraries and other interested users.

Catalog—a set of bibliographic records that describes the resources of a collection or library.

Content designation—the codes and conventions established to explicitly identify and further characterize the data elements within a record.

Heading—the structured form of a name, subject, uniform title, or series placed at the beginning of a bibliographic record to provide access to the record and thus the catalog. The heading also helps provide structure for the catalog. It differs from a descriptor or term in a thesaurus, which is usually limited to subject and which, in its unstructured form, does not contribute to the structure of the file to which it provides access.

Integrated (or total) system—a system developed to handle multiple functions. The various components of the system work together to produce a unified result.

MARC (machine-readable cataloging)—the standard format developed for online searching and retrieval of bibliographic and authority records. It consists of a set of codes and content designators defined for encoding a particular type of machine-readable record.

Series—a group of separate works issued in succession and related to one another by the fact that each bears a common, collective title. Each individual work in the series represents a bibliographically independent item with its own unique title on its own distinctive chief source of information (e.g., a title page). Each item within the series, thus, has both a collective title and a distinctive title. A series differs from a serial in that the various parts of a serial are not bibliographically independent nor do they have distinctive titles. Each part of a serial is dependent upon the collective title of the whole for its identity.

Tag—a three-digit label used to identify the various fields in a MARC record.

Topical subject—a subject heading consisting of a general, scientific, or technical term as opposed to a personal or corporate name.

Uniform title—the particular conventional or filing title by which a work that has appeared under varying titles is to be identified for cataloging purposes.

USMARC format (sometimes used interchangeably with LC/MARC)—standards for the representation of bibliographic and authority information in machine-readable form for use in the United States. Developed to enable the Library of Congress to communicate its bibliographic records to other institutions.

Validation—a machine or manual process in which the data and the content designators of a record are matched against standards and notification is given of any errors or inconsistencies detected.

Bibliography

"Agreement Is Reached on LSP Priorities and Issues." *Library of Congress Information Bulletin* 45 (December 15, 1986): 403.

American Library Association. Subject Analysis Committee. Ad Hoc Subcommittee on Library of Congress Subject Authority Control: Scope, Format, and Distribution. Library of Congress. *Subject Authority Control: Scope, Format, and Distribution: A Final Report.* 1982. (Unpublished report.)

Anderson, Dorothy. "An International Framework for National Bibliographic Development: Achievement and Challenge." *Library Resources & Technical Services* 30 (January/March 1986): 13–22.

———. *Universal Bibliographic Control: A Long Term Policy—A Plan for Action.* Munich: Verlag Dokumentation, Pullach, 1974.

Anglo-American Cataloguing Rules. 2nd ed., 1988 revision. Chicago: American Library Association, 1988.

Auld, Larry. "Authority Control: An Eighty-Year Review." *Library Resources & Technical Services* 26 (October/December 1982): 319–330.

Authorities: Persons, Corporate Bodies, & Series. Audiotapes from the 100th Annual American Library Association Conference, San Francisco, Calif., June 1981. Tapes 81107-341–344.

"Authorities Phase of LSP Completed by RLG and LC." *Library Journal* 112 (September 1, 1987): 124.

"Authority Control in the Online Environment." *RTSD Newsletter* 12 (Winter 1987): 8–9.

"Authority Control or the Key to Survival in the Eighties." *Law Library Journal* 73 (Fall 1980): 929–957.

Authority Control Symposium: Papers Presented During the 14th Annual ARLIS/NA Conference, New York, February 10, 1986. Edited by Karen Muller. Occasional Paper No. 6. Tucson, Ariz.: Art Libraries Society of North America, 1987.

Authority Control: The Key to Tomorrow's Catalog: Proceedings of the 1979 Library and Information Technology Association Institutes. Edited by Mary W. Ghikas. Phoenix, Ariz.: Oryx Press, 1982.

"Authority Files." In *How to Catalogue: A Practical Handbook Using AACR2 and Library of Congress,* by Liz Chapman, pp. 17–20. London: Clive Bingley, 1984.

"Authority System Is Revised." *Library of Congress Information Bulletin* 43 (April 23, 1984): 138–139.

"Authority Systems: Papers Given at the Sessions of the Section of Cataloguing Which Took Place During the IFLA Congress in Copenhagen, 1979." *International Cataloguing* 9 (January/March 1980): 10–12; (April/June 1980): 19–20; (July/September 1980): 34–36; (October/December 1980): 45–48.

"The Automated Name Authority File and Music at the Library of Congress." *Music Cataloging Bulletin* 11 (December 1980): 4–5.

Avram, Henriette D. "Authority Control and Its Place." *Journal of Academic Librarianship* 9 (January 1984): 331–335.

———. "The Linked Systems Project: Its Implications for Resource Sharing." *Library Resources & Technical Services* 30 (January/March 1986): 36–46. (Also published in *Collection Management* 9 [Summer-Fall 1986]: 39–54.)

———. "The Role of Authority Files in a National Bibliographic Network: A Proposal to the National Commission on Libraries and Information Science." In *Toward a National Library and Information Service Network*, edited by Henriette D. Avram, pp. 27–41. Washington, D.C.: Library of Congress, 1977.

———. "The Role of the Library of Congress in the National Bibliographic Network." *Journal of Library Automation* 10 (June 1977): 154–162.

———, and Wiggins, Beecher. "The Role of the Linked Systems Project in Cooperation and Resource Sharing among Libraries." *Journal of Academic Librarianship* 13 (May 1987): 4 p. inserted between p. 100 and 101.

———; Maruyama, Lenore S.; and Rather, John C. "Automation Activities in the Processing Department of the Library of Congress." *Library Resources & Technical Services* 16 (Spring 1972): 195–239.

Baecker, Edith K., and Senghas, Dorothy C. *A Little-Brief Authority: A Manual for Establishing and Maintaining a Name Authority File*. Norwood, Mass.: DeDoss Associates, 1978.

Baer, Nadine L., and Johnson, Karl E. "The State of Authority." *Information Technology and Libraries* 7 (June 1988): 139–153.

Baker, Carolyn W. "Name Authority and Arkansas Academic Libraries." *Arkansas Librarian* 40 (March 1983): 8–9.

Baldwin, Paul E. "The Transition to AACR2 Through the Shared Authority File Development." In *AACR2 Seminar Papers*, edited by Ralph W. Manning, p. 111–119. Ottawa: Canadian Library Association, 1981.

Bankole, Beatrice. "Problems in Establishing a Name File for Nigerian Authors." *International Cataloguing* 9 (April/June 1980): 19–20.

Bates, Marcia J. "Subject Access in Online Catalogs: A Design Model." *Journal of the American Society for Information Science* 37 (November 1986): 357–376.

Bausset, Jaye. "Authority Files and the Online Catalog." *RTSD Newsletter* 6 (November-December 1981): 65–66.

Bernard, Patrick S. "Name Authority Activities and the Building of the National Union Catalog Database at the Library of Congress." *RTSD Newsletter* 13, no. 1 (1988): 6–7.

"Bibliographic Targets for '84 Defined: Goals Include Standards, Authority Service." *CLR Recent Developments* 9 (August 1981): 3–4.

Blair, David C. "Indeterminacy in the Subject Access to Documents." *Information Processing & Management* 22, no. 2 (1986): 229–241.

Boss, Richard W. "Interfacing Automated Library Systems." Library Technology Reports 20 (September-October 1984): 615–703.

"British Library and RLG to Cooperate." *American Libraries* 16 (February 1985): 83.

Buchinski, Edwin J. *Initial Considerations for a Nationwide Data Base*. Washington, D.C.: Library of Congress, 1978.

———; Newman, William L.; and Dunn, Mary Joan. "The Automated Authority Subsystem at the National Library of Canada." *Journal of Library Automation* 9 (December 1976): 279–298.

———. "The National Library of Canada Authority Subsystem: Implications." *Journal of Library Automation* 10 (March 1977): 28–40.

Bulaong, Grace. "Authorities and Standards in a Changing World." *International Cataloguing* 11 (July/September, October/December 1982): 35–36, 41–43.

Burger, Robert H. "Artificial Intelligence and Authority Control." *Library Resources & Technical Services* 28 (October/December 1984): 337–345.

——. *Authority Work: The Creation, Use, Maintenance, and Evaluation of Authority Records and Files.* Littleton, Colo.: Libraries Unlimited, 1985.

——. "NACO at the University of Illinois at U-C: A Narrative Case Study." *Cataloging & Classification Quarterly* 7 (Winter 1986): 19–28.

Cain, Jack. "Authorities and Authority Control." In *AACR2 Seminar Papers,* edited by Ralph W. Manning, pp. 105–109. Ottawa: Canadian Library Association, 1981.

"CDS to Distribute Machine-Readable Subject Authorities." *Library of Congress Information Bulletin* 44 (August 19, 1985): 231–232.

Chan, Lois M. "The Principle of Uniform Heading in Descriptive Cataloging: Ideal and Reality." *Cataloging & Classification Quarterly* 3 (Summer 1983): 21–35.

Chernofsky, Jacob L. "Authority File Service." *AB Bookman's Weekly* 65 (June 16, 1980): 4634, 4651.

"Citation of Sources in Subject Authority Records." *Cataloging Service Bulletin* 33 (Summer 1986): 56–62.

Clack, Doris Hargrett. "Authority Control and Linked Bibliographic Databases." *Cataloging & Classification Quarterly* 8, no. 3/4 (1988): 35–46.

——. "Authority Control: Issues and Answers." In *Libraries in the '80s,* pp. 127–140. New York: Haworth Press, 1985. (Also published in *Technical Services Quarterly* 3 [Fall/Winter 1985/1986]: 127–140.)

——. "On Becoming an Authority on Authorities: A Working Bibliography." *Florida Libraries* 33 (January/February 1983): 13–18.

Clements, Charles R. *Automated Authority Control at the Genealogical Society of Utah.* Arlington, Va.: ERIC, 1979 (ED 186 001).

Cochrane, Pauline A. *Improving LCSH for Use in On-line Catalogs.* Littleton, Colo.: Libraries Unlimited, 1986.

——. "Is Compatibility of Authority Files Practicable?" In *Information Systems Compatibility,* edited by Simon M. Newman, pp. 69–81. Washington, D.C.: Spartan Books, 1965.

Cole, Jim E. "Unique Serial Title Entries." *Serials Review* 7 (October 1981): 75–77.

"Computers Will Link via Standard Network Interconnection." *CLR Recent Developments* 10 (March 1982): 2.

"The Continuing Saga of Authority Control." *Illinois Libraries* 65 (May 1983): 329–336.

Cook, C. Donald. "Headings for Corporate Names: International Standardization under *AACR2*." *Library Resources & Technical Services* 28 (July/September 1984): 239–252.

"Cooperative Automated Name Authority Project." *Journal of Library Automation* 13 (March 1980): 66–67.

Council on Library Resources. *Twenty-fourth Annual Report, 1980.* Washington, D.C.: The Council, 1980.

Coyne, Fumiko H. "Automated Authorities Maintenance at the Western Library Network." *Technical Services Quarterly* 5, no. 1 (1987): 33–47.

Crawford, Walt. *MARC for Library Use: Understanding Integrated USMARC.* 2nd ed. Boston: G. K. Hall, 1989.

"Cross Reference Structure in the LC Automated Subject Authority File." *Cataloging Service Bulletin* 33 (Summer 1986): 62.

Cutter, Charles Ammi. *Rules for a Dictionary Catalog.* 4th ed. rewritten. Washington, D.C.: Government Printing Office, 1904.

Daily, Jay E. "Authority Files." *Encyclopedia of Library and Information Science,* vol. 2, pp. 132–138. New York: M. Dekker, 1964–1969.

Davison, Wayne E. "The WLN/RLG/LC Linked Systems Project." *Information Technology and Libraries* 2 (March 1983): 34–46.

Denenberg, Ray. "Linked Systems Project, Part 2: Standard Network Interconnection." *Library Hi Tech* 3, no. 2 (1985): 71–80.

———. "Standard Network Interconnection." *Information Technology and Libraries* 5 (December 1986): 314–323.

———, and McCallum, Sally H. "RLG/WLN/LC Computers Ready to Talk: Three Disparate Bibliographic Systems Will Link Up This Fall." *American Libraries* 15 (June 1984): 400–404.

Descriptive Cataloging Manual. Washington, D.C.: Descriptive Cataloging Division, Library of Congress, 1918(?)–.

Dillon, Martin; Knight, Rebecca C.; Lospinuso, Margaret F.; and Ulmschneider, John. "The Use of Automatic Indexing for Authority Control." *Journal of Library Automation* 14 (December 1981): 268–277.

Dio, Makiko. "Establishing the Subject Authority File." *Unabashed Librarian* 6 (Winter 1973): 27–28.

Duke, John K. "NAF Card: A Microcomputer-Based Reference Card Generator." *Technical Services Quarterly* 1 (Summer 1984): 73–82.

Elias, Cathy Ann, and Fair, C. James. "Name Authority Control in a Communication System." *Special Libraries* 74 (July 1983): 289–296.

Epstein, Susan Baerg. "Automated Authority Control: A Hidden Timebomb?" *Library Journal* 110 (November 1, 1985): 36–37; 111 (January 1986): 55–56.

Evans, M. J. "Authority Control: An Alternative to the Record Group Concept." *American Archivist* 49 (Summer 1986): 249–261.

Farmer, Linda. *Alternatives to Full Authority Implementation: A Discussion Paper.* Prepared for the Management Committee's Working Group on Authorities. Toronto: Office of Library Coordination, Council of Ontario Universities, 1979.

Fayen, Emily Gallup. "The Online Public Access Catalog in 1984: Evaluating Needs and Choices." *Library Technology Reports* 20 (January-February 1984): 7–59.

Fenly, Judith G. "Name Authority Co-op (NACO) Project." *North Carolina Libraries* 43 (Winter 1985): 228–232.

———, and Irvine, Sarah D. "The Name Authority Co-op (NACO) Project at the Library of Congress: Present and Future." *Cataloging & Classification Quarterly* 7 (Winter 1986): 7–18.

Franklin, Laurel F. "Preparing for Automated Authority Control: A Projection of Name Headings Verified." *Journal of Academic Librarianship* 13 (September 1987): 205–208.

Funabiki, Ruth Patterson; Mifflin, Ingrid; and Corlee, Karen. "Use of the WLN Authority Control System by an ARL Library." *Library Resources & Technical Services* 27 (October/December 1983): 391–394.

Funk, Carla. "When a Catalog Isn't a Catalog: Bibliographic Compromises in a Shared Automated Circulation System." *Illinois Librarian* 62 (Summer 1980): 606–609.

Gabriel, Erna; MacDonald, Clarice; and Vojta, Vilma. "The Vocabulary Control System of the Washington Library Network." *Proceedings of the ASIS Annual Meeting* 19 (1975): 14–15.

Grady, Agnes M. "Online Maintenance Features of Authority Files: Survey of Vendors and In-House Systems." *Information Technology and Libraries* 7 (March 1988): 51–55.

"Grants Underpin First Steps Toward Nationwide Authority File Service." *CLR Recent Developments* 8 (April 1980): 4.

Gray, Carolyn M., and Wetherbee, Louella V. "Amigos: The Growth of a Network." *Serials Librarian* 5 (Fall 1980): 59–63.

Grisham, Frank P. "The Link." *Solinews, the SOLINET Newsletter* 14 (May 1987): 1.

Grosch, Audrey N. "Computer-Based Subject Authority Files at the University of Minnesota Libraries." *Journal of Library Automation* 5 (December 1972): 230–243.

Hagler, Ronald, and Simmons, Peter. *The Bibliographic Record and Information Technology.* Chicago: American Library Association, 1982.

Havens, Carolyn. "The Networks Merger and Serials Control." *Serials Librarian* 14, no. 1 (1988): 33–40.

Henderson, Kathryn Luther. "Great Expectations: The Authority Control Connection." *Illinois Librarian* 65 (May 1983): 334–336.

Herzog, Kate. "The Technical Reports Authority File." *Science & Technology Libraries* 2 (Spring 1982): 35–51.

Hill, Janet Swan. "The Northwestern Africana Project: An Experiment in Decentralized Bibliographic and Authority Control." *College & Research Libraries* 42 (July 1981): 326–332.

Hisatsune, Kimi. "Authority Control—Beyond Global Switching Headings." *Technical Services Quarterly* 1 (Fall 1983): 121–127.

Holley, Robert P., and Killheffer, Robert E. "Is There an Answer to the Subject Access Crisis?" *Cataloging & Classification Quarterly* 1, nos. 2/3 (1982): 125–133.

Howard, Joseph H. "LC Authority Project." *Library Journal* 105 (November 15, 1980): 2358.

Howerton, Paul W. "Organic and Functional Concepts of Authorities." In *Information Systems Compatibility,* edited by Simon M. Newman, pp. 47–54. Washington, D.C.: Spartan Books, 1965.

Hudson, Judith. "Bibliographic Record Maintenance in the Online Environment." *Information Technology and Libraries* 3 (December 1984): 388–393.

Hunn, Nancy O., and Wright, Jean Acker. "The Implementation of ACORN Authority Control at Vanderbilt University Library." *Cataloging & Classification Quarterly* 8, no. 1 (1987): 79–91.

"In-depth: University of California MELVYL." *Information Technology and Libraries* 1 (December 1982): 350–380; 2 (March 1983): 58–115.

"An Inexpensive 'User-Oriented' Authority File." *Unabashed Librarian* 21 (1976): 5–6.

"An Integrated Consistent Authority File Service for Nationwide Use." *Library of Congress Information Bulletin* 39 (July 11, 1980): 244–248.

International Federation of Library Associations and Institutions. Working Group on an International Authority System. *Guidelines for Authority and Reference Entries.* London: IFLA International Programme for UBC, 1984.

Jamieson, Alexis J.; Dolan, Elizabeth; and Declerck, Luc. "Keyword Searching vs. Authority Control in an Online Catalog." *Journal of Academic Librarianship* 12 (November 1986): 277–283.

"Japan: Authority File for Japanese Authors." *International Cataloguing* 9 (January/March 1980): 2.

Jaramillo, George R. "Authority Control: Is It Needed for the 80's?" *Colorado Libraries* 11 (Spring 1985): 24–28.

Jones, C. Lee. "Planning for Governance at the National Level." *Bulletin of the American Society for Information Science* 6 (June 1980): 10–11.

———. "Summary Recommendations from Subject Access Meeting." *Information Technology and Libraries* 2 (March 1983): 116–119.

Kellough, Patrick H. "Name Authority Work and Problem Solving: The Value of the LC Name Authority File." *Technicalities* 8 (June 1988): 3–5.

Klemperer, Katharine. "Authority Control in MELVYL." *DLA Bulletin* 4 (June 1984): 6–7.

Knutson, Gunnar. "Does the Catalog Record Make a Difference? Access Points and Book Use." *College & Research Libraries* 47 (September 1986): 460–469.

Kochen, Manfred, and Tagliacozzo, Renata. "A Study of Cross-Referencing." *Journal of Documentation* 24 (September 1968): 173–191.

Krumm, Carol, and McDonald, Beverly I. "Libraries on the Line." *Technical Services Quarterly* 1, no. 1/2 (1983): 117–120.

"LASP, NAFS Projects Related in Authority Efforts." *CLR Recent Developments* 9 (August 1981): 5.

Lawrence, Gary S.; Matthews, Joseph R.; and Miller, Charles E. "Costs and Features of Online Catalogs: The State of the Art." *Information Technology and Libraries* 2 (December 1983): 409–449.

"LC, Three Universities Work on Authority Project." *Library Journal* 105 (June 1, 1980): 1246.

"LC, Three University Libraries Agree on Name Authority Cooperation." *Library of Congress Information Bulletin* 39 (February 15, 1980): 53.

"Library Launches Retrospective Name Authority Project." *Library of Congress Information Bulletin* 39 (April 4, 1980): 116.

Library of Congress. Descriptive Cataloging Division. *Descriptive Cataloging Manual. Z, Name Authority Records.* Washington, D.C.: Library of Congress, 1983– . (Unpublished procedures manual.)

———. Subject Cataloging Division. *Library of Congress Subject Headings.* 11th ed. 3 vols. Washington, D.C.: Library of Congress, 1988.

Likins, John. "How I Run My Authority File Good." *Unabashed Librarian* no. 33 (1979): 25–26.

"The Linked Systems Project: Impact on Bibliographic Networks and Systems." *LITA Newsletter* 26 (Fall 1986): 1–2.

Linking the Bibliographic Utilities: Benefits and Costs: [A Report from Battelle-Columbus Laboratory.] Washington, D.C.: Council on Library Resources, 1980.

Ludy, Lorene E. "LC Name Authority Tapes Used by Ohio State University Libraries." *Information Technology and Libraries* 3 (March 1984): 69–71.

———. "OSU Libraries' Use of Library of Congress Subject Authorities File." *Information Technology and Libraries* 4 (June 1985): 155–160.

———, and Logan, Susan J. "Integrating Authority Control in an Online Catalog." *Proceedings of the 45th ASIS Annual Meeting* 19 (1982): 176–178.

———, and Rogers, Sally A. "Authority Control in the Online Environment." *Information Technology and Libraries* 3 (September 1984): 262–266.

MacIntosh, Helen. "SHARAF: The Canadian Shared Authority File Project." *Library Resources & Technical Services* 26 (October/December 1982): 345–352.

Maclean, Ian A. "Collocation, Consistency and Cleanliness: Authority Control and the Computer-based Catalogue." In *AACR2 Seminar Papers*, edited by Ralph W. Manning, pp. 21–28. Ottawa: Canadian Library Association, 1981.

Malinconico, S. Michael. "Bibliographic Data Base Organization and Authority File Control." *Wilson Library Bulletin* 53 (September 1979): 36–45.

———. "Circulation Control Systems as Online Catalogs." *Library Journal* 108 (June 15, 1983): 1207–1210.

———. "Mass Storage Technology and File Organization." *Journal of Library Automation* 13 (June 1980): 77–87.

———. "The Role of a Machine-Based Authority File in an Automated Bibliographic System." In *Automation in Libraries: Papers Presented at the CACUL Workshop on Library Automation, Winnipeg, June 22–23, 1974.* Ottawa, Ont.: Canadian Library Association, 1975.

MARC Conversion Manual—Authorities (Names): Content Designation Conventions and Online Procedures. 2nd ed. Washington, D.C.: MARC Editorial Division, Processing Services, Library of Congress, 1984.

MARC Conversion Manual—Series Authorities. Washington, D.C.: MARC Editorial Division, Processing Services, Library of Congress, 1985.

"MARC Distribution Service—Subject Authorities." *Cataloging Service Bulletin* 32 (Spring 1986): 71.

Markey, Karen, and Vizine-Goetz, Diane. *Characteristics of Subject Authority Records in the Machine-Readable Library of Congress Subject Headings.* Research Report Series, No. OCLC/OR/RR-88/2. Dublin, Ohio: OCLC Online Computer Library Center, 1988.

Martin, Susan K. "Authority Control: Unnecessary Detail or Needed Support." *Library Issues* 2 (January 1982): 2–3.

———. "Upgrading 'Brief and Dirty' Data." *American Libraries* 10 (April 1979): 212, 214.

Matson, Susan. "Desiderata for a National Series Authority File." *Library Resources & Technical Services* 26 (October/December 1982): 331–344.

Matthews, Joseph R. "Competition and Change: The 1983 Automated Library System Marketplace." *Library Journal* 109 (May 1, 1984): 853–860.

———. "Online Public Access Catalogs: Assessing the Potential." *Library Journal* 107 (June 1, 1982): 1067–1071.

Matthews, Karen L. "Authority Control." *Colorado Libraries* 6 (June 1980): 156–200.

McCallam, Sally H. "Linked Systems Project: Implications for Library Automation and Networking." In *Advances in Library Automation and Networking.* Vol. 1, pp. 1–20. Greenwich, Conn.: JAI Press, 1987.

———. "Linked Systems Project in the United States." *IFLA Journal* 11, no. 4 (1985): 313–324.

———. "Linked Systems Project, Part 1: Authorities Implementation." *Library Hi Tech* 3, no. 2 (1985): 61–70.

———. "Linked Systems Project Will Facilitate NACO Procedures." *Library of Congress Information Bulletin* 43 (March 5, 1984): 59–60.

———. "MARC Record-Linking Technique." *Information Technology and Libraries* 1 (September 1982): 281–291.

———. "Using UNIMARC: Prospects and Problems." (Unpublished paper presented at the IFLA General Conference in Nairobi, Kenya, August 1984.)

———, and Godwin, James L. "Statistics on Headings in the MARC File." *Journal of Library Automation* (September 1981): 194–201.

McCarthy, Constance. "The Reliability Factor in Subject Access." *College & Research Libraries* 47 (January 1986): 48–56.

McCombs, Jillian. "Public and Technical Services: Disappearing Barriers." *Wilson Library Bulletin* 61 (November 1986): 25–28.

McCoy, Richard W. "The Linked Systems Project: Progress, Promise, Realities." *Library Journal* 111 (October 1, 1986): 33–39.

McDonald, David R. "Data Dictionaries, Authority Control, and Online Catalogs: A New Perspective." *Journal of Academic Librarianship* 11 (September 1985): 219–222.

McGill, Michael J.; Learn, Larry L.; and Lyndon, Thomas K. G. "A Technical Evaluation of the Linked Systems Project Protocols in the Name Authority Distribution Application." *Information Technology and Libraries* 6 (December 1987): 253–265.

McKinlay, John. "Concerning Subject Authority Catalogues." *Library Resources & Technical Services* 16 (Fall 1972): 460–465.

McPherson, Dorothy. *Authority Control in the University of California Union Catalog.* Division of Library Automation Working Paper, No. 9. Berkeley: Division of Library Automation, Office of the Assistant Vice President, Library Plans and Policies, University of California, 1980.

Miller, Dan. "Authority Control in the Retrospective Conversion Process." *Information Technology and Libraries* 3 (September 1984): 286–292.

Miller, R. Bruce. *Name Authority Control for Card Catalogs in the General Libraries.* Austin, Tex.: University of Texas at Austin, General Libraries, 1981.

Millican, Rita. "Authority Control." In *Online Catalog: The Inside Story,* edited by William E. Post and Peter G. Watson, p. 33–39. Chico, Calif.: Ryan Research International, 1983.

Mosey, Jeanette Gail. *Name Authority Work in OCLC Libraries: A Survey of Practices and Expectations.* 1980. (Unpublished dissertation, University of California.)

"NACO Celebrates Tenth Anniversary." *Library of Congress Information Bulletin* 47 (January 25, 1988): 27–29.

"NACO Changes Its Name." *Library of Congress Information Bulletin* 46 (January 26, 1987): 44.

"NACO Libraries to Contribute Series Authority Records." *Library of Congress Information Bulletin* 45 (September 1, 1986): 306.

"NACO/LSP Contribution Begins with Yale." *Library of Congress Information Bulletin* 46 (October 12, 1987): 438–439, 442.

"NACO/LSP Success Continues: OCLC Contribution Begins." *Library of Congress Information Bulletin* 47 (July 11, 1988): 290.

"Name and Series Authority Records." *Cataloging Service Bulletin* 24 (Spring 1984): 25–55.

The Name Authority Cooperative/Name Authority File Service. Task Force on a Name Authority File Service, Bibliographic Service Development Program. Washington, D.C.: Council on Library Resources, 1984.

"Name Authority File Service Planning Document Issued." *CLR Recent Developments* 9 (April 1981): 5.

"Name Authority Records Put in Machine-Readable Form." *Library of Congress Information Bulletin* 37 (December 1, 1978): 726.

"National Library Name Authority Files." *National Library News* 8 (January-February 1976): 2–3.

"Need for Network Authority File Implemented." *Law Library Journal* 73 (Spring 1980): 516–517.

Oddy, Pat. "Name Authority Files." *Catalogue & Index* no. 82 (Autumn 1986): 1, 3–4.

O'Neill, Edward T., and Vizine-Goetz, Diane. "Computer Generation of a Subject Authority File." In *Proceedings of the ASIS Annual Meeting* 19 (1982): 220–223.

Palmer, Joseph W. "Subject Authority Control and Syndetic Structure—Myth and Realities." *Cataloging & Classification Quarterly* 7 (Winter 1986): 71–102.

Payne, Charles; McGee, Rob; Schmierer, Helen F.; and Harris, Howard S. "The University of Chicago Library Data Management System." *Library Quarterly* 47 (January 1977): 1–22.

Perreault, Jean M. "Authority Control: Old and New." *Libri* 32 (June 1982): 124–148.

Potter, William Gray. "When Names Collide: Conflict in the Catalog and *AACR2.*" *Library Resources & Technical Services* 24 (Winter 1980): 3–16.

Preston, Gregor A. "Coping with Subject Heading Changes." *Library Resources & Technical Services* 24 (Winter 1980): 64–68.

Prichard, R. J. "Access Points for Serials." *Library Review* 30 (Summer 1981): 74–77.

Reisner, Phyllis. "Construction of Authority Files." In *Information Systems Compatibility*, edited by Simon M. Newman, p. 55–68. Washington, D.C.: Spartan Books, 1965.

"RLG and LC Cooperate to Provide Up-to-Date Authorities File." *Research Libraries Group News* 15 (January 1988): 6.

"RLG & Washington Network to Build Authority File." *Library Journal* 105 (June 1, 1980): 1245.

"RLG and WLN Undertake Authority File." *Wilson Library Bulletin* 54 (June 1980): 618.

"RLG's RLIN Authorities Subsystem Ready for Searching." *Information Technology and Libraries* 2 (June 1983): 218.

Romero, Nancy, and Wajenberg, Arnold. "Authority Records and Authority Work in the Online Catalogue." *Information Technology and Libraries* 4 (December 1985): 318–323.

Rosenthal, Joseph A. "Planning for the Catalogs: A Managerial Perspective." *Journal of Library Automation* 11 (September 1978): 192–205.

Ross, Ian C. "A Cataloger's Authority List Maintenance System." *Journal of the American Society for Information Science* 27 (July-August 1976): 224–229.

Roughton, Karen G., and Tyckoson, David A. "Browsing with Sound: Sound-based Codes and Automated Authority Control." *Information Technology and Libraries* 4 (June 1985): 130–136.

Rule Interpretations. 2nd ed. Washington, D.C.: Descriptive Cataloging Division, Library of Congress, 1989–   .

Runkle, Martin D. "Authority Control: A Library Director's View." *Journal of Academic Librarianship* 12 (July 1986): 145–146.

———. "Authority in Online Catalogs." *Illinois Libraries* 62 (September 1980): 603–606.

Salmon, Stephen R. "The Union Catalogue: Functions, Objectives and Techniques." *Cataloging & Classification Quarterly* 2, nos. 1/2 (1982): 21–44.

Schmidt, Judith G. "Name Authority Co-op." *Library of Congress Information Bulletin* 41 (April 2, 1982): 105.

Schmierer, Helen F. "The Relationship of Authority Control to the Library Catalog." *Illinois Libraries* 62 (September 1980): 599–603.

Sears List of Subject Headings, edited by Barbara Westby. 13th ed. New York: H. W. Wilson, 1986.

Seba, Douglas B., and Smith, Pat. "Simple Logic for Big Problems: An Inside Look at Regional Databases." *Database* 5 (December 1982): 68–71.

"Serial Record Division." *Library of Congress Information Bulletin* 41 (January 8, 1982): 25.

"Shared U.S. Authority File System" [Report of the Meeting of the Bibliographic Utilities and National Libraries]. *IFLA Journal* 6, no. 2 (1980): 189–190.

Sheehy, Eugene P. *Guide to Reference Books*. 10th ed. Chicago: American Library Association, 1986.

Shore, Melinda L. "Variation Between Personal Name Headings and Title Page Usage." *Cataloging & Classification Quarterly* 4 (Summer 1984): 1–11.

Smirnovs, Marie. "Authority Files and Their Problems: Report to the CLANN Technical Committee." *LASIE* 8 (September/October 1977): 23–27.

Smith, Barbara G. "Online Series Authority Control in the Integrated Library System." *Technicalities* 6 (July 1986): 3–5.

Spalding, C. Sumner. "Music Authority Files at the Library of Congress." *Music Cataloging Bulletin* 10 (October 1979): 4–6.

"Standards, Data Base Access and Highlights of Program Review." *CLR Recent Developments* 8 (November 1980): 1–2.

Stevens, Patricia A. "The Authorities Project: A Status Report." *LS/2000 Communiqué* 9 (Fall 1986): 6–7.

Stevenson, Gordon. "Descriptive Cataloging in 1982." *Library Resources & Technical Services* 27 (July/September 1983): 259–268.

"Subject Authority Products." *Cataloging Service Bulletin* 31 (Winter 1986): 77.

"Subject Cataloging." *Cataloging Service Bulletin* 27 (Winter 1985): 54–63.

Subject Cataloging Manual: Subject Headings. 3rd ed. Washington, D.C.: Subject Cataloging Division, Library of Congress, 1989.

"Subject Headings." *Cataloging Service Bulletin* 16 (Spring 1982): 52–67.

A Survey of Authority Files and Authority Control Systems for Catalogue Headings: First Report. Prepared by the IFLA International Office for UBC. London: International Federation of Library Associations and Institutions, International Office for UBC, 1978.

Svenonius, Elaine, and Schmierer, Helen. "Current Issues in Subject Control of Information." *Library Quarterly* 47 (July 1977): 326–346.

"System Links Promote Nationwide Bibliographic Data Base." *UNESCO Journal of Information Science* 5 (April 1983): 132.

Tauber, Maurice. *Technical Services in Libraries.* New York: Columbia University, 1954.

Taylor, Arlene G. "Authority Files in Online Catalogs: An Investigation of Their Value." *Cataloging & Classification Quarterly* 4 (Spring 1984): 1–17.

———. "Staying Open in 1981." *HCL Cataloging Bulletin* 39 (1979): 11–15.

———; Maxwell, Margaret F.; and Frost, Carolyn O. "Network and Vendor Authority Systems." *Library Resources & Technical Services* 29 (April/June 1985): 195–205.

Thomas, Catherine M. "Authority Control in Manual versus Online Catalogs: An Examination of 'See' References." *Information Technology and Libraries* 3 (December 1984): 393–398.

Thomson, Mollie. "Authority Files." *LASIE* 9 (January 1979): 5–21.

Tillett, Barbara B. "1984 Automated Authority Control Opinion Poll: A Preliminary Analysis." *Information Technology and Libraries* 4 (June 1985): 171–178.

Tillin, Alma M., and Quinly, William J. *Standards for Cataloging Nonprint Materials.* 4th ed. Washington, D.C.: Association for Educational Communications and Technology, 1976.

Toward a National Library and Information Service Network: The Library Bibliographic Component. Preliminary ed. Prepared by the Library of Congress Network Advisory Group. Edited by Henriette D. Avram and Lenore S. Maruyama. Washington, D.C.: Library of Congress, 1977.

Tseng, Sally C. "Online Catalog with Authority Control." *Journal of Educational Media and Library Science* 20 (Spring 1983): 189–201.

Udoh, D. J. E., and Aderibigbe, M. R. "The Problems of Development, Maintenance, and Automation of Authority Files in Nigeria." *Cataloging & Classification Quarterly* 8, no. 1 (1987): 93–103.

Van Pulis, Noelle, and Ludy, Lorene E. "Subject Searching in an Online Catalog with Authority Control." *College & Research Libraries* 49 (November 1988): 523–533.

Wajenberg, Arnold S. "The Use of LC Authority Records in the On-Line Catalogue of the University of Illinois at Urbana-Champaign." *Illinois Libraries* 65 (May 1983): 331–333.

———, and Gorman, Michael. "OCLC's Database Conversion: A User's Perspective." *Journal of Library Automation* 14 (September 1981): 174–189.

"Washington Library Network, the Research Libraries Group, and the Library of Congress Complete First Phase of the Project Designed to Link Computer Systems: Targets for Second Phase Established." *Information Hotline* 14 (February 1982): 4–5.

Watson, Mark R., and Taylor, Arlene G. "Implications of Current Reference Structure for Authority Work in Online Environments." *Information Technology and Libraries* 6 (March 1987): 10–19.

Way, William. "Subject Heading Authority List, Computer Prepared." *American Documentation* 19 (April 1968): 188–199.

What's in a Name? Control of Catalogue Records Through Automated Authority Files. Proceedings of the Workshops sponsored by National Library of Canada et al. Edited and compiled by Natsuko Y. Furuya. Toronto, Ont.: University of Toronto Library Automation Systems, 1978.

Wiggins, Beecher. "How Important Are Unique Access Points?" *RTSD Newsletter* 9, no. 7 (1984): 88–89.

Williamson, Nancy J. "Is There a Catalog in Your Future? Access to Information in the Year 2006." *Library Resources & Technical Services* 26 (April 1982): 122–135.

Wilson, Louis Round, and Tauber, Maurice F. *The University Library: The Organization, Administration, and Functions of Academic Libraries.* 2nd ed. New York: Columbia University Press, 1956.

Wilson, Mary Dabney. "Back to the Concept: Perspectives on Series Authorities." *Information Technology and Libraries* 7 (March 1988): 779–783.

"Work on System Links Progresses." *CLR Recent Developments* 11 (January 1983): 2–3.

Index

Compiled by Kristina Masiulis

Doris Hargrett Clack is a professor in the School of Library and Information Studies at Florida State University, and has also served as senior cataloger at the Library of Congress. She received her A.M.L.S. from the University of Michigan and her Ph.D. from the University of Pittsburgh. In 1987 Clack was the recipient of the Florida State University Teaching Award.